A Million and One
LOVE STRATEGIES

Everyone knows that in affairs of the heart the French lead the field. Marie Papillon, the glamorous world-renowned love and relationships expert, here reveals her secrets for each stage of a relationship – from finding your perfect partner to getting the ring on that finger!

A Million and One
LOVE STRATEGIES

♥ ♥ ♥

Marie Papillon

Thorsons
An Imprint of HarperCollins*Publishers*

Thorsons
An Imprint of HarperCollins*Publishers*
77–85 Fulham Palace Road,
Hammersmith, London W6 8JB

Published by Thorsons 1992
1   3   5   7   9   10   8   6   4   2

This Thorsons edition is a translation
and enlarged version of the original
French-language edition, *Mille et Une
Stratégies Amoureuses*
Translated with the help of Janet Adams
and Johanne Sorrentino

© Friendship International Inc. 1992

Marie Papillon asserts the moral right to
be identified as the author of this work

A catalogue record for this book
is available from the British Library

ISBN 0 7225 2767 5

Typeset by Harper Phototypesetters Limited
Northampton, England
Printed in Great Britain by
HarperCollinsManufacturing Glasgow

This book is dedicated to the millions of people around the world who want to attract the one they admire; to all those in love who want to shower their loving partners with attention and romance; and to all those whose relationships have been born of love and caring, brought up on passion and filled with starry nights of romance – and who want to keep the feelings flowing! Live – and love – passionately!

Note: Throughout the book, please take 'she' to mean 'he or she' and so on – these strategies apply equally to both sexes!

CONTENTS

INTRODUCTION

♥ ♥ ♥

Some people can approach others, young or old, and engage them in conversation – seemingly effortlessly! However, most of us are intimidated by meeting new people, talking with them, and making a good impression. Going to a party where you don't know anyone? Sheer torture! But if you don't accept the social invitations that come your way, how can you manage to introduce yourself to potential love partners?

Part One of this book – A Million and One Love Strategies for Meeting Your Perfect Match – will help you become assured and confident in chance meetings as well as in planned social encounters. You will learn how to initiate meetings and conversations, keep the action going, and walk off with the top prize: a terrific someone to love.

This section is filled with tips on how to take that important first step in approaching people, and what to do and say once you have met them. It includes up-to-date information, coupled with highly effective strategies, actual conversational openers, and anecdotes drawn from real life, to help to transform the socially shy into social butterflies!

People at all stages of their social lives will find this section very helpful. The intriguing, highly effective tips will open your eyes to many new ways of meeting – and *places for* meeting – that ideal date/mate you have been dreaming about!

You may be meeting lots of people, but are they people you're attracted to? Are you compatible with them? Are you dating interesting prospects, or do you keep dating the wrong type of person? Do you know how to talk to people in such a way that they will be interested in *you*? Part One will help you unearth a gold mine of dating possibilities, and will provide techniques for meeting the right candidates for *you*! Wouldn't it be incredible to be able to enjoy good relationships that could lead you to your ideal love?

Flirting is an art that will help you meet people and make a lasting impression on them. Part Two of this book – A Million and One Strategies for Becoming an Irresistible Flirt – reinforces the strategies of Part One on how to meet people by providing you with amusing ways of attracting the attention of that 'interesting someone'.

Have you always wanted to be a social butterfly, outgoing and unafraid of interacting with others? This section of the book will give you the added confidence and positive self-image that will help you to attract the right person for you. It will show you how to develop a personal style of flirtation through verbal and non-verbal strategies that, by enhancing your qualities and talents, will lead to close encounters of a romantic kind. With this guide, *you* can become an *irresistible flirt!*

Discover the game of flirting and all of the benefits it will bring to your life as a single person. This section offers unique advice for dealing with social dilemmas. With the techniques described, you will look forward to social events instead of being apprehensive about them!

The lessons of Part Two will eliminate the qualms you may have about flirting. For example, did you know that flirting will improve your social skills? . . . Will help you be yourself in social situations? . . . Will draw people out of their shells? Did you know that dancing is a form of flirting?

Flirting helps you relate to people. This section will teach you how to make your advances sizzle with excitement! You will learn how to 'flirt with perfume', how to 'flirt with a kiss', and how 'mirroring' someone can make him or her flirt with you!

Your interpersonal strategies, combined with the power of the self-confident individual you can become, will transform you into a *superflirt!*

Courtship is a delightful stage of a relationship. It is a time when you become intimately involved with your love partner on an emotional level, and when you prepare the foundation for a lasting relationship that will enrich both of your lives. But it doesn't just happen magically after you meet the right person. There are key points along the way that determine whether two people who are attracted to each other will evolve into a couple.

Part Three of this book – A Million and One Love Strategies for a Terrific Relationship – offers many proposals that will help you to develop a warm, loving, nurturing relationship. It teaches you how to know yourself by putting together a 'self-portrait', so that you realize what you can offer to a love relationship. A comprehensive self-portrait also helps you identify the type of relationship you should be looking for at this stage of your life.

Do you always fall for the same type of person, someone who always turns out to be the wrong one for you? Have many of your previous involvements ended in a painful breakup? This section will show you how to identify your ideal love partner, help you to understand why you have chosen the wrong people, and give you courtship strategies for developing a strong, loving relationship.

Even if you have found your perfect mate and are in a happy relationship, this section will point out strategies that will spark your awareness of what being a couple is all about. It will show you how you can improve your love relationship and enrich your life, as well as that of your ideal partner.

Remember when you first met? Life seemed to shimmer with love. Everything looked bigger and brighter, food tasted better, and everything you saw, smelled and touched was marvellously scintillating! It was as though you were floating on air . . . you never got tired or bored . . . your outlook was optimistic . . . and you felt wonderful, even beautiful. You felt connected to the universe, floating through a new dimension – the realm of romantic love! The hours you spent with your newly-found ideal partner were timeless, and you felt you had known each other all your lives!

The sheer newness of a relationship can inebriate you with passion. While you are courting your ideal partner, romance fills your hours together. But once the sweet sting of Cupid's love arrow has diminished, keeping the glow of romantic love in your relationship will require new strategies.

Is romantic love an illusion? Part Four – A Million and One Love Strategies for Keeping Passion in a Romance – will show you how to recapture the glorious passion of your early encounters as well as how to keep love's enchantment brightening all your days together. This section of the book will teach you how to fill your relationship with romantic moments, bringing joy, happiness and enduring passion to you and your partner in love. It will cater to the needs of every type of relationship and give practical hints for all budgets. This section includes true stories of ultra-romantic deeds, such as that of the man who jettisoned 200 pounds of flowers over his girlfriend's house! You will learn how to send your partner 'love vibrations', how to prepare a 'romantic menu', and how to turn 'pesky errands' into 'romantic interludes'.

This section will prove a soothing balm for a waning courtship as well as an inspiration for the best of relationships. Anyone who is romantically involved will benefit from this treasure trove of romantic strategies.

So get ready for the fireworks – you are about to travel through the enchanted worlds of initiation, flirtation, courtship and passionate romance!

♥ 1 ♥

A Million and One Love Strategies
for Meeting Your Perfect Match

♥ ♥ ♥

Develop an approach that suits *you*.
This section of the book offers a wide array of love strategies
for meeting other people. Although the majority of the tips will
appeal to you, some might not suit your temperament or your
personality. For example, two of Cecily's single friends placed
ads in the 'personals' column of a local newspaper. They were
so successful that Cecily – who also wanted very much to meet
someone new – was encouraged by her friends to try a
personal advertisement.

In less than a week, Cecily was overwhelmed by 56 replies!
She couldn't believe it! Unexpectedly, she was disturbed by
having to read so many letters from all types of men *and* having
to decide which ones to contact. Finally she narrowed the
choices down to ten – all unknown to her, of course. Faced
with making the initial phone calls to introduce herself, Cecily
became so anxious and nervous that she decided to drop the
whole exercise. Obviously, this strategy was not for her!

Although Cecily was prepared to meet a potential partner,
she felt ill at ease with having to resort to the use of a personals
advert. She might have felt more comfortable with a dating
service or a chance meeting at a ballroom dance class, or even
while waiting in the supermarket queue, or at the dry cleaners!
Of course there are people who go to extravagant lengths to
announce their love, like the man who placed an advert on a
hoarding in the centre of town! On the other hand, many people
have difficulty with the simple act of leaving their business card
or calling card because they are so timid and reserved.

Recognize what style of social encounter *you* feel comfortable with, then you can select those strategies that appeal to you. Identify which approaches might be a problem for you – those that make you feel ill at ease or don't suit your personality – and don't use them. You shouldn't try to become a different person: be yourself! Your first objective is to develop a method that is uniquely yours, one that gives you confidence and natural poise. Try the techniques described in this part of the book, but give them a personal twist. Your confidence will develop with each new success and you will soon find that you are able to enjoy meeting new people – and they will love meeting *you!*

Multiply your chances of finding your ideal love by using different ways of meeting new people!

It is wise not to put all your eggs in one basket! Why not proceed like the commodities broker when you are in the market for a love partner? Put together a portfolio of possible love interests and develop a plan of action accordingly. Just like the financial planner, you will be diversifying your assets and increasing your chances of winning big!

Try all of these strategies to see which ones suit you best. By experimenting with different methods, you will learn which ones work for you as well as 'feel right' for your various situations. You will also learn to develop the right approach to attract your 'ideal person' while still leaving you open to other exciting possibilities! And you certainly don't want to close the doors on possibilities! One attraction may lead to another more interesting person . . . so keep an open mind! Once you have discovered which techniques work best for you, you will be on your way to fascinating meetings with potential partners!

A good way to meet a wide range of people is to vary the places where you practise your many love strategies. Instead of just waiting passively for answers to a personals advertisement, flirt at work, at cocktail parties, at intimate get-togethers with friends, or during classes and seminars. Smile at everyone you pass on the street! By being open-minded and receptive, you will be actively pursuing your dream of love!

Develop the art of meeting people . . . step by step.

You *can* develop the art of meeting people! Work at it step by step and you will soon become professional at it. Don't expect immediate results. You weren't born a diplomat! Grace and charm are acquired by being involved in many social situations. As with any other skill, you will become more competent with each experience.

How can you develop your 'people' talents? By becoming involved in as many social activities as you can! The social graces are talents like any others. Just as an exceptional singing voice is perfected through lessons, or just as a budding artist might attend an art school to become a professional, social graces develop best through practice, namely through extensive social contacts. Take full advantage of every opportunity to socialize, and watch your skills grow!

Not everyone will react to your advances in the same way. People who are outgoing may well be delighted that you took the first step in meeting them; on the other hand, shy or reserved people may not appreciate your approach, and may even think you're arrogant! But in general, your attempts to meet people will be welcomed. All you have to do is make the effort to go out and mingle! Take every opportunity to make contact with people – you might even go so far as to 'accidentally' bump into someone you are attracted to! The strategies listed here will provide amusing ways to meet others. Experiment with a few strategies at a time and you will soon become a 'strategies Grand Master'!

There is no magic recipe for finding your love partner, and there is no foolproof way of getting the right response from someone you're interested in. You must be persistent. Practice makes perfect! Sample different strategies and you will surely reach your goal. It is important to work towards your objectives without becoming fanatical about reaching them in a hurry. Enjoy yourself instead! For example, if marriage is your goal, the worst thing you can do is to scare off every person you meet by letting on you are eager to 'tie the knot'. Take your time in getting to know people . . . discover their little quirks and delights! Let your search for the love of your life unfold like a splendid fairy tale!

Take control of your life.
Yes, you can wait for destiny to fulfil your longings, but you can
also help it along. Take advantage of unexpected occasions to
meet people and increase your chances of finding your ideal
partner. Accept all the social invitations you possibly can,
especially ones to parties where you don't know anyone. What
an opportunity to meet someone excitingly new! During the
party, take the time to introduce yourself to everyone – it is a
great way to practise your social skills while making new
friends of both sexes.

Be alert to all possible places and events where you may meet
interesting people. Follow the social columns in your
newspaper, as well as the entertainment section. Read
newsletters, organizational bulletins, all those flyers and posters
advertising upcoming social events. Don't rely on only one
method to encounter new people. Be open and receptive to all
possibilities. You can take charge of the direction of your life by
being aware of and choosing from those myriad, tantalizing
social possibilities shimmering on your horizons!

**How much time are you willing to spend each week
looking for your ideal partner?**
How much time are you willing to invest every day . . . every
week . . . every month . . . in the search for the love of your
dreams? Think about it: the more time you devote to your
quest, the better your chances are of finding your ideal partner
in a short time! Finding your love is comparable to finding a
job. How many applications would you send out every week?
Your 'love search' requires just as much time and effort – and
it's far more pleasant! Take a decision as to how much time you
will schedule – an hour a day? Two nights a week? And stick
to your resolve! If finding a terrific love match is really
important to you, the old excuse 'I haven't the time!' should
never enter your mind!

Become a social success!

What is a social success? Someone who will take the necessary steps to meet people . . . anywhere, anytime. Someone who is not restricted by conventional thinking when planning a social encounter; a person who will go all out to meet that enchanting someone he is attracted to. Confident and self-assured, this person will introduce himself and begin a conversation, then ask the right questions to get a sense of the other person's personality as well as to prolong the discussion.

In a nutshell, a social success is a person who has the will and savvy to go out and meet people of the opposite sex without fear of rejection! Are you a social success? You will be, after you read this book!

Are you making excuses for not meeting people? Do any of these sound familiar?

Have you been wondering why you are still alone? Perhaps you should take a look at your particular reasons. Do you find they seem to fall into lists of excuses, other priorities, or fears? See if any of the following comments sound like yours!

- I have so much work to do that I have no time for love . . . my career comes first . . .
- I enjoy my lifestyle, my personal habits and comfort. Why should I make an effort to go out and meet new people? I like being single!
- I always find something about my partners that annoys me . . .
- I'm not sure whether I want a relationship or not. I guess it depends on how I feel at the time . . .
- I'm afraid to lose my freedom, my independence. I'll feel caged in a relationship!
- I hesitate to commit myself in case I then meet someone I like even better . . .
- I'd rather drink beer and watch sports with my buddies.
- It's too hard to meet other singles. Singles organizations? Those clubs are for losers.

- Who can you trust these days? So many people are superficial.
- There aren't enough single men out there.
- I'm so shy about meeting people . . . I was brought up to be reserved and quiet, and I'm really not comfortable with people at social affairs or meetings where I don't know anyone.

If you recognize yourself in any of the above statements, it may be a good time to look at what you could do to make your life more exciting as well as more fulfilling.

Reading this is a good starting point. The advice you will find in these pages will help you develop the confidence you need to widen your social contacts, while supplying a multitude of strategies for meeting people. Forget excuses! That lovely person you see on your way to work or in the corner shop may be only a smile and a 'hello' away from becoming your dream lover!

Do you feel that you have other, more 'pressing priorities' than meeting people?

There are singles who insist they have urgent matters more important than meeting people and finding a possible love partner. Of course, you realize that these 'other priorities' are only disguised excuses?

Some people think they must lose weight . . . or earn more money . . . or move to a nicer neighbourhood, flat or house . . . or get a promotion . . . or start their own business . . . or who knows? before they can meet the right person. For them, the perfect situation – in all respects – must exist before they can even begin looking for their ideal partner! Acquiring a particular social status . . . a new car . . . a house straight out of *House and Garden* . . . a seaside resort or quaint weekend getaway chalet . . . All this must pre-date a date with the love of their life! They forget that the right person is ideal because she will accept them for what they are, the way they are. A fairy-tale lifestyle doesn't guarantee a magical love. People with this attitude always find something missing . . . life is never quite right.

Achieving your dreams and goals with someone special is more satisfying and a lot more fun than doing it alone!

You want love, but not right now? Ask yourself this question: 'If I meet the right person, when will I be ready for a serious relationship?' Be honest with yourself when you choose an answer!

- In a year . . . after I receive my degree.
- In two years . . . after I build my mountain home.
- In four years . . . when my kids are grown!
- In a few years . . . after I have sown my wild oats!
- *Never!* I want to keep my independence, my freedom, and the power to make my own choices for the rest of my life!

Should you find that you genuinely want to achieve 'greater things' before becoming involved and possibly settling down with a person, go ahead and follow your ambitions. But when your ideal partner comes along, you may find yourself happily exchanging your 'excuses' for a strong, loving relationship!

Keep a budget just for meeting people.
If you want to meet new people, you have to go out! Of course you want to be magnetically attractive, and that means looking your best. You certainly won't look appealing with greasy hair and a torn shirt! A budget will help you determine how much money you will have to set aside for your clothes, toiletries and all the other details you need to feel attractive. In addition to looking good, you should set up a budget for entertainment: dinner in a nice restaurant, drinks, entertaining at home, going to the theatre, etc. How much money can you afford for these activities? Plan carefully: it's better to be in the black at the end of the month and still be able to meet someone new, than dateless and in the red!

Are you looking in all the right places?

People have a tendency to go to places where they feel comfortable. Sometimes men like to go to sports events or other social gatherings where they can talk 'man-talk' without women around, while some women like afternoon get-togethers with other women, or going shopping with close friends, or spending their evenings with a group of women friends. If you're looking to meet someone of the opposite sex, this is not the way to go about it!

If you want to meet men, why not take a course in auto repair? You'll have men flocking around you in no time! Take judo, kung fu or karate lessons; be adventurous and go parachuting, flying, water-skiing, scuba-diving or mountain climbing! Or, if you're looking for the right woman, why not try a cooking class, or instruction in massage, flower arranging, interior decorating, sewing, or aerobic dancing? You might discover a new talent or a whole new career – *plus* a lovely new someone!

Of course, you want to choose activities according to your interests, not to join any old class in the hope of meeting a member of the opposite sex. Strive to enjoy yourself . . . expand your horizons! If you are having fun, people around you will notice and will want to have fun with you!

Take the first step in an encounter.

Be daring! Take a chance. Go up to that attractive stranger and start a conversation. Times have changed. The 'social graces' have taken a giant leap forward: women no longer sit back waiting for their Prince Charming . . . and men are becoming more direct. In these more permissive nineties, you can approach someone you find attractive! Too shy? Then disguise your advances: ask for the time . . . or for directions. If you know someone is an expert on sound systems, ask him/her to help you choose one. Instant contact! – *Plus* the opportunity to get to know that person without the pressure of a real date!

If you don't take that first step you may never have another chance to meet that person you find so attractive, and he might have been your ideal partner! Nothing ventured, nothing gained: take the dare and meet people!

When you're 85 years old, thinking back on your life, you will be glad that you took chances instead of crying over missed opportunities.

Yes, that first step *is* a giant step – yet it could change your life. Take a deep breath, reach for the stars and make that first contact! Whether you have a negative or a positive reaction, the important thing is to persevere, to continue to 'play the game'! The more interpersonal contacts you initiate, the better chance you have of meeting the love of your life!

Set a time frame for meeting potential love partners.
Aim to meet one new person a week for a period of one year. Meeting this goal will certainly increase your chances of finding your ideal partner. Variety is supposedly the spice of life: it is definitely what you need to make comparisons! Make sure you list five to ten of your essential criteria in choosing a love partner, and compare each person you meet to this list. Remember, you can compromise on the qualities you hope for, but not on 'essential' criteria! Keep your senses sharp and your eyes wide open. Be a love detective!

For example, suppose you are going to buy a new car in six months or so. You begin your research well in advance of the actual purchase by visiting several showrooms in order to make the best choice. You look at different models, study the facts about several makes, compare prices – in other words, you take your time in order to take a good look at all the possibilities offered to you. Naturally you would not choose a car only for its appearance or its terrific hub caps or smooth ride! You take into consideration the performance levels, the length of the guarantee, etc. – and the size of the down-payment!

Obviously, when choosing a love partner, taking your time is of far more importance than when choosing a car – particularly when looking for a relationship that will last a lifetime! Certainly you should take all the time you need – and then some!

One last bit of advice. Put your priorities in the proper order: having a marvellous love partner is certainly far ahead of owning a terrific car!

Be 'visible'! If you want to succeed in meeting the person of your dreams, you *must* be seen and heard – out there, in the real world!
Get out of the house! How on earth are you going to meet new people if you stay home all the time? It is truly amazing how many intelligent, charming people stay home on Saturday nights with a frozen dinner, popcorn and the television for company! There is no such thing as 'singles radar'! People driving past your house are not going to know there is a 'single' person inside looking for a date! So make the effort to get up and go out: set your VCR to record those programmes you feel that you just can't miss. Meeting people is much more exciting than watching TV!

As you go about your daily tasks, keep your eyes open!
Look around you wherever you may be! When you're out shopping and you happen to spot an alluring stranger, do something to attract his/her attention! Drop your packages . . . ask for directions . . . be impulsive and creative . . . just meet him/her! No matter what your activities may be, notice the people around you. Life will be much more interesting when you focus on others. You will find that everyday, unremarkable places are perfect for meeting remarkable people – maybe even the right partner for you!

Change your routine. Are you in the habit of going to the market every Saturday? Try a Thursday night: you'll see a sea of new faces! Launderette on Tuesdays? Sunday might be a better bet! If it's difficult to change the day in your busy schedule of things to do, change the time of day! Go to the gym on Tuesdays at 4 p.m. instead of noon . . . you'll see members you never knew existed! Go to places where you can encounter as many new people as possible . . . the bus stop . . . the underground . . . the newsagent's!

Make a game of your 'people search'. List the love candidates you have noticed. For example, for three weeks you have been going to the bank on Fridays at four instead of your usual Thursday. You've seen this lovely woman walk in at precisely four o'clock. And who is that handsome man who rides the same bus as you every morning? Make a list of what attracts you, then use the strategies in this book to help you approach those people who fit the description. Once you make contact, you will have more intimate details to add to your list! Take that first step . . . go out, meet new people and enjoy getting acquainted!

Carry or wear a conversation piece.

Wear something that will make you stand out – a brightly coloured shirt or blouse, or an unusual piece of jewellery. Or carry a provocative book – like this one! It's bound to attract the attention . . . of singles!

The idea is to make yourself highly visible. The object in question should encourage curiosity and inspire conversation. 'I see you're reading *A Million and One Love Strategies* . . . I've heard it sizzles!' Just imagine the discussions you can initiate!

Be inventive. Wear an amulet around your neck. When asked about it, you have a chance to talk about the meaning of amulets . . . and perhaps go a step further and tell the other person what she should carry to attract beautiful people the way you just did!

Another way to be visible is somewhat complicated, but it really works! Set up a telescope in a public park. Who can resist wanting to take a look when you have obviously gone to some trouble to choose the best location to see – who knows? – undoubtedly, something fascinating!

A single person must make him/herself stand out in the crowd. Be creative: wear clothes with whimsical designs and bold colours. Men could sport a wild tie with matching braces. Try a boldly painted scarf or wear an amusing T-shirt . . .

people are sure to stop and ask where you bought it! When they do, start up a conversation: offer to get them the same piece of jewellery, scarf, etc.: 'My friend makes costume jewellery . . . Would you like me to get you one like it?' Seize every opportunity to make contact – plus conversation – with new people!

You're playing the 'notice me' game, so why not sit in a pub or a café or even a park reading or carrying an outstanding book or pamphlet that will pique the curiosity of an onlooker? It might be something controversial, or something exciting like a travel brochure for exotic holidays!

And what is more natural than reading a book while basking in the sun on a beach? But don't be a bookworm . . . you'll never meet anyone with your nose buried in a book! Carry a love story with a seductive cover – and read it casually, while taking a quick look around to see if anyone interesting is watching you. If there is . . . flash him/her a sensuous smile!

Make sure your conversation piece is large enough to be seen across the room by that intriguing person who has just looked your way – again!

Be different! For singles, originality is vitally important. Attract people with your outrageous apparel, your unusual umbrella, or quirky watch! Be imaginative in your dress and manner. Use your creativity to develop an image that is uniquely you: show the world what a special person you are!

Before getting involved in a relationship, make sure that you are psychologically, emotionally and financially independent.
Be your own person. Don't search for someone to be your meal ticket or your reason for living . . . live for yourself! Think of a love partner as dessert . . . the icing on the cake . . . an already substantial cake that can stand deliciously alone! You have your own life. A loving partner is there to share the joys and to ease the sorrows. As an independent, self-sufficient person, you will be more likely to cultivate a satisfying love relationship – one of respect and happiness. You won't have a need to blame your

partner for the failures in your life . . . or anyone for your successes! Your achievements will enhance the strengths of your relationship and enrich your mutual love life!

A confident, self-reliant person will be better able to choose a suitable partner without compromising. Thank goodness we live in the nineties when the implications of the expression 'better half' have literally become obsolete!

Are you afraid of rejection?

Each of us has, at one time or another, faced rejection. Not being chosen for the lead in a school play, being left out of games by playmates, or not being invited to a special party are all familiar examples. When these momentarily hurtful experiences can be outweighed by other, good happenings, the pain of the situation passes harmlessly. When, however, a person's general sense of self-worth is poor, even minor rejections become major episodes of self-recrimination and feelings of sadness and anger. Most damaging of all, these episodes can lead to a fear of rejection.

Since fear of rejection is based on negative thinking and the painful experiences of the past, it can be overcome by mentally correcting the illogical line of thought that begins with this interior dialogue: 'I am not a worthwhile person and so I am going to meet with rejection all my life.'

Such negative thoughts transform themselves into stress, anguish and anxieties, which is all the more regrettable because there is no real basis for the negativity.

Just because someone said 'no' to you is no reason to feel that it was your fault. A rejection certainly does not mean you are a reject. The decision probably had nothing to do with you! Perhaps this person refused to take you somewhere simply because he did not have enough money. Maybe he had recently broken up with someone and wasn't ready to start dating again. It is possible you just didn't fit the selection criteria, and you could certainly not have known that beforehand!

Furthermore, there are people who don't meet your selection criteria and yet you know they are perfectly nice people – they just don't interest *you*! So you see, there are many reasons why someone might say 'no' to you. It is important not to feel that you have to re-evaluate yourself every time someone does say 'no'. To feel rejected does not indicate that you are worthless or a social misfit!

But what about that anxiety engulfing you . . . turning your stomach? It stems from fear of rejection and of being hurt. When you are rejected, you feel devalued, diminished. Every time you give in to this feeling, you are allowing a stranger to decide whether you are a winner or a loser. Tell yourself that that privilege is reserved for you and only you!

So before you become involved with someone, make sure that you have these feelings well in hand. Be absolutely positive that you consider yourself a valuable person, no matter what anyone said about you or how anyone made you feel.

So that you can better understand the 'rejection phenomenon,' let's use a 'palatable' analogy!
Suppose you are a chocolate cake . . . part of a grand buffet that offers a variety of dishes . . . salads, potatoes, quiche, boeuf bourgignon, paté de fois gras, peach pie, Bavarian cream dessert, hazelnut torte, fruit and more.

The first eleven people serve themselves huge slices of peach pie. Did they overlook the chocolate cake, thinking it wasn't any good? Of course not: the pie lovers simply preferred peach pie to chocolate cake!

The buffet represents society. Each dish can be compared to an individual. Each person has her own particular flavours that please the tastes of some while leaving others flat!

The twelfth person at the buffet chose an enormous piece of chocolate cake! Was this because the chocolate cake wasn't good before, but has now suddenly become too deliciously enticing to pass up? No! It was chosen because it pleased that person's tastebuds. Just as someone will choose you according to her personal likes and dislikes, you, too, have specific tastes! So when someone overlooks or rejects you, it has absolutely nothing to do with your worth as a person!

If you let your anxiety overwhelm you, you are encouraging rejection. Don't think that because one person rejected you, everyone else will do the same. Those who don't appreciate what you have to offer can only influence your self-esteem *if you let them*!

Don't make the mistake of saying, 'How can such a terrific person be attracted to me?' You are placing the other person on a pedestal and diminishing yourself. People are drawn to you because they recognize some aspect of your personality that charms them. Whether you are blond, blue-eyed, dark-haired, brown-eyed, short, tall, fat or thin, these concepts can't categorize you, for it is impossible to define what attracts different people. To each his own! How else can you explain someone's preference for peach pie over chocolate cake? It is simply a matter of personal taste!

Say 'hello' to as many people as you can . . . don't be afraid to greet everyone you run into!
When you pass someone on the street, smile and say 'Hi, how are you?' It's a simple enough greeting, but it will help you to become more open and friendly with people in general. Furthermore, those persons who see you regularly will start to feel comfortable with you and end up being friendly in return.

Do you often enter a full lift? What an opportunity to meet people and to project a welcoming personality! Try saying 'Good Morning!' with a lilt to your voice and a smile on your face. You'll undoubtedly be pleased with the response once people get over the shock of having someone being pleasant to them first thing in the morning!

According to statistics, the average person crosses the paths of 100 people a day. So why are you alone? Because most people go about their business anonymously . . . without caring about their fellow human beings. Why not take the first step: greet people . . . be friendly . . . get people's attention by being cordial!

Dare to be humorous! People will remember you if you make them laugh! Think of the world as your oyster and a smile as the grain of sand that will develop into a pearl. Smile at everyone: your goodwill will be returned to you as pearls of friendship . . .

Try not to restrict yourself to one category of people – one age group or sex. Talk to, nod and smile at everyone – even to grandmothers – they might just have a granddaughter or grandson to introduce you to!

By the same token, don't limit your attention to people who 'look' nice or friendly . . . you can't judge a book by its cover! You may be pleasantly surprised to discover that the one person you thought preoccupied and cranky is really very witty, once you get to know him.

Why greet everyone? It will give you confidence. And the next time you see someone who really attracts you, you will be confident enough to take the first step . . . and who knows? He might just be your ideal partner. You can make a game of saying 'hello' to as many people as possible when you are out with friends: the person who greets the most people wins . . . in more ways than one!

Develop your conversational skills by chatting with many people.
Have you ever met someone you are so smitten with that you freeze-up . . . stutter . . . and splutter nonsensically, practically paralysed and speechless with anxiety? It happens to the best of us and this is all the more reason to talk to people of all ages no matter what their sex or physical appearance. Becoming a great conversationalist is as simple as talking with as many people as you possibly can. Become a one person talk-a-thon: chat up a storm!

Remember that strangers are only strangers until you talk to them! All of your friends were once strangers, right? So even if you are sometimes unsure of approaching someone, make the effort . . . she may end up becoming your best friend . . . or, better still, your dream lover!

Conquer your fear! Say 'hello' to everyone . . . without thinking 'Here is my new love interest!' Concentrate on a friendly image: smile brightly and compliment people about their apparel . . . or ask where they found a particular item they may be carrying. Be inventive and open to people . . . the rest will follow! Don't be shy or show them you are insecure: focus on having a nice chat. Assume they are interested in hearing what you have to say and in spending a few minutes with you.

Be enthusiastic and you will capture the other person's attention. Project your enthusiasm through your words, your voice, your gestures, your eyes. On a subconscious level your tone and attitude are saying: 'I am thrilled to be talking with you, I have been dying to meet you, you are just the person I want to be with!' – all thoughts you can't verbalize at this point, having just met!

Treat the person you are talking to as a rare jewel. Make her feel as though you have never treated or talked to anyone the way you are treating and talking to her. Make her feel good with a compliment or two. Send her 'feeling waves' with your conversation and gestures . . . waves of either warmth or excitement or mystery!

Talk to be remembered. Don't just chatter away for the sake of talking. Choose dramatic words and phrases, delivered in your own inimitable style. Let the force of your presence make conversational encounters memorable. Of course you have to consider where you are having this great talk: you wouldn't want to tell funny stories at a serious gathering – such as a wake – or satirize a political debate at a wedding!

Be a good listener. The best conversationalists know when to listen!
On the other hand, it is not wise to keep quiet and let the other person do all the talking, either. Strive for a comfortable balance by concentrating on what the other person is saying. You will be able to respond in a way that keeps the conversation going, *plus* you'll pick up feelings and intentions hidden in the other person's words and gestures.

You can motivate people to open up and get personal by doing just that yourself. Casually drop a few intimate details and comments that will cause the other person to divulge information. Phrases to try are: 'Is your wife with you tonight? . . . or 'I'd love to meet your wife and get her viewpoint on that!' If the person is not married, he will certainly correct you at once! *Voilà!* You've just found out his marital status without directly asking the question . . . wasn't that easy?

The art of conversation can only be mastered through practice. Take the time and opportunity to talk with as many people as you can get to listen to you. In a short time, you'll be talking up a storm and captivating the hearts of countless numbers of people!

Encourage brief conversational encounters to build up your courage and skills.
Does carrying on a conversation seem overwhelming? Strive for brief interludes: facing something you think is going to be unpleasant can be tolerated when you know it will be over quickly. If you are nervous about meeting people, don't think of long encounters: you aren't going to spend a whole evening with the person . . . or a whole lifetime! Be cool, nonchalant. Set a time limit before you go up to someone, and then say, 'We haven't been introduced, but may I have ten minutes of your time?' You have just broken the ice by specifying that you will not bother her for too long. You've just made yourself feel better *and* assured the other person that you will not corner her for hours! That tactic should earn you a very pleasant reception! You don't have to set a stop-watch, but when approximately ten minutes are up, politely excuse yourself by saying something like, 'It was nice talking to you . . . see you later!' and be on your way. If your appealing stranger is indifferent to you, you will have left with dignity. If she is attracted to you, you will have created an aura of mystery!

Sue is a skilled conversationalist, but at a party she wants to maximize her contacts. She manages this by setting everyone up for a 'brief encounter.' Her repartee goes something like: 'Hi, I'm Sue, can I talk with you for a few minutes?' When she judges the time to be up, she thanks the person: 'It was nice chatting with you. Perhaps we'll have a chance to talk more later on!' and she's off to the next person! A social butterfly? Perhaps, but an effective user of the brief encounter!

Learn the art of making 'small talk'.
Good conversationalists can talk about everything and nothing in particular. In other words, they always find something to say! Your first conversation with a stranger should be light: forget philosophical musings on how the world began or the metaphysical implications of the Seven Wonders of the World. Subjects like the weather are safe – but terribly boring. Talk about something amusing you've read – perhaps a tip from this book! – or mention the latest art exhibit . . . what's going on in the local singles' scene . . . things of general interest. Relax and be your charming, interesting self!

There is at least one thing you have in common with the person you meet for the first time – the place! If you meet someone at a party, you can talk about the house, the food being served or the neighbourhood: 'I've never been to this part of town before . . . it's very pretty!' At a university you can talk about your courses . . . at the library inquire about books. Every place has a multitude of subjects to discuss. You can even talk about the décor: 'Did you notice the woodwork in this place? Magnificent!' Just make small talk to break the ice, and before you know it you'll be right in the middle of a spirited discussion!

Discover the art of asking the right questions!
As important as it is to initiate a conversation, it is equally important to keep it going. One way of doing this is by asking questions – the *right* questions! Those the other person has to answer in full sentences, not just with a 'yes' or a 'no'. Instead of saying, 'Did you see the film, *The Godfather*?', try 'What did you think about the film, *The Godfather*?'

Listen carefully to answers: they will tell you a lot about the other person. The right questions will help you better to understand the other person's true feelings. Good questions require personalized responses involving an individual's own point of view. Asking the right questions is like solving a mystery – the mystique of a personality.

How to approach someone who is talking to others.
You've spotted someone you want to talk to, but he is already deep in conversation with others. Walk over to them and stand about five feet away. Look straight at the person you want to speak with. Smile at him when he notices you, but don't interrupt. If the conversation is too involved, walk away for a while and come back later. Keep an eye on the little group from afar. If, on the other hand, the conversation is light, look for an opening. Make sure you address your comment to the one you admire . . . use your eyes to direct your intentions. Once you have met the one who enticed you, you can bring the other people back into the conversation . . . unless of course they left you and the charming stranger alone together!

Be diverse: collect trivia and learn about different subjects.
You can talk about lots of interesting facts if you know a little about many different subjects. Pick up interesting tidbits by reading popular magazines such as *Reader's Digest*, *Private Eye*, or *Paris Match*. You can use these eye-opening facts in conversation to impress that interesting person you have just met. There's no need to collect facts that will change the world . . . trivia will do: – great ice-breakers at a party!

Remember to research subjects that will be interesting to the people you want to get interested. Pick up a sports or car magazine, or a copy of *Vogue*, *Vanity Fair*, or *Cosmopolitan*. Imagine you're at a party and you hear a group of women talking about fashion . . . if you've just read a leading woman's magazine, you can easily join in the discussion. No doubt these women will be impressed!

Keeping abreast of current events is always impressive. It says: 'I'm a person with my fingers on the pulse of the world . . . I'm interested and interesting!' Don't forget to read the sports section of the newspaper – at least to find out who won last week's football match! Remember, too, that the woman of the nineties has changed. She works outside the home and is interested in more than sewing and cooking . . . so read up on environmental issues, legal cases, trends in the stock-market, etc . . . be as interesting as she is!

Be well informed!
If you can't take the time to read the newspaper end to end, at least read the headlines every day. Listen to news reports on the radio or on television. Get a general sense of what is happening in your town . . . in the country . . . in the world! The point is not to appear ignorant of current affairs . . . after all, you don't want to seem like you're from another planet!

Build a network of friends – of different ages and sexes.
Friends are there for you when you need them. They won't be insulted if you use them to fill dateless times: friends enjoy the pleasure of your company. Besides, you can have a lot of fun going out with them, which gives you visibility among new people in a friendly, carefree atmosphere. The more close companions you have, the more chances you have to be a part of different types of activities . . . all of which leads to more people in your network!

But how do you build a network? You can start with your school friends, your colleagues, cousins, brothers, sisters . . . don't forget the friends of your cousins, sisters, brothers, and colleagues! Make a habit of getting the telephone number and address of people you meet on trips, acquaintances you meet at a friend's house . . . and use them . . . call them or write to them on a regular basis . . . visit them when you are in their town, entertain them when they are in your neighbourhood.

This way you will build a solid foundation of friends and contacts. One of them may introduce you to an absolutely fabulous new love!

Everyday situations can also help you to meet new people. Think of the many times you have needed assistance or advice and a friend has offered: 'Give me your phone number, and I will ring you back with the name and address of the person who can help you.'

Keep adding to your network of friends. It is inevitable that you will lose track of some people, so it is important continually to add new ones to your current list. Think of the process as if it were like banking: try to deposit new addresses and phone numbers regularly . . . this method could reap unexpected dividends – like the *right one* for you!

When you go out for an evening, make having fun a priority!

Go out with a positive attitude and with the intention of having fun. If you don't see anyone who attracts you immediately, don't write off the entire evening: you can still have fun just being around other people and doing something other than sitting at home. Sure, meeting someone would be a bonus, but don't feel slighted if that doesn't happen. Enjoy these moments with friends and have a good time!

If one of your friends wants to set you up with a blind date, accept – but go with an open mind . . . and above all with a positive attitude! If you are determined to enjoy yourself, even if the blind date isn't what you had hoped for, you will! Be glad you are single and free to live life to its fullest. Your spirit and zest for life will give you the air of a person who is fascinating to be with. Before you know it, you will be surrounded by potential love partners!

Have an agenda in which you write the precise dates of rendezvous with yourself, for those activities that interest *you*!

Set aside specific times for activities you enjoy doing by

yourself. Don't give in to pressure and take someone else with you. If you decide to go out every Tuesday and every Saturday, for example, write it in your agenda, plan for the evenings and don't let anything keep you from your appointments with yourself! Choose an notebook for your agenda that gives you enough room to write a complete account of your activities. There are different types of notebooks available: with space to make notes by the day, week or month. A little one for your handbag or pocket is perfect for your social calendar.

Go out and do something just for you . . . something you enjoy doing! Love to walk in the woods and contemplate nature? Go window shopping? Do you long for the quiet and serenity of going fishing? Just do it! Keep an agenda of your special outings with yourself – *and stick to it*! Just as you wouldn't break a date with someone else, don't break one with yourself!

Taking care of yourself is a way of building your self-esteem. It is important to realize that before you can love someone else, you have to love and accept yourself. Conversely, if you can't stand your own company, don't expect anyone else to tolerate you! Besides, if you are out alone, doing something you enjoy, you will radiate peace and happiness – which is sure to attract very interesting people!

Find out where the 'in' meeting places are, as well as information on special events for singles!
Generally, you will find weekly or monthly publications on cultural or artistic events scheduled for different areas of your town or city. Check on the availability of courses and seminars, too! Weekend papers also provide good information on what is going on in and around the city. There's more to do out there than you think! So look in the newspapers . . . cut out the special events calender . . . pin it on your refrigerator! A free evening and nothing to do? Consult your refrigerator door! Choose an interesting event . . . you will encounter new and interesting people!

Are pubs good places to meet people?

Many people have met their present spouses at pubs, while others feel that pubs are disreputable 'pick-up' places. The fact is that you want and need to meet *only one right person!* If you worry about the clientele in general, you will never spot that special someone. All kinds of people go to pubs: including the respectable types you want to meet!

'I don't drink, so I have no business in a pub.' This is a popular misconception. Can you tell the difference between water and gin? Not likely! Today, there are many different types of pubs ranging from a basic neighbourhood tavern to elegant wine bars with décor to match. You probably already know which are the 'trendy' pubs in your area, where all of the 'socially-wise' people gather. There is usually a cover charge in these places and the dress code is strictly *elegant*!

There are also hotel bars where you are likely to meet out-of-towners or people commuting on business. Beware: you are more likely to meet a married person in these pubs! Other pubs catering to commuters are usually situated in railway stations or near public transportation – often in the middle of a city's business district. The majority of their clientele are the relaxing-after-work crowd. If you are smitten by a fellow commuter over cocktails, at least you don't have to drive home!

Neighbourhood pubs are often small, casual and friendly. Special bar stools or tables are sometimes reserved for local customers. You are more likely to encounter someone you've seen around the neighbourhood, so these may well be opportune spots to get acquainted with someone you've met and admired. Usually a wide variety of people come and go in these pubs, making them a good place to meet interesting people.

Then there are those quaint little places with lots of hanging plants and flowers. Many kinds of people are attracted to these pubs, making them a great place for you to frequent!

Another major category, 'singles' pubs, cater specifically to the 'unattached-but-looking' relationship-seekers. Be fore-warned: the competition is generally fierce and the pressure to be 'matched' with someone – even for the evening – may be overwhelming! Choose the pub – or pubs – you want to go to according to your level of self-confidence as well as to the type of crowd you expect to encounter.

Plan on a fun evening! Dress up and make a grand entrance . . . you're sure to dazzle quite a few people with this positive attitude!

All in all, pubs are not bad places to meet people: it all depends on your perspective. You'll find plenty of variety in pubs to make your quest for an ideal mate a spicy affair. Pubs offer a relaxed atmosphere for practising your social skills. You don't have to drink hard liquor: soft drinks are also available, you just have to pay more for them – and for the ambience!

A word of warning: pubs are also frequented by alcoholics. When you meet people, notice how much they are drinking and how it affects them. You certainly don't want to become involved with anyone who has a drinking problem.

Take a day and explore your city as though you were on holiday.
When you are on holiday, you are eager to discover new places and you aren't afraid to go alone. And yet in your own city you don't really like the idea. You tend to show a lot more courage – particularly about meeting new people – when you are away on holiday than you do when faced with your own city. Logically, it is much more practical to meet someone from your area whom you could go out with regularly.

And what happens with possible love interests you meet while on holiday? When you become attached to a person who lives in a far-away city, your romance has to be conducted 'long-distance'. Loneliness is a real threat to this romance in spite of the best intentions!

What better reason for taking a 'holiday' in your own city than having the same chance of meeting someone? Particularly when you haven't far to go to see them again!

Go out by yourself!
Choose a place near home for your first time out alone. You

needn't go for the whole evening, but spend a little time there, at least. In the beginning, particularly for the first half-hour, you will find being alone a little difficult. You will no doubt say to yourself, 'Why did I come here?' and later, 'I am not dressed right for this place!' Take a deep breath and relax. Try to look as if you were enjoying yourself. Perhaps you will meet someone with whom you will spend a pleasant evening – someone new you can add to your group of friends!

Change your 'night out on the town' habits: you haven't always got to go with someone. Women have a tendency to go out in groups or with a girlfriend. This can intimidate men because they will not approach a group of women chatting at a table. Men feel awkward joining the conversation. If a man is attracted to one of the women in the group, he will be reluctant to approach her. So, if you insist on going out with the girls, make sure that you circulate alone throughout the evening. Plan to meet your friends in the Ladies' at a particular time to decide whether you will leave together or not . . . maybe you got lucky and found an interesting someone to have a nightcap with!

Make a list of the places where you feel at ease.
You will feel more comfortable going out alone if you select a few spots from your favourite list of restaurants, pubs, discos and clubs. After going to these places a few times you will get to know the staff . . . the maître d'hôtel will greet you . . . the waiters will call you by your first name . . . you will feel at ease in a familiar atmosphere where you can relax . . . and be comfortable meeting new people.

One major advantage to becoming an *habitué* of a place is that the staff and management will feel they know you well enough to introduce you to other 'regulars'. Another advantage might be that the terrific person you always notice on Thursday nights will strike up a conversation . . . at least he shares your choice of an interesting place to spend some leisure time.

Patronize the businesses in your neighbourhood . . . have breakfast at that quaint little café down the street . . . buy your newspapers and magazines from the same newsagent's every week. Before long you will have a new network of people who will greet you with a smile, ask how things are going for you, etc . . . and before you know it, they are telling you about this nephew . . . or niece . . . or cousin of theirs you simply *must* meet!

Make a list of the sports that you excel in or that interest you.
Do you play tennis? Volleyball? Do you swim? Join a sports club or association: you'll meet a lot of people who share your interests! You could even start your own group or club with an original slant: a skiing club just for singles, perhaps . . . or a 'singles only' cycling team!

Carry your business cards at all times!
You haven't a business card? Have some printed immediately! Business cards are absolutely crucial – they are indispensable in planning many of the most successful love strategies! You can have very nice business cards printed in small quantities at reasonable rates. In some places you can even get them in minutes from a coin-operated machine! These automated card outlets have a rather limited range of designs compared to commercial print shops, but for a small number of business or personal cards, they are very convenient and inexpensive.

You can even create a business to put on the cards. For a small fee, you can register a business at the proper local government office. Why not choose something really attractive to singles: like an errand service for singles, pet care for singles, cooking for bachelors . . . the possibilities are endless!

What is the most common question asked when you first meet someone? Usually it is 'What type of work do you do?' A perfect opportunity to present your card! Impressive! Whether the card lists your own business or not, the fact that you have one shows stability. Presenting a crisp business card from a lovely card-case is much more refined than scribbling your telephone number on a serviette!

Business cards are like a safety net. You are giving a stranger your business number instead of your home number – which is a very good idea at this stage of the game, as after all you don't really know this person. It also gives you the opportunity to write down your home number, if you so choose, on the back of the card – an action that clearly states: 'I'm single! You may phone me at home!' And by the same token, when you ask someone for her card, you are clearly stating: 'Don't worry, I'm not prying into your private life. I'll be in touch during your day at work, not ringing you up in the middle of the night!'

When you introduce yourself, always give your business card! By offering your business card and suggesting that the person gives you a ring, you will show that you are polite enough to let that person decide if further contact would be pleasant. People will be *so* intrigued!

If someone gives you a business card, you might want to verify the home number by ringing before agreeing to anything more involved . . . just as a precaution. If a voice you don't recognize answers and you have the nerve to go on, you could say that you are ringing for a business survey and have some market research questions to ask. You can invent from there, but the object is to find out whether the person in question is really single!

Get in the habit of collecting business cards: you can buy attractive, practical booklets for your collection. Even though you may be involved with someone presently, accept the cards offered to you. Who knows? It is possible that in the coming months you might find yourself free again, and among those unassuming little cards you may well find a terrific friend! A business card gives you the chance to get back in touch with likely love prospects! Keep collecting!

Personal calling cards are also suitable.
Even if you have a business card, a supply of personal cards listing your full name, home address and phone number are

also suitable – particularly for those occasions when you are sure you want the recipient to be considered a part of your 'inner circle' of friends.

Personal cards can also have catchy phrases or be adorned with astrological symbols or lovely flowered borders: it's all up to you as to what image you want to present.

Establish your credibility as soon as possible. Don't be secretive; cultivate an honest, open image.
Don't hesitate to volunteer certain details about yourself. When the other person knows a bit of your background, she will be more likely to divulge confidences of her own.

This doesn't mean you have to go into lurid details of your Aunt Sarah's fifth divorce. Make light comments such as, 'I finally graduated from university last spring, and now I'm working in a law office as a researcher and I love it!' or 'All four of my brothers have straight brown hair: I had to be the one with the frizzies!'

Drop hints that you are single.
In the course of conversation, subtly mention that you are single. For example, if you live alone you can say: 'I love to cook, but when I get home from work I haven't the incentive to cook just for me.' Or: 'I prepare all my dinners for the week on Saturday and freeze *individual* portions'. Now she knows there is no one special in your life!

You could also slip references into your conversation about the small size of your flat – just right for one person – or how you enjoyed decorating it to suit your individual taste. Furthermore, the fact that you didn't hesitate to give your home telephone number signals beyond a shadow of a doubt that you are not currently sharing your life with anyone!

Don't wear confusing rings on your fingers!
Are you wearing a ring on the finger that signifies a married person? Or someone who is engaged? Be careful which finger you choose for a favourite circlet! You don't want to discourage or misinform possible love interests!

Act natural.
Don't try to be 'superman' or 'superwoman' or give the impression that you can do everything well. Be natural: let others see that you are a normal human being with strengths and weaknesses, good qualities and faults – traits that make you unique and interesting! You know the old saying, nobody's perfect! So just be yourself . . . a little silly . . . a little serious . . . a little shy . . . very human!

Act 'desirable'.
In order to project the image of a 'desirable' person, above all you have to feel you are desirable! It's a state of mind. Being desirable does not necessarily have sexual connotations; basically, it is a feeling you have about yourself, a sense of confidence that you are pleased with yourself and can therefore be pleasing to others. You can bolster this self-image by pampering yourself with simple things like relaxing in a bubble bath, or sipping a hot cup of fragrant tea while reading a favourite book or magazine.

Indulging in 'little niceties' like wearing luxuriously comfortable clothing, having your hair done in a new way, or using beautifully scented soaps will give you a renewed sense of self. Regular physical exercise will condition and help maintain your sleek, energetic body. Any and all of these activities will make you feel wonderful – and deserving of a wonderful 'someone' in your life!

Remember, you are unique; you have qualities that others do not have . . . there is only one you! If you believe firmly that you are desirable, you will radiate confidence and comehitherness! If you need a little nudge, pin notes up around the house that say: 'I am a wonderful, loving person. I deserve respect and happiness.' Stick this memo-to-me on your bathroom mirror and repeat it every day while brushing your teeth! Place other self-affirming notes all over the house: on your phone, under your pillow, on the refrigerator! Before you know it, you will feel terrific, invincible . . . desirable!

Do things that make you feel good: read a great book, watch your favourite film, take a sauna, buy yourself something frivolous! Make yourself feel special! But beware, you are only human . . . don't expect to feel desirable 24 hours a day, 365 days a year! Seize the moments when you can . . . do things that make you feel special, and repeat them often. Make a list of your qualities and read it to yourself often. Be kind to yourself . . . and you will attract a kind-to-you partner!

Project the image of a fun-loving, happy person.
Whom do you prefer to be with . . . a fun-loving, happy-go-lucky person, or someone who is constantly complaining about his life? No contest! Everyone loves an amusing, entertaining and cheerful person. So be one yourself! Show your sense of humour – laugh at yourself and the world will laugh with you!

Project the image of a well-rounded person who has an interesting life.
How can you be interesting if you spend all of your time at home in front of the television set? That is no way to meet people! You want people to think of you as an interesting, active person . . . so become one. Go out with friends . . . make an effort to socialize at work and at play. Keep abreast of current affairs, of new films, of special events!

If you act as though you are satisfied with your life and with yourself, people will flock to you. If you act despondent, people will ignore you. Think about it: which type of person would you rather spend your time with?

Let things happen in their due course. If you try to rush or force events, you will lose in the end. A true story that demonstrates this fact goes as follows: a woman, who was old enough to know better, blurted out on her first date with an eligible young man that she was 39 years old and had a very great desire to get married soon! 'I want a family! My biological clock is ticking away . . . I have no time to lose! If you don't want a wife and family, then we should say good-bye right now!'

Maybe her date did want the same things, but certainly not with her! Not when she delivered an ultimatum on their first date! The poor woman might have had all she was looking for so desperately, if she had only shown a little patience and let the relationship develop at its own pace!

A far better way to begin a serious relationship is to pretend that you are not looking for the love of your life. Be nonchalant, not anxious! People who desperately seek a love partner usually end up being used by the very people they attract. So, just relax . . . act cool and debonair. If your weekend date turns out to be your ideal partner – fine! If not, you'll have had a good time! And that is what enjoying life is all about: welcoming the gift of every moment of happiness!

Ask your friends and acquaintances to introduce you to someone they think you will get along with.
Your friends and colleagues know you, they know your personality, and they are in an excellent position to introduce you to compatible people. Friends are probably surprised to hear that such a fun-loving, interesting person as you needs a date! Let them know that you are always ready to meet new people . . . that you love to socialize! Without making a pest of yourself, remind them delicately every once in while . . . they may have just met someone who is absolutely perfect for you! – perhaps a new colleague . . . or a friend who has recently become single!

John met the woman of his dreams after a weekend alone. He went into the office on Monday morning and said to his friends as they stood around his desk, 'I had a great weekend. I went sailing on Saturday, then on Sunday I saw this great film. But . . . I don't know, there was something missing . . . I realized that I was doing all that great stuff alone! It would have been so much nicer if I had had someone to share it with. Do any of you have any prospects for me?' You can do what John did: ask your friends, colleagues, parents, cousins – everyone you know – if they know any interesting singles you could meet. And keep checking every few months: they may not know anyone at the moment, but circumstances do change, and someone they know may be divorced or widowed or have just moved in next door or may suddenly be alone again!

Your eccentric aunt rings you one day and says she has the perfect partner for you . . . don't refuse . . . seize the opportunity. Go out on the blind date with a positive attitude. Don't expect to meet the person of your dreams: after all, your aunt may not have the same idea of perfection as you! Don't expect anything – just go out with the intention of having a good time . . . you never know what can happen!

Offer a cash prize to the person who finds you a love partner.
This idea came from a rich American who offered a thousand dollars to the person who would find his future wife for him! Sure enough, someone did: he is still married! It is an outrageous idea, but it worked for him! Why don't you try being that creative? If your bank account can't handle a thousand dollars, try offering a reward you *can* afford. Use your imagination: offer a gourmet dinner . . . or an all-expenses-paid weekend for two to some romantic resort . . . with the right luck and contacts, you might be there, too!

You may have to change some of your non-essential criteria for selecting a love partner.
Don't be so picky! You want to share a life with a real person

. . . not some paragon of all virtues! Drop your stereotyped ideas. Stop looking for someone 'perfect' and start looking for someone 'nice'. If you have been drawn to a particular type of person over the years and for some reason a relationship never developed, it may just be high time to adjust your expectations!

For example, if you have always dated high-flying businesspeople, but ended up leaving them because they devoted too much of their time to work and not enough to you, then maybe it's time you went after another type of person. Similarly, the person who dates only blondes, but never seems to have a satisfying relationship, may be well advised to date a brunette . . . or maybe even a redhead. What about the tennis fan who must have a tennis enthusiast for a date? The point here is that the broad categories of blondes, businesspeople or tennis players are not 'essential criteria' . . . they may be preferences, but they should not limit your choices.

Typecasting your love partner limits the choices available. Keep your perspective: Snow White and Prince Charming exist only in fairy tales! Realizing that you are not perfect, but certainly a perfectly desirable person, will help you to keep an open mind and an open heart. Before long, your fairy-tale partner will come charging into your life!

Identify your biggest obstacles to meeting people.
Are you shy? Have you trouble exchanging romantic glances? Do you freeze up or act like you are in another world on a date? Are you afraid to propose a second date for fear of being rejected? Have you trouble keeping up your end of a conversation? The sooner you confront your fears, the sooner you will be rid of them! Take the time to identify and work on your social weaknesses. By exchanging these problem areas for a confident, positive attitude, you will soon be looking forward to meeting people!

Get rid of your negative thoughts, complexes and fears!
Negativity is bad for you psychologically and interferes with

your relationships. When you think about it logically, your anxieties exist only in your mind. A negative attitude will influence the way you interact with people you meet, and may well keep you from taking the first steps towards meeting someone who attracts you.

Fear of rejection, fear of commitment, fear of intimacy . . . these are obstacles that you must overcome before becoming involved in a relationship. Conquering these negative fears will free you to experience a sense of renewed happiness in your social life – and that will lead to happy relationships!

A study done in the United States confirmed how a state of mind can become a bad habit that will influence our lives negatively. They placed a large fish in an aquarium – ordinarily the large fish was fed a small fish – but the scientists separated the big fish from the small fish with a glass plate. When the big fish went to eat the small fish, it banged its nose against the glass. After a while, the scientists removed the glass – only to find that the big fish did not approach the small fish for fear of smashing its nose against the glass!

You, too, may have developed fears from past experiences, but remember, your fears and complexes are only illusions that you allow yourself to believe. So why not exchange your negative attitudes for optimistic ones? Positively wonderful things are bound to happen!

Don't let rejection get you down; make your imagination your greatest ally.
If you have suffered a number of rejections recently, take a break. Take time to reaffirm your confidence in yourself. And remember not to take rejection too personally – very often a person will spurn an advance because of her own misgivings . . . it is not necessarily because she doesn't like you . . . you may simply not have been her type. You can't please everyone all of the time, but you can please yourself!

If you need to boost your spirits, think about the nice things your friends say about you. Remember an ex-beau who may have complimented you on your beauty or intelligence. Look only at the positive aspects of your life – you are in the rebuild mode! Do things to make yourself happy – buy yourself some incredibly good chocolates if you have a sweet tooth . . . buy that coat you've been wanting . . . give yourself a facial . . . go fishing . . . indulge in one of your favourite pastimes!

Your imagination is a very powerful tool. Use it to visualize your life the way you would like it to be. Every day – at least once – sit down quietly and picture in detail your ideal life. Would you like to live in the country? Imagine the countryside . . . your garden . . . the house . . . feel yourself in the scene! Of course, you won't forget to include your loved one in this exercise!

Actively pursue your positive feelings. Refrain from thinking you are not good enough to have someone worthy in your life. Don't even whisper things like, 'I can't talk to that person, she'll think I'm boring.' Never assume what others are thinking . . . you might be very surprised! Keep a positive outlook: say, 'I'm going to go and talk to that person . . . she'll like meeting me!' If you think highly of yourself, others will, too!

Make the first call!
A few days ago you met someone nice. You exchanged telephone numbers. Now you feel like talking to that person . . . so ring him! It's as simple as that! Why wait for him to phone you? After all, you are just ringing to say hello, or to ask him to a film or dinner, not to marry you!

If the person is busy or not home, don't sit around chewing your nails until he phones you back! Go on about your business, have a good time – he probably is! Never waste your life away waiting for the phone to ring, for the weather to get better, for something fun to happen: there are many interesting things to do and many, many terrific people waiting to meet you!

Be prepared for telephone calls . . . buy an answer phone.
Why miss a call because you're not home? Today's technology

provides every convenience. An answer phone is particularly useful for singles. There are a variety of models with different functions. Having a remote control so you can ring in for your messages is an interesting feature. If you live alone, you might want to invest in this little 'extra' – unless you have a cat trained to answer for you!

Another nice feature: an answer phone can also be turned on when you are home so that you can screen your calls.

It's important to leave an upbeat, unusual message on your answer phone, emphasizing: 'Your message is important to me.' But it is equally, and perhaps even more, important to leave an appealing message on someone else's machine. Remember, you are registering your emotions on a person's tape. Your voice echoes how you are feeling at that very moment: are you sad the person is not home? Are you surprised? Your voice will reveal these emotions!

One way to create a good impression is to prepare yourself to leave a message. Think about why you are ringing: to find out how the person is? How her day went? How work is? Did you phone to ask for a date? To invite her to a party? To ask a favour? Identify the intention of your call, then add the right words! But remember, your voice is the key! It must be poised . . . it is like a melody suspended in time! . . . make it alive with the passionate timbre of a violin or the sweet notes of a harp!

When you ring someone, always be ready to leave a message on an answer phone.
Today, many people are equipped with an answer phone. So be prepared to leave a message or ring off. Whatever you do, don't sputter incomprehensible nonsense! Write your message down beforehand if you must . . . and don't forget to leave your name and phone number! Be courteous and add the best time to reach you. Or keep control of the situation by leaving a message like, 'Hi! It's Gayle. I'm hard to reach, so I'll ring you back tomorrow night between six and seven!'

Leaving an amusing message is always a great way to attract attention. You might say 'Hi! Douglas here. Remember? – the tall, thin guy with the pipe who bumped into you at the railway station and spilled your juice all over your coat? Just rang to say I'd like to buy you another juice . . . I promise this time I won't spill it!'

Be assertive and self-possessed: a chuckle on an answer phone is as winning as a smile in person!

Go to dances and socials.

You'll be going for the same reason as everyone else – to meet people! Check the newspaper, especially the Saturday edition, for events of interest to singles. Telephone the organizers to ask them the general age of those attending. Find out if the ratio of men to women is favourable – to you! Is there a welcoming committee to introduce people? Is there pre-arranged seating?

When you get to the event, circulate! If you go with a group of friends, split up. Sit at different tables and smile sweetly at the people who look your way. Show that you are accessible, available and approachable . . . you never know when Cupid is drawing his bow!

Go out for breakfast.

Breakfast is the most important meal of the day . . . for your health and love life! Check your mirror before you go out and make sure you look fresh and that your hair and clothes are perfect. On weekends, many singles go out for brunch because it's an inexpensive way to meet people and a great way to start the day!

But why reserve only weekends for breakfast at a restaurant? Your city must have cafés that serve bargain breakfasts during the week. Or you can find bakeries that serve croissants or home-made crumpets with coffee, or even traditional breakfasts. If you must read a newspaper, raise your head occasionally to check out the crowd . . . you may just spot someone interesting! You might even offer him a muffin!

Go out for coffee and dessert.

There are so many charming little pastry shops that offer exotic teas such as herbal or fruit, as well as extravagant coffees such as cappuccino or espresso along with an assortment of luscious pastries. A perfect place to take someone you have just met! Great for meeting someone, too, as many singles go to such places just to get out of the house after dinner. Definitely an excellent choice for an inexpensive evening in nice surroundings, with soft music and mood lighting: the perfect spot to invite someone for that first evening together! Or drop in solo: you might just pick up something sweet!

Art galleries, libraries, book shops, video shops and newsagents are great meeting places!

Art galleries are made to order for singles: Particularly during a special exhibition. Think of the advantages: you have a built-in topic of conversation – you can discuss the paintings, the artist's personality, the latest gossip about the artist's exotic love life – and you needn't stay for a long time: fifteen minutes if it is hopelessly boring – or if there are only avant-garde artists wearing berets and beards and chain-smoking . . . or two hours if you meet someone enticing, articulate, debonair . . . who knows?!

When you attend public exhibitions, ask to be placed on the mailing list even though you doubt you will ever return. You could have a change of heart . . . and interests!

Visit trade shows, go to conferences . . . to auctions, street fairs!

Have you ever gone to a trade show? There seems to be one for almost every business you can name! Among the major ones are those that feature boats, sports equipment, computers, antiques, home furnishings – even ones for *singles*! A number of major cities worldwide have hosted special shows and seminars for single people; there may even be one coming to your city soon! Check the newspapers for these and other shows, seminars, exhibitions, etc. that interest you and join in on the fun!

You can meet a lot of people by visiting a trade show that interests you. Do you like computers? There are usually several trade shows a year – plus conferences and seminars on how to use the latest hardware and software. You'll encounter all kinds of new equipment and ideas – and people who share your interests – maybe even in love!

An auction can be great fun! Many people go to be entertained: an auctioneer in full cry is quite a sight! People at auctions are usually in a lighthearted mood and quite receptive to the advances of a magnetic person such as yourself! Will your heart be going, going, gone?

Take a walk with your dog! You haven't got a dog? Borrow one!
You'd be amazed how many people will stop to talk to a dog. In fact, these furry creatures are about the best-ice breakers you can find – as long as they aren't trained to be aggressive!

Increase the attention-getting action of your dog by putting a multicolour 'bandage' around its tail! Imagine how many people you'll attract walking a dog that is sporting a flashy fuchsia 'bandage' on its happily-wagging tail!

This strategy worked for Suzanne. She had tried for a year to meet someone nice before finally giving up. One day she went to the shop to buy flour and brought her dog along. When she came out of the shop, there was a handsome young man petting and talking to her dog. Today, Suzanne and Clark – the dog admirer – are married and living happily . . . with the dog that brought them together!

If you haven't a dog, or can't borrow one, why not walk a cat on a leash? Or a tiny monkey?

Talk to people who are out walking their pets.
The conversation could go something like: 'What a cute dog, what's his name?' 'Fido.' 'And what's Fido's telephone number? . . .'

Do you jog? Go cycling? ... Do it where people congregate!

You'll meet a lot more people if you practise your sport on crowded paths ... and they'll probably have the same interests, too!

Are you an ace at pinball or video games? If you are, impress someone with your prowess at the arcade. Many adults play these new-age arcade games, and if you are new to the scene, they can be interesting to watch and a way to meet the top players! Simply stand close to someone you'd like to meet and watch her play. Then when she's racked up a high score, say something like: 'Impressive! This game looks exciting – could you teach me how to play?'

Car dealerships are great places to go shopping for potential love partners!

Choose the kind of dealership according to the type of person you are looking for: a sharp dresser and 'sporty' person might drive a sports car. If it's top-drawer luxury you have set your sights on, then visit a Mercedes-Benz or Jaguar. Why not take a test drive in your dream machine? A prospective buyer might even go with you!

Do your laundry at the launderette!

Even if you have a washer and dryer at home, stop asking your mother to do your laundry: go to a launderette! It truly is a terrific place to meet people! Think about it: people have to wait around for the washing and drying cycles to finish, so what do they do? They chat! You can play helpless and someone for help separating your colours and whites! Or find out when you should use fabric softener ... which detergent is the best? How much soap should you use in soft water? Isn't it great to have built-in topics of conversation?!

Alternatively, you can offer your assistance to that attractive person who is just about to throw a woollen jumper in the dryer! Or that one putting a red shirt in the same wash with white socks! Offer advice, and maybe a helping hand!

In some parts of the world, launderettes have become very 'in' meeting places for singles. So much so, that some people who have met there decided to hold the wedding ceremony and the reception at 'their' launderette!

In Los Angeles and other major American cities, cocktail and snack bars have been set up alongside the laundering area . . . what an incentive for doing your laundry there!

Why limit yourself to one launderette? Go to several different ones throughout the month . . . you'll meet new people. Just imagine! You'll have clean clothes *and* a good time!

Investigate those seminars and courses given for singles and couples in relationships. Check for personality development courses.

There are all kinds of workshops available to singles to help them to come out of their shells and improve their social skills, thereby increasing their chances of meeting their ideal partner. More and more organizations are offering this type of adult education. Some of the course/seminar titles can be quite spicy: 'How to Meet a Much Younger Man', for example.

Choose a course title that looks like it will help your personal development. Better read the course description carefully . . . titles can be misleading. Check the instructor's credentials and find out how long the course has been running as well as the attendance rate. High attendance several semesters in a row is a good sign!

You may truly enjoy or benefit personally from these seminars and workshops, but the main reason for attending is to meet someone. And to discover what *other* singles do! You never know what you may learn about other singles in the process!

Join a charitable organization.

Of course you want to join an organization you believe in, but regardless of whether its objectives are to help the homeless, care for children or build hospitals, it is a brilliant way to meet people. Many volunteers are single . . . they are people who have time to give. By participating in charitable work, you can help others and yourself. Take a close look at this opportunity to improve your social skills and meet respectable, generous people.

Join a political organization.
Political groups always have a large number of members. They also sponsor a number of events – conferences, meetings, socials – where you can meet many singles. Be bold and volunteer for a place on the executive committee . . . you will lead the way, and they will follow!

Join a professional association.
Most professions, jobs and businesses are represented by an association or a syndicate. Why not join the one that applies to you? You will meet lots of people with the same training and values as you have through the many events put on by these organizations. Introduce yourself to all the members . . . create a network . . . maybe even run for a position on the executive committee! Your commitment will increase your self-worth while allowing you to meet many new people.

When you go to a museum, don't forget to visit the gift shop or the restaurant.
There's more to do at a museum than look at the displays. What about all the people who go for a coffee? Why don't you go along, too; it's easy to strike up a conversation. There's so much to talk about: the exhibitions, the artists, the architecture of the museum! And don't forget the gift shop . . . all that bric-à-brac offers built-in ice-breakers for approaching new people!

Take advantage of the interval!

When you go to the theatre, the opera or to see your favourite entertainer, don't stay seated during the interval, go out to the lobby for a drink or a snack. If people have congregated around the bar, join them and take part in the conversation . . . which will no doubt be about the performance – past, present and anticipated! Practise your social skills by contributing some trivia about the stars on stage . . . you may end up sharing the exhilarating remainder of the performance with a 'star' of your own!

The best place to stand at a party is near the bar or at the hors d'oeuvres table!

Why? Because these areas get the most traffic: people are always popping back and forth for drinks and food! If you are at a hotel affair, stroll over to the hat check counter . . . a lot of people come and go in that area, too: some to get a breath of air . . . or to get away from the crowd . . . or they may also be in search of a potential love partner . . . perhaps you will meet each other!

If someone boring monopolizes you at these prime locations, excuse yourself politely and move away . . . find another busy location . . . perhaps circulate a little first. Remember, you promised yourself you would meet as many people as possible tonight! But if someone you are attracted to captivates you, smile and say: 'Would you care to continue this conversation next Tuesday night, over dinner?'

Pay close attention to the type of person you are talking with – particularly to things he likes . . . and use your imagination to suggest a date he is likely to accept . . . a ballroom dance contest? A marathon? Old horror films? By being attentive and friendly you will interest the person you have just met . . . and he will be excited to see you again!

Be receptive to people and they will gather wherever you are standing!

♥ ♥ ♥

When travelling by train, eat in the dining car.

You could pack a boring box lunch and eat alone, but why not visit the dining carriage? It will make your journey seem shorter and much more enjoyable . . . especially if you meet several interesting people! Perhaps your future love is going your way!

Make a point of going out to eat or for a walk at lunchtime!

Even if you bring your lunch to the office, go out for coffee, or for dessert, or even just for a breath of fresh air. Get out of the office or classroom . . . at least you'll get to see some different faces, and your work day won't seem so long. Stretch your legs in the park . . . go people-watching. Maybe someone will notice you and surprise! surprise! . . . introduce herself! Now that would really make taking a break worth while!

Go to boutiques and department stores.

If you'd like to meet a woman, try visiting the women's perfume counter at department stores. If you see an attractive woman buying perfume, you could approach her by saying: 'What an exquisite perfume! I have to buy my sister a birthday present. How can I tell if she might like the one you have just tried?' Always ask questions that require full-sentence answers, not just a 'yes' or a 'no'. With this one sweet question, you have met a new person and shown her that you are thoughtful and caring . . . great strategy!

If you're looking for that special man, go to a men's clothing shop. No doubt you'll spot someone buying a tie! Why not ask him for his advice? 'Excuse me, but you look a lot like my handsome brother, and I noticed that your eyes and hair are the same colour as his. I'm trying to decide on a tie for him. What do you think of this one?' He will, of course, be flattered that you are asking for his advice; and now that you have met, you can introduce yourself. You also may want to compliment him on his apparel . . . adding that his jacket and shirt . . . have inspired other ideas for a present for your brother!

The trick is to prolong the conversation. Once you are merrily chatting along, who knows what topics will come up? You may find out that you have a lot in common . . . and that this 'interesting shopper' has all the possibilities of an ideal love partner! Perhaps both of you will discover more about each other over lunch?

A good place to shop for potential partners is in shops that attract them. You may not need a thing at a computer or a DIY shop or from the sporting goods department, but it's well worth a trip because you'll find an assortment of people there!

You may think the only time to step into a florist shop is to buy a bouquet for your mother's birthday, but what about that shop as the ideal place to meet someone special – anytime? No matter what kind of shop you are in, keep your eyes open for attractive shoppers . . . be impulsive and ask one for assistance! If one of the shoppers intrigues you, casually stroll over next to her and pretend to be interested in the same type of merchandise she is examining. Be bold and strike up a conversation . . . 'Excuse me, do you know if this brand is any good?'

If you are in the market for a particular item, you could also ask questions of a customer who is browsing or shopping in that department. Emphasize the close relationship of the person you are buying for . . . your mother, your brother, your sister . . . and the person you approach will be flattered that his help is important to you. The mere fact that you are inquiring about certain items – perhaps a special saw your brother wants – is an opportunity to meet people. You never know when an attractive stranger will overhear your inquiry and flirtatiously offer to assist you in your purchase! More often than not, willingness to ask questions about a possible purchase is a great opener for meeting interesting, exciting people! Next time you are in a shop, try it and see!

Dialogue is the key to a memorable first contact!
You can convey your values, your preferences and your personality through your comments. Conversation with other

shoppers helps you to establish a personal rapport. Asking a fellow customer about an item can lead to other subjects, and before you know it, you are having a discussion with a stranger! Consider the clientele of all the shops you usually go to, and you will realize that ordinary, everyday shopping is also a great way to 'shop' for someone special!

Enrol in night classes.

What better way to meet interesting people than to take evening classes at the local university? Not only will you widen your horizons, you will have a built-in group of people to introduce yourself to and ready-made topics of conversation!

Universities and trade schools will send their catalogue of courses upon request. While choosing topics that you find exciting or that you would like to learn more about, pay attention to those having particular appeal for the kind of people you'd be interested in.

Perhaps you'll end up taking a navigation or mechanics course? Or a class on sewing or gourmet cooking – more than one person is sure to come to your rescue when you try to separate an egg!

So why not be educated and popular? You can count on meeting lots of people when you take classes. Taking courses opens up a multitude of social situations: snacks between and after class with a few classmates . . . or maybe one in particular! Then there are study groups . . . the library . . . seminars . . . special projects . . . and let's not forget celebrating completion of the course! The object is to take the type of class that attracts the people you find attractive!

Dare to cross traditional gender lines: learn something that will make you stand out from the crowd.

Paul took this advice when he learned how to knit. 'When I learned to knit, during college, my intentions were strictly therapeutic. I was a fidgety student, and knitting was a pleasant change from my previous 'therapy' – incessantly biting my nails. Under the circumstances, I didn't expect to attract more than mild interest. I was wrong. Whenever my knitting surfaced, so did an appreciative – largely female – audience. During the month or more that I worked on a yellow cardigan, I even held my own against the jugglers and street musicians outside the student union! A knitting needle in male hands, I soon discovered, isn't merely a curiosity, it's non-threatening to women, is admired by them and is certainly a great way to get them interested!

'I'm constantly amazed at the near-breathless admiration a woman will heap on a man who makes his own jumpers. The moment I take my knitting out of the bag, any thoughts of "What is a man doing with knitting?" are instantly lost in a torrent of pure admiration! The insanity reaches almost comic proportions when I visit a yarn shop, where male customers are generally treated like lost children who've wandered in looking for their mums! Even in the neighbourhood yarn shop where I'm a regular, they can't help me enough! Female shoppers will wait patiently at the checkout counter while all three saleswomen wait on me. "What a sweetheart," I hear them say as I leave. "He'll make someone a wonderful husband!" . . . I love it.'

Join a health club!

Before joining a health club, shop around. See what type of people frequent the place. Are there more women or men? Do you recognize any celebrities? Taking a good look around is an excellent way of meeting people. While you are examining the facilities, talk to members . . . question them on the cleanliness of the club . . . the instructors, the social activities, the classes and so on. Do it flirtatiously and you may end up with a date!

Your main reason for wanting to join a health club may be to get and/or to stay in shape, but capitalize on its use as an outlet to socialize, too. After your workout, amble over to the juice bar and ask that very fit-looking stranger sipping a tall glass of carrot juice, 'What exercise regime gave *you* such a ravishing body?' You might get some personal instruction on the spot!

By enrolling in a health club, you can meet new people while improving your health and moulding your body into a firm, svelte physique that will stop traffic!

Spend the day at a sports centre: a tennis club or a golf course.
Sports centres are always teeming with activity . . . and energetic singles with athletic style whose zest for life shows! Even if you don't golf or participate in a sport, go and watch the activities . . . and the people! Who knows? Maybe a charming single will tee off right into your life!

Go to weddings, family get-togethers, birthday and other anniversary celebrations, school reunions, conventions . . .
You never know whom you're going to meet! All the gatherings listed above offer the perfect atmosphere for meeting a wonderful range of new people. In your favour, people will be in a mood to party and to socialize, and will definitely be receptive to new faces!

Steven is a stellar example of how this strategy works. He went to a wedding with his mother and met Louisa, the cousin of the groom. They hit it off immediately! A year later, Steven and Louisa were married!

Why pass up an opportunity to meet a marvellous partner because you think no one new will attend? What if you don't go and *the one* was there? Got an invitation? Get dressed up and *go*!

Take a good look at your place of work for potential love partners.
Times have changed, and in the nineties there are almost as

many women as men in the workplace, so the office has become an ideal place for singles to meet. Since people spend so much time at work, it's possible to become attracted to colleagues. Take a good look at the place where you work. Keep an eye open for a possible love interest among the people you work with every day.

What about other offices on your floor? or at the canteen? . . . that terrific-sounding person you speak with often on the telephone? There was a joint office party last year for all the branch offices; did you go? And the group formed from all the offices in your building to go carolling; did you join them this year? And your company's recreational club, are you a member? Did you participate in the last annual employees' golf tournament? Keep your eyes open for all such opportunities. You'll meet interesting people and perhaps one of them will be *it*!

There are a number of advantages to an office romance. Although an office romance can be a problem if the relationship sours or others in the office are jealous, there are advantages to being in the same place at the same time. Here are some of them:

- Generally, you are both well-dressed and looking your best while at work.
- Your love interest is not going to just 'disappear' from your life the next day.
- You know whether the person is married or single, and you know about other 'credentials' such as his career and educational levels.
- You have the opportunity of observing his behaviour, how he reacts to stress, whether he gets along with other people in the workplace, and if he is generally pleasant and cheerful.
- You have the perfect opportunity to assess your love interest's aspirations, ambitions and career possibilities as well as observe whether he is punctual, well-organized and generally a responsible person.

- You can get to know this new person in your life gradually, five days a week, eight hours a day. If you are able to tolerate this much togetherness, your relationship probably has a good chance of enduring!

Some pointers on keeping your 'office romance' and your career balanced.
The last thing you want to encounter in an office romance situation is gossip, criticism, jealousy and general ill-will. You can avoid these pitfalls by keeping the following pointers in mind.

- Always act very professionally on the job so your colleagues or supervisors will have no reason to blame your romance for a drop in productivity.
- Make your career goals very clear to your co-workers. Let them know you are taking self-improvement courses or specific subjects to further your career.
- Make a point of going to lunch with your colleagues more often than you go with your love interest.
- When attending meetings or seminars, don't sit next to each other.
- Avoid cute nicknames, quick kisses, hand-holding or other overt signs of affection during business hours.
- If both of you are travelling on a business trip, take rooms on different floors of the hotel or check in at different hotels.
- Don't always leave the office together at the end of the day or arrive together in the morning – unless you are both in the same carpool!

Today, in most companies an office romance no longer has the stigma attached to it as it had in the past. Although many employers have formal policies against office 'partners', there are some firms who hire married couples. Know your company's policy if you have marriage in mind!

To make the most of the possibilities at your work place, find out who is single in your department and among the people you deal with on a regular basis. You have the added advantage of observing behaviour – likes and dislikes – before you actually approach someone new.

Be aware of the implications of an office romance.
How will you react to the other person after an argument? What about authority – is your lover also your boss? Be realistic about an office romance . . . you don't know where it will lead . . . what if you eventually break up? How will you forget him if you have to see him every day, and you are constantly reminded of the pain of breaking up every time you walk into the office? Your career may be in jeopardy if there is obvious bitterness between you.

Bear in mind that any work-related problems might be blamed on your office romance, so don't rave to co-workers about your dates or shower affection on each other during office hours! Keep the romance side of the relationship private and outside the office . . . *never neglect your work!*

Suppose you really love your job, and your career is finally taking off. Then a new person enters the office scene and you are really attracted to her. The feeling is mutual, and you go out to the cinema and for dinner. By the end of the evening you realize this relationship will not be worth the risk of losing a great job. How to handle this? The next day, be pleasant, but keep from committing yourself to more dates with her.

Be especially careful about dating married colleagues . . . your reputation will be irreparably damaged by the consequences. Be aware that an office romance is never really secret: there is always someone around who will 'spill the beans'! Sooner or later, no matter how careful you are, someone will find out and all kinds of rumours will sweep the office.

So, go ahead and check out your office for potential love interests . . . just be prepared for any repercussions!

What to do if your 'sweet romance' falls apart and you still have to work at the same place.

The course of true love never runs smoothly – according to an old saying. But what if the turbulence strikes when you are involved with someone at your office? Don't panic! Be polite, civil and keep your sense of humour. Above all, don't let your feelings show during office hours – even if you see red at the sight of your ex-interest! This is not the time or place to make a scene. By retaining your professional composure, you distance yourself from the whole 'affair', and at a later point in time when your emotions are under control, you will be able to decide if you wish to continue the relationship.

By conducting yourself in a smooth, professional manner, higher-ups will notice your ability to function under stress, and that transfer or promotion you have been wanting may materialize and solve your 'How can I possibly work in the same place with *that* person?' problem permanently!

What if your supervisor or boss makes unwelcome advances? How to handle sexual harassment.

Handling this situation with tact and resourcefulness is difficult when your first instinct is to either laugh, run, burst into tears or slap him! However, by keeping your calm, cool professional manner intact, you can keep the situation not only under control, but make it work positively for you.

You can counter a request for a date without hurting his 'ego' with an answer that shows you are a serious, ambitious person: 'I really haven't any leisure time at the moment because I am taking night classes so I can further my career. The homework load leaves me no time for romance in my life right now.'

If he asks you out persistently, make your position clear with a firm 'No'. Don't say anything you may regret, or try to humiliate him – you may jeopardize your career. By responding pleasantly but firmly, you will gain respect. And he can keep his self-respect because you took his feelings into consideration when rejecting his approach. Above all, act business-like and make a point of never socializing with him after office hours – even to go for a snack or a drink.

How to get to know someone who works in your building but whom you know nothing about!

She works in your office building . . . you see her every day . . . in the lift or in the corridor, but you don't know a thing about her! She does say 'hello' whenever you bump into each other, but you're dying to get to know her better! How can you make it happen? Play detective! Watch what floor she gets off at. Try to find out which office she works in . . . whether she is single or not . . . do you know someone who knows her? Be discreet while trying to get this information. Get a business card from the company where she works . . . call up and say you spoke to someone but can't remember her name, giving the receptionist a description of her. Imagine how intrigued she will be when you call her by her first name the next time you see her!

Bewitch her with personal comments. For example, you found out she owns a sailboat. So, the next time greet her with: 'It was a great weekend for sailing, eh Denise?!' Or ask her a nautical question! Create intrigue . . . and before you know it, she'll be asking about you!

If you want to meet people you've got to go out . . . and *cruise*!

Go to clubs . . . jazz clubs, sports clubs, restaurants . . . get out of the house! Clubs and restaurants that feature spectator sports on giant screens are particular favourites of many people. If you go to these clubs you'll definitely meet people, but woe to the person who tries to make small talk during a match! True sports fans will be very upset if their concentration on the match is interrupted! Listen to the match and learn as much as possible about it, so you can interject an occasional intelligent comment or question. Better wait until half-time or until after the match to try any real conversation!

Throw a party with a sports theme!

Since spectator sports are so popular, why not have a party? Invite a group of single people who love soccer, cricket – or whatever sport is on TV – to watch the match on *your* set. Have everyone bring something – a main course, dessert, soft drinks, lager, wine – and set up an informal smorgasbord. Keep things casual: don't go to a lot of bother fussing with fine china and silver; use paper plates and serviettes and plastic cutlery. The purpose of this party is to watch the match! The people you've invited are *big* fans. When the match is over, the real partying begins – either to celebrate the victory or to console the losers!

Host a 'blind-date' party!

This is a really fun party idea for singles, and it's the latest rage. To arrange your event, invite an equal number of men and women for early evening drinks at your place. Then everyone is 'paired' for a dinner on their own. You can either draw names from a hat using one hat for each sex, or have the women go in one room and the men in another, close the doors, and then have one person at a time exit the room and be 'paired' with the person who comes out the other door. Great fun! Arrange for everyone to meet after dinner at a local club where notes can be compared over drinks. A really fun evening! And a terrific way to meet someone new!

Arrive early to have the choice of the perfect spot at a cocktail party or disco.

Arriving early can help keep you from suffering from the party jitters . . . no need to 'make an entrance' with all those people watching you!

However, arriving late has its advantages, too! You might want to cause a stir and have heads turn as you dazzle guests with that striking ensemble chosen expressly for the occasion! Since the party will already be well under way, you will walk into action! . . . instead of standing around waiting for things to happen!

You've come to the party dressed in your best – so show off! Stand where you will be noticed . . . and where you can have a good look at the rest of the crowd as they arrive. Your objective is to be highly visible so that someone will come over and strike up a conversation, or ask to be introduced . . . or ask you to dance!

A word of caution: some people who go to clubs and discos on week nights already have partners and are just looking for a one-night love interest . . . so be discriminating! There are, of course, those who choose mid-week to go to discos just to groove to the music . . . or at least that was their first intention until memorable *you* showed up!

Go on holiday alone! An organized tour for singles can be a great way to meet 'availables'.
Choose an 18–30 or similar resort holiday at locations that offer a wide range of recreational activities and where the accent is on singles . . . learn how to sail while you charm the first mate . . . inquire about special 'Singles cruises' from major cruise lines . . . book a room at that exclusive mountaintop resort the 'jet set' frequents . . . Don't give up a trip because you are alone; on the contrary – it's more interesting! People will approach you more readily, figuring that you are available! . . . You won't be alone for long! A person travelling solo is also more receptive to meeting people . . . you don't have anyone holding you back, or frowning, or influencing you. If you choose to bring a friend along, make sure he understands that you will not spend all of your time together, that you want to meet new people. Suggest activities he can enjoy without you. Both of you realize that you are travelling together to economize.

When you are making trip reservations, you can ask your travel agent to request sharing a room with a person of the same sex who has similar interests and lifestyle. If you don't hit it off with your roommate, at least you'll have saved some money on accommodations! If you really can't stand to be in the same room with a stranger, you can always ask the steward or manager to find you another room or roommate!

Whatever type of holiday you choose, don't give up a trip just because you are by yourself . . . people all alone attract other lone people!

If you haven't time or money for a holiday, you can always go away for a weekend.
You can meet plenty of people in just two days. It all depends on your attitude. Be positive . . . even if you don't meet *the one*, at least you will have a chance to practise your social skills and to enjoy a change of scenery for a while! Join in as many activities as possible – you're not there to sleep, you're there to party! At mealtimes, sit next to the one you admire most. Forget the competition! Take every opportunity to get to know more about a prospective partner. Give your phone number to any interesting people you meet – they may introduce you to others! But if someone really appeals to you, make sure that he lives a reasonable distance from you . . . a long-distance romance can really turn out to be a very lonely romance!

A weekend by yourself, away from work and other daily distractions, is a worthwhile strategy for meeting people. Try it . . . you may end up coming back to the same hotel or resort next year – to mark your first anniversary with Mr or Ms Right!

Learn how to dance.
Do you have to refuse invitations to dance at parties because you don't know how? Take lessons . . . learn how to dance the cha-cha, the rhumba, the two-step! It will open a world of new people to you. You'll have a great time whirling gracefully around the dance floor with entertaining people who enjoy being pleasant and lively!

Now that you know how to dance, you can go to dance halls and dance the night away! Some fabulous dance 'palaces' are so large and lavish that they can accommodate a few thousand people . . . imagine meeting hundreds of new people in one evening! Surely one of them will sweep you off your feet!

Throw a singles party!
A singles party has a two-for-one formula! You don't just invite singles: as their 'admission ticket', every person you invite has to bring another single person! The object of the game is to build up your 'singles bank.' You haven't that many single friends? Don't worry: invite a couple with the stipulation that they bring two available, unmarried people to the party!

Throughout the evening, everybody must introduce their single friends to everyone at the party. In such a highly charged atmosphere, the mood is almost Cinderella-magical! Everyone is sure to have a great time! A singles party is certainly a wonderful way to meet prospective partners! You will have so much success with this kind of party, you'll want to give one every month! Unless you meet your perfect match at the very first one!

Become an entrepreneur: arrange a 'singles night'.
What great fun! Be innovative in organizing your party for singles. Advertise publicly on flyers and in the social events section of the newspaper. Why not make it a theme night? Party-goers could come dressed as their favourite character from a romantic film. A Roman theme is often popular, and the costumes are simple: flowing togas and tunics with sandals! Charge enough for tickets to defer your costs of food, hiring a large room, advertising, etc. You may want to include a bit of profit for yourself for all your efforts and build it into a lucrative 'business of the heart'!

You can be as elaborate as you wish: put on a casino night, have a wine and cheese party, be casual or elegant – your party will be a success if you plan games to encourage participation and conversation. You might organize a mock forum with a provocative subject: 'What is the most romantic thing you ever did?' and give everyone a chance to express themselves! Have a welcoming committee introduce people and give each person a name tag. If you are hosting a 'sit down' dinner, make sure everyone changes places at least once throughout the evening. If two people wish, they can always change tables together! At the end of the evening, have a list of names and telephone numbers available for people to take home so that they can ring their new friends!

These types of personalized singles events are well liked because they are given by people – not agencies. Because these 'singles evenings' are highly effective for meeting new people, you could have a new career *plus* a new 'bank' of possible partners!

Set up your easel in the park.
There you are in the park, painting a still life at your easel . . . passers-by are flocking around you, admiring your work . . . what a great way to meet people! Haven't you ever noticed how curious people are, gathering around an artist, fascinated by her drawing or painting? No matter if the artist is using watercolours, or oils, or charcoal, crayons or acrylics, the creative process in action attracts people like flowers do bees! Your creation can have the same effect: you have managed to attract a gathering and you don't even have to talk about yourself – your brush talks for you!

You don't know how to paint a landscape? No problem, abstract art can be anything you want it to be. Experiment with bold blocks of colour or a minimalist white on white! Paint away just as seriously as the artists, and you will attract people every time!

Be sure to go one step further and use your special 'arts' to find out if any of your aficionados are single!

Use your talents and your professional station in life to meet people.
All of us have special talents we can use to meet people. If you have a beautiful phone voice, then leave witty messages on the answer phones of people you've just met – your sultry voice and clever words are sure to appeal to them! Are you a popular public speaker? Use your ability to tell funny stories at social

affairs – you will undoubtedly be the life of the party! Are you
a marketing genius? Then use your imagination to capture the
attention of someone who fascinates you. If you have a special
ability, use it in your love life! Impress that terrific 'someone'
with the imaginative, talented *you*!

It is important to give a possible love partner a second chance.

If you meet someone you are not sure stands up to your
'essential criteria', it is possible that he may be nervous about
meeting you, giving you a false impression of himself. It is
normal to be nervous, and stress increases when one is really
attracted to the other person and wants to make the best
impression possible . . . our words and feelings may not come
out the way we want them to. Give your admirer another
chance!

First encounters are fraught with a sense of uneasiness – a
fear of the unknown. This anxiety often leads to erratic or
downright silly behaviour! Did your love interest act
dimwitted? Or ultra-cool and unsociable? Give her a chance to
calm down and try again. You may well see a tremendous
difference in behaviour – now that she knows you a little
better. How many times have you been nervous and unsure at
a first rendezvous, and wished you had a second chance to
project your true image – a chance which, quite often, you
never got?

Nervousness does cause people to act out of character. More
often than not, the loud-mouthed, seemingly insensitive, crude
individual just can't get a grip on his emotions! So if you meet
someone who laughs in a rude manner at your jokes, spills his
drink all over himself *and* you, then says your eyes are as green
as his bowling shoes . . . don't run in the opposite direction –
that seemingly 'unpolished' manner may be a nervous
reaction, hiding a terrific 'diamond' of love!

Keep in mind that we are all human. Forgive your partner for
her ineptness. Try to ease the atmosphere by appearing relaxed.
Your attitude will be appreciated and certainly rewarded. A big

hug would be good!

There are types of people who truly deserve a second chance. These people try too hard to impress during the first meeting . . . you know, the ones who talk incessantly at speeds that could get them arrested if driving? Of course, life would be enchanting if everyone could be a Romeo or Juliet when they first meet, but that scenario is, unfortunately, not reality! You can't set romance like the dials of a clock: time to be romantic, so here I am poised, charming and ready!

Yet there are those times when, no matter how the other person acts, it's love at first sight! You meet someone new, and click! your intuitive radar goes into high gear and signals *this is the one!* Go for it!

Don't write someone off just because he approached you with a cliché.

A stranger comes up to you and says: 'You look like a Pisces . . . am I right?' or 'Haven't we met somewhere before?' These clichés might annoy you, but at least give the person credit for making the first move! His lack of imagination may simply be due to nervousness . . . you may be intimidating and not even realize it! Or maybe he is feeling drained by his fruitless search for a person to love. Be receptive . . . talk to him for a little while – you may be pleasantly surprised!

Express your admiration.

There is nothing sweeter than receiving a kind word or a lovely compliment. Who doesn't like to be complimented? For the exceptionally good-looking it can be bothersome, but for the rest of us, it is refreshing and very welcome! A compliment is an excellent way to approach someone. A well-placed compliment can go a long way towards making the other person feel desirable . . . and we all need to feel wanted!

Compliment someone by drawing attention to something noticeable about her person. You needn't make elaborate claims like, 'Your eyes are so big and beautiful, deep pools of dark water strewn with stars!' Sometimes a simple compliment is more flattering. So just look at the other person and be honest about what strikes you! Such a compliment will give both of you pleasure!

Of course, when you don't know someone, you can compliment him only on his appearance!
The person you just met is attractively dressed. Tell him so! Go the step beyond thinking a compliment and say it! Since you can't compliment him on his work, cooking, or singing voice, or admire his philosophy of life because you don't know him well enough, you can still mention personal impressions. If this possible future partner – let's hope! – has nice hair, why not tell him you've noticed? A compliment doesn't cost a penny, and makes the recipient feel like a millionaire! Passionate response may be expected: *kiss me* springs to mind!

A compliment says you are observant and want to know the other person better. So drop your shyness and heap on the praise! You will be thought of as a considerate, caring person – one who is loving and lovable!

Learn the fine art of accepting a compliment.
Are you one of those people who turns away a compliment? Does this sound familiar . . . 'You have lovely hair.' 'How could I? I haven't had it cut for six months!' Or . . . 'What a nice dress!' . . . 'This old thing? . . . I've had it for years!' You are not only putting yourself down, you are insulting the person offering the compliment. Try to realize that the person complimenting you is doing her best to be nice . . . perhaps to get you to notice her in return! A polite, positive response to her attempts would be a simple, 'Thank you! How nice of you to notice! And the colour of your shirt is very becoming to you!' . . . Be prepared for a big smile . . . or more!

Be adaptable to last-minute arrangements and changes.
He invited you to the pictures and now, at the last minute,
you're going to visit some of his friends instead! Don't lose your
cool! The theatre will still be there tomorrow, but this golden
opportunity to meet his friends probably won't be . . . *plus*
you'll be meeting new people!

Change your routine!
Are you stuck in a dull routine? Change your habits! You'll see
your life go from dull to exciting. Take a chance: go grocery
shopping on Friday night instead of Saturday morning . . . you
might just run into some very interesting people! Why stay
home on Wednesday to watch the soap opera you've been
watching for ten years? Dare to miss an episode . . . you might
meet a potential love partner during your evening out! After all,
you can always tape the programme and watch it later – with
that great new person you discover!

Change every little habit . . . leave for work 15 minutes earlier
than usual – in case you encounter your perfect match along
the way! You could be driving along and suddenly you see this
great-looking person in your rear view mirror. She's in the car
directly behind yours. Stop your car, jump out, and pretend you
have engine trouble. Wave at Ms Dreamy-looking. Now you see
why it was a good idea to leave home early!

Go someplace different for lunch . . . change! change!
change! . . . that's how you'll see new faces and meet new
people! Go to different shops; alter your schedule so that you
can be in different places at different times. Isn't it refreshing
to see all those new people with another wide range of hopes,
dreams and ideas for you to discuss and explore?! And you
already know a number of strategies for meeting them from
reading this book!

You say you are satisfied and comfortable with your present
routine? Everything is going smoothly? Well, no, you haven't
met anyone special lately. What are you waiting for? Would you
rather be comfortable or have an exciting life? Looks like the
quality of your life could stand a boost! Start with little changes

to your routine; be more active – walk instead of driving to work or to the shops. Gradually, your interests and new experiences will lead to a whole new perspective on life! . . . and you will have immeasurably increased your chances of meeting the love of your life!

A perfect example of a tied-to-routine person is the husband in the film, *Shirley Valentine*. He had a fit when Shirley served him eggs on Tuesday instead of his usual steak. He made another fuss when his tea wasn't ready at precisely 6.15 one evening. Shirley pointed out that maybe if he had his tea at 6.20 one night, his life would become more exciting. The rest of the film deals with change and positive consequences. Surprising how a tiny, seemingly inconsequential change can completely rejuvenate our lives. The French author Pierre Reverdy wrote: 'We must start early to develop good habits, especially the ones that help us to change our habits often!' Change something in your life today!

Wear vibrant colours . . . ones that flatter you and earn you compliments!

Colourful clothes attract attention . . . and different colours stimulate different responses. For example, purple is *the* most powerful of all colours. It symbolizes leadership – definitely the colour to wear when you want to project a strong image!

Red is exciting! Festive! It stimulates happy feelings! People smile at the colour red. The use of red in a work environment stimulates creativity and arouses the senses. Because red has a positive effect on appetites, many pubs and restaurants use this colour. Think *red* when you want to attract people with your vivacious appearance! Be desirable . . . be that lady (or gent) in *red*!

Psychiatrists have noted that pale blue has a calming effect. Because blue is a restful colour, like the blue of the sea and the sky, it is many decorators' top choice for bedrooms. You can always spice up your boudoir décor with red satin cushions!

It is important to wear colours that are flattering. Why not have a professional 'do' your colours? A colour analyst or an image consultant can tell you what your 'season' is. If you have a rose/bluish complexion you are probably a 'summer' or 'winter'. A golden tone to the skin can be either 'spring' or 'autumn'. The colour consultant/analyst can tell you your exact 'season' and recommend a palette of colours which best suit your complexion, as well as suggesting the most flattering garments, shapes and cuts that will enhance your figure. Their guidelines are important when choosing items for your wardrobe. By following this advice, your colour choices and styles will be most becoming!

Brighten your moods with colour! . . . If you wake up one morning feeling a little dispirited, wear something red to stimulate happy feelings – for yourself and all who see you! Or you might choose an emerald green shirt to reflect the brilliance of a bright spring morning! On grey or rainy days, stay away from neutral colours like beige or grey . . . colours that will definitely not brighten a rainy day! Be bold and vibrant in your choice of wardrobe colours! Your energy and dynamism will surprise and delight all who see you! Make an impression – in colour!

Romance and tobacco don't mix well according to today's social code.
Dating agencies report that more and more people are requesting non-smoking partners. This means that the potential number of partners for smokers decreases proportionally as the number of non-smokers increases. The latest polls indicate that fewer people smoke today than ten years ago. You will notice this phenomenon in the personals column of the newspaper. Count how many ads request non-smokers!

A survey by the Boston, Massachusetts agency Lunch Date showed that 89 per cent of their clientele preferred non-smokers, and 47.9 per cent of this number categorically refused to meet a smoker. Smokers were judged even less desirable than overweight people or very short people!

You must realize how intolerable it is for a non-smoker to be with a smoker . . . even more so for an ex-smoker! So do yourself a favour . . . *stop smoking*. You'll not only save money, your health will improve! And you will increase your 'bank' of potential partners. Smoke-free breath is much more inviting than tobacco-tainted breath! Why let a budding romance go up in smoke?

Place an advert in the personals: it's worth a try at least once in your life!

Choose a newspaper that is read by people like yourself. It's important to write a very specific advert. Why try to save money by writing a short advert that barely describes you or the person you want to meet? This is one instance where being 'wordy' can be the winning strategy! It's better to receive 30 letters from people who fit your criteria than 100 that don't even come close. Of course you should include what type of relationship you are looking for: an adventure? a fleeting romance? a solid relationship that might lead to marriage? . . . and children? Be precise!

Statistics show that women receive fewer letters than do men – particularly in the over-40 age category. So a woman should not feel rejected if she receives only 40 replies when her male friend who also ran an advert receives 100!

Personals adverts are particularly useful for people who are worried about some aspect of their appearance. It is a great way of avoiding the stress of meeting people in person! Describe yourself clearly, but don't put yourself down unnecessarily. You may receive fewer replies, but at least you will know that your correspondent is responding to you, and that you sound acceptable to them!

Never exaggerate your appearance. At some point in time you will have to face your prospective admirers . . . it is wise to be honest from the start!

Be ready to answer your letters and calls, and be prepared to go on dates.

Many people don't plan their time properly and find

themselves torn between a desire to meet new people and the lack of time to handle responses to their personals advert! A lovely dilemma, but one that can cause you a lot of unwelcome stress!

Ring those who answered your advert and get them talking. The longer you speak to them the more you will learn about the kind of people they are. It will also sharpen your social skills and your ability to discriminate between candidates. Keep in mind that many people exaggerate their good points and even their lifestyle when they answer personals adverts, so be inquisitive! Don't be surprised at the number of phone calls you will have to make before you hit on one that sounds even close to a 'possible'! Statistics show that a minimum of 8 to 10 replies need to be responded to before you actually contact a candidate with love potential! Keep ringing! The next one may be *the one!*

You've seen dozens of personals adverts: why not answer one of them? The only costs are the price of a stamp and paper!
You've made the decision to go for it! Now to be original and creative. You are in competition with dozens of other letters. Answer a personals advert in the same way you would reply to a job application! Tell the person why you chose his advert. Don't waste your time responding to adverts that you know you won't have a chance at. For example, if the advert asks for a non-smoker and you have all of the other qualities, but you do smoke, forget it. Rule number one: recognize a lost cause! From many dozens of responses, why would a smoker be chosen over several non-smokers who are also otherwise just right? Better to go on to other adverts that aren't so exacting.

Increase your chances of finding a love partner: cut out a number of adverts that interest you and develop some kind of filing system for each one, so that when a person returns your call, you can quickly refer to her advert. This system will avoid embarrassing mix-ups. If you are unsure, ask the respondent to recite part of her text or her reference number when you have her on the telephone.

Do not send photocopied form letters when answering adverts! Two brothers, Peter and Neil, were horrified to find that half the responses they received to their adverts, which had been placed months apart, were exactly the same – form letters! Needless to say, both Peter and Neil threw those away!

Do you have some really nice stationery? Use the best you have when answering an advert. You want to attract favourable attention to your reply. Which letter would you read first? . . . One on ordinary, looseleaf paper, or one written on high-quality paper? An amusing card is a great way to make sure your response gets attention. Short, to the point, with just the facts, thanks! A nine-page letter? You really don't want a call! If the advert asks for a photograph, choose a flattering one: in focus, please! Lush landscape as a backdrop? A castle in Spain? Include a caption and a few lines describing the photograph: 'Here I am on the French Riviera; I would have had a better time if you had been along!' That should give the recipient an incentive to ring you!

Write your letter by hand; it might be wise to brush up your penmanship! Computer printout? Typewritten? Those formats are strictly for business letters! You want to create an impression . . . a personal one! Your first contact with this unknown person will be your letter – make it count favourably!

Don't get discouraged if your replies remain unanswered! A young American persevered right through her 96th attempt – the only one who then wrote back! Today she is married to this man whose advert was the 96th she'd responded to. So you're writing reply 39 and counting? Keep going! You too can get lucky!

When answering adverts, give an honest account of yourself . . . after all, wouldn't you expect the same consideration from the person who placed the advert? When you reach the telephone stage of the process, find out as much as you can before you even meet the person. You probably won't come right out with a direct question like, 'What are your faults?' but you can get him to admit to some, if you use the right strategy.

Invent a friend who met people through adverts and was disappointed because the person she met was always complaining about everything, particularly where they went on dates! Then ask what he likes to do on a date – and *listen!* You will hear a lot about his good points, so test his honesty. Ask him to describe himself physically. Ask him about previous relationships: how long did they last?

It is important to get down to the nitty-gritty before you even meet a person. Elizabeth's experience confirms this point. She talked several times to a respondent of her advert. Over several telephone calls, Elizabeth discovered that Anthony had only been separated for three weeks . . . was not divorced . . . and had been married 18 years! Elizabeth severed the contact immediately without even meeting him in person . . . she did not want love on the rebound!

It is important to know what you want from a relationship before you answer a personals advert.
Your answer should also reveal what *you* want. When you describe yourself, your likes, your desires, don't just scribble them half-heartedly, *express* yourself! Have you got a good sense of humour? Show it with a line like, 'When I read your advert, I thought to myself, "now that sounds like a nice woman . . . the kind my mother always wanted me to bring home!" But I wondered whether you would like a perfectionist who is about as adept in romance as a flea and has a jumble of idiosyncrasies: can't sleep through hammering . . . never leaves the cap off the toothpaste tube . . . and must have coffee before waking up!' A letter like that would certainly get attention . . . and a chuckle! If you can make someone laugh, you have made a friend!

You don't necessarily have to meet someone after the first telephone conversation. If you feel uncomfortable or feel that you don't know enough about the person, tell her that this is a new experience for you and that you will ring back in a few days . . . after you have had a chance to mull things over. If your intuition tells you not to see the person, nobody is forcing you

. . . you are still completely free to do as you please!

It is true that you can't always tell what a person is like until you meet him. Caroline found this out when she received 46 replies to her personals advert. She decided that since all these people took the time to answer her advert, she would take the time to meet them. She arranged the rendezvous in order of preference – from what she could tell from the letters. She was not impressed with numbers 1–45, but Number 46 – who had written only three lines – was the one for her! They have been married for seven years . . . and going strong!

Is the love of your life hidden in the personals? Should you write an advert yourself? Why not? At least you'll have an amusing time reading all those letters!

Try a dating service.
Before you say no, remember that turning to a dating service is not a desperate act. It is a constructive way to meet people! A dating agency can handle your search for interesting, compatible people very well. An average of half the people you'll meet through a good professional dating service generally prove to be interesting – a much better bet than the personals, which may yield one quality candidate out of every eight! Most of the people who sign up at dating agencies genuinely want to meet their ideal partner for a meaningful relationship. A professional dating service is a costly proposition, so people who join are serious about finding a partner . . . they don't want to waste time or money!

How do you choose a good professional dating service?
You will want to check them out thoroughly before you join. Check their business record with your local office of consumer affairs agency. You don't want to be involved with a fly-by-night operation! When you ring a dating service, find out how long they have been in operation. Ask them how many members they have. You should only consider joining those with 500

members or more, and make sure that they give you the number of members in *your* city, not in the whole county or nation!

Are there branch offices elsewhere? Do they have more than one office in your city ? Ask them if only one counsellor is assigned to you for the duration of your contract. And what about that contract? What if you find the love of your life – on your own – two weeks after you join the dating service? Do you get a refund? What if you sign up for a year and you meet someone after six months? Are you reimbursed for the remaining six months?

What if they don't find you a partner: how does their contract work? Is there a dissolution clause? Ask whether the agency organizes socials or information nights. How long must you wait for your first date? How long are the intervals between dates?

One very important factor: what is their male-female ratio in the age bracket you are interested in? If you are a man, and they tell you they have more women than men, and then they tell a female friend of yours that they have more men than women, something is very wrong!

In general, a good, reputable dating service is more costly, but you can verify their standing by inquiring how long they have been around. Also find out if you have the privilege of seeing the interview video of your prospective dates. This service is usually available at an additional cost, but it is well worth the expense! After all, if you wanted a blind date, you could ask Aunt Flo to introduce you to her bridge partner's nephew!

Videos can be misleading: the average person is not a star of stage and screen, so he may be nervous and answer questions stiffly. However, a video does give you an idea of what a person looks like, and you can always go on from there!

Shop around for your dating agency.
It is wise to choose your professional dating agency the same way as you would any major purchase. Shop around! There are many sophisticated agencies, also known as 'head-hunters'.

Be on your guard! Dating agencies are out to make money! Does the dating agency you are considering give you their rates over the telephone? They should. Check whether the rates for men are the same as for women – often they are not! Choosing a professional dating agency that pays its counsellors a commission is risky – you may get more dates, but ones with people you would never have an interest in!

Another question you will want to ask the agency concerns the average age groups they deal with and the prices charged for different age categories. It is an unfortunate fact of life that age makes a difference: the older we get, the more single women there are in relation to single men. Sometimes dating agencies will put on 'specials'. In this case, check to see exactly what kind of discount you are getting.

Having located a well-organized, reputable dating service, give it a try! Found two? Double your chances by joining both of them! You might have an experience similar to Nancy's. She fell in love with an agency video of Marc, and a meeting was arranged. They had a perfect romance for three years, got married and are living passionately ever after!

Meeting someone you don't know for the first time? Be well-prepared: make sure you look good and follow certain basic rules.
Plan your date in advance over the telephone, taking the following points into consideration:

- Meet in a public place – one that is popular. Since you are essentially meeting a stranger, a certain amount of caution is necessary!
- Have your own transportation. Don't be dependent on the other person. What if you don't like her at all . . . you certainly wouldn't want her to have to take you home! You had better make sure that she has her own transportation too, so that you won't have to drive her home!
- Make the first meeting a short one! Suggest going for a cocktail from 5–7 p.m., or perhaps for tea, coffee and

dessert. Brief meetings in casual places are more likely to be successful, yet they don't waste too much of your time if the two of you end up being completely incompatible. If the person turns out to be a dreamboat, you can always order another tea or coffee . . . *and* plan another date!

- How are you planning to recognize each other? You can always describe what you are going to wear, but what if you decide on another outfit at the last minute? Why not suggest something more unusual or amusing? Such as each of you carrying something exotic . . . a red flower perhaps? Just so it's something not everyone would carry. A newspaper wouldn't stand out, but a cardboard cutout or small ceramic animal would! A tiger could be fun! Be original!

- Try *not* to imagine what the other person will look like . . . you may be disappointed. If you are dissatisfied when you see him, try not to show it; don't take a big step backwards or look horrified. Keep your cool . . . you're not there for long. Smile and say hello . . . maybe he has a terrific personality, and once you get to talking, you won't even remember that he didn't appeal to you at first glance!

- It is undeniably true that the first impression people have of you is based on your appearance. So make an effort to look great! Wear something becoming . . . *not* your faded, torn jeans and stained T-shirt! Clothes may not make the man – or woman – but they certainly do help to make that first impression a good one!

A note of caution, especially for women: always let one of your friends know where you're going on your first date – especially if it is in answer to a personals advert. Tell your friend what time you are expected home, so that if you have a problem, at least one person will be aware of your whereabouts.

Imaginative suggestions for 'maxi-fun' get-acquainted 'mini-dates'!

If you have been trying to think of something different for a first date, doing something or going somewhere that won't be expensive or involve a full day or evening, you might want to try one of the following 'mini-date' suggestions. At least you won't be caught for hours with a crashing bore: your experience will simply be a 'mini-disaster'!

- Lucky you! There is a street carnival in a nearby neighbourhood. The two of you can people-watch and sample exotic food while you walk around and get acquainted. Lots of topics for conversation and no pressure to be entertaining!
- Buy a couple of throw-away cameras and suggest that the two of you become top-notch photographers for an afternoon. Delight in snapping quick shots of exotic birds or catching the antics of monkeys at the zoo. Landscaped gardens offer beautiful 'photo opportunities' and the air is filled with the scent of tropical flowers: a lovely prelude to a long evening – if the chemistry is right!
- Shades of your childhood! Rollerskating at the local rink! Not a good idea if you've never been on skates before, but a good bet if you are shy: the music and noise make conversation difficult, so you have a chance to smile a lot while you give her the once over. Later, if all is going well, you might offer to share a giant soda or a double banana split at the local ice-cream parlour!
- Combine exercise, nature appreciation and companionship by suggesting a bike ride or a walk along a well-frequented scenic or historic route. Take along some fruit or a few soft drinks to show what a thoughtful, considerate person you are.
- Is there a special exhibition at a local art gallery? That would be a fun outing if you both like the artist or the style of work. Check out the local book shops – a famous author might be having a book-signing session. Or there could be a lecture on film-making at the library. Being in public places among other people is the key to keeping these first dates on a 'comfortable' basis.
- Take a guided bus tour of your city or a walking tour of an interesting old section. Most towns have a local tourist attraction that residents often have not bothered to visit.

Arrange to meet there and discover its unique history – and each other's, of course. Lunch at a café would be a nice break, and a chance to assess mutual interests.

- If it's spring or early summer, the two of you might enjoy picking wildflowers or wild fruits. Being out in the sunshine and fresh air will do wonders for your spirits even if your date isn't fascinating!

- Bird-watching and -feeding or hunting for butterflies to photograph or collect is another 'fresh-air' date that will encourage smiles and a sense of wonder at nature's beauty. A compliment on yours would be great, too!

- There are half-day or one evening 'mini-cruises' that appeal to the adventurous types. Or go along on a one-day archaeological dig or a horseback trek to an interesting site.

- The autumn is a lovely time to walk in the woods admiring the glorious colours. If Halloween is approaching, you might want to buy some pumpkins at a farmer's market and go to a nearby park to carve imaginative pumpkin heads. Be environmentally-conscious and take along rubbish bags for the cleanup.

- If you are both tennis, badminton or racquetball players, challenge him to a match. Be a real sport and offer to bring soft drinks and a light snack.

Participate in religious activities and ceremonies.
All religions have festivals, parades or social gatherings for their members. Some faiths even organize special events for their singles. Whatever your faith, you can be assured of making friends with people who are in tune with your beliefs when you attend functions associated with your religion. These potential love partners you might meet there will understand and respect the same traditions and any forms of worship as well as observances and restrictions to which you are required to adhere. Your faith, your religion and your place of worship can give you a marvellous sense of 'belonging' and of self-worth. When the love of your life shares the same religious beliefs, you have a good base for a strong, lasting relationship.

Join a choir or an amateur dance group.
Do you love to sing? Play a musical instrument? Dance? Then
join a choir . . . a band . . . a quartet! A folkloric dance group
is a lot of fun – as well as hard work! Best of all, you have a
chance to learn more about a specific culture and to meet
people you ordinarily would not encounter in your own social
circle. A big plus is that some of these groups are semi-
professional, and they travel the world! What an opportunity
to meet even more people!

Are you *too* beautiful?
Some people are so shy and self-conscious they have difficulty
talking to anyone who is very good-looking. For example, three
young men walking in the park noticed a gorgeous young
woman sitting alone on a park bench. They talked about her
among themselves: maybe she was a model or a TV star . . .
she certainly was gorgeous! But not one of them approached
her. She was so beautiful she intimidated them.

Have you this problem? And it is a problem, in spite of what
others may think! You are good-looking, yet often alone? Then
you will have to take the initial step; if people don't come to
you, you must go to them. Approach them, show them you are
a simple human being . . . flesh and blood . . . and with the
same types of fears and hopes. Smile and be pleasant, make
small talk. People will soon feel relaxed and begin talking with
you as they would an old friend!

**You have been involved in several relationships, but now
you are taking some time for yourself. You can sit back,
relax and say: 'Hooray! There is no one in my life right
now – I'm single and happy to be that way!'**
What a great feeling! Now you have time to do all those things
you have been putting off: a trip to your favourite beauty salon
for a full day of pampering – including a manicure, pedicure,
body wrap and facial; shopping for things that please *just you*;

reading the books stacked up on the coffee table; renewing old friendships. This is a time for relaxing and getting back in tune with yourself and what you really want from life.

Being alone can be a lot of fun! Have a party with yourself. Appreciate your free time and use it to get rid of everything that has negative memories of past relationships. This is a time just for you, a recharging of your physical, mental and spiritual batteries. And, of course, it is the perfect time to plan your next romantic move.

Oh, oh! Somebody is ringing your doorbell!.

Learn from your mistakes. Use them to redirect your behaviour and your choice of partners . . . learn not to make the same mistake twice.
It is a fact that we learn more from our mistakes than from our successes. Fumbled a relationship? Consider the whole episode a learning experience! Use it as an opportunity to reflect on your choices of partners. Do you really consider compatibility when you choose a partner? After all, similar goals are the most important factor in a long-term relationship!

And what about the emotional scale? Have you chosen partners who have as much respect for your feelings as you do for theirs? Maybe it's time for you to change your perspective, to try a different type of person. Do you really take the time to analyse your partner before you jump into a relationship? Re-evaluate your strategies so that you won't make the same mistakes.

You can rely on your friends when you're feeling low. Real friends are there during the bad times as well as the good. They see you in a different light and rarely judge you as harshly as you would judge yourself.

Everyone has vulnerabilities and feelings of insecurity from time to time. At such times a sympathetic friend is so very valuable. Friends help you to face the need to change the things you can and to accept those facets of your life that you can do nothing about. With their support, you can keep from repeating past mistakes as you move on to newer and more fulfilling encounters of a loving kind.

Persevere: you have to open many oysters before finding that rare pearl!

Perseverance is the key! Even if your search seems like looking for a nugget of gold in a mountain of sand, you'll find the right love partner if you persist. How many people must a salesman see before he makes a sale? Seven, ten? How many goals does the athlete miss for every goal scored? You can't win every time – not in sales, not in sports, and not in love! Keep looking, keep the faith: among all the single people in the world, there is surely one special pearl for you!

♥ 2 ♥

*A Million and One Love Strategies
for Becoming an Irresistible Flirt*

THE STRATEGIES

What is flirting?
Flirting is a delightful exchange of looks, body language and innuendos – frankly sexy, yet camouflaged in innocence. Anyone who has lifted his eyes over an up-raised glass, or smiled invitingly or winked conspiratorially, has engaged in the pleasures of flirting. There are so many nuances to the game – for a game it is, and a delightful one, at that!

Flirting is an appreciation, a way of saying 'you attract me' without further involvement – unless the overture is returned! In that case, the flirtation continues – with an upward spiral of subtle body movements accompanied by double-edged wordplay and leading to an electric physical contact: a stolen kiss, a quick caress, or who knows?

There are verbal and non-verbal flirting techniques.
When you use double meanings or cute phrases while talking with someone, you are using verbal techniques to get your subliminal 'I find you very attractive' message across.

A wink, a certain stance, a provocative gesture, a lingering look – all are examples of non-verbal methods of letting that special person know he is interesting. Both verbal and non-verbal types of approach should be in a successful flirt's repertoire!

Flirt before, during and after you meet the love of your life – with your lover, of course!

Flirting is more than the initiation of a relationship, it is a way to keep it interesting and fun. If you are already in a relationship, your flirting days are not over! You must continue flirting with your loved one, because other people will! The couple that plays together, stays together! Flirting will help keep the spotlight of love on you and on your feelings for each other. However, once you have found the love of your life, limit any other flirtatious behaviour to light, amusing repartee, and save seductive flirting for your partner in love.

Flirting is a delightful, light-hearted game!

Flirting is a game, an amusing 'I dare you!' exchange. There is no set of rules for flirting – you can be as dramatically enchanting, devilish, demure, inventive and sophisticated as you dare! Flirting is a whimsical pastime dedicated to winning a response: finding true love is a bonus! Happy flirting!

Dispelling the myths about flirting.

If you are conservative in manner and thought, you probably have more than a few qualms about flirting. You think flirting with strangers is too dangerous. It could be if you let it go beyond a simple game . . . a diverting way to meet someone new . . . a way of telling a stranger you are interested. Flirting in itself is not the dangerous part, provided that you are in a public place and not alone with the person. You can determine the level of danger by the type of response you receive. No aggressive, bullying behaviour wanted here! What you do *after* you're noticed is up to you!

Some of the most common questions about flirting are listed below.

How can I know the person I am flirting with is available?

You can't know for sure. Short of a wedding ring or of someone telling you the person is single, there is no way of knowing at first glance. If the person responds favourably to your flirting, you can drop a reference during your conversation like 'Are you here with your wife/husband?', 'Are you waiting for your boyfriend/girlfriend?' or 'Your wife/husband is a lucky woman/man.'

I'll be embarrassed if the other person realizes I'm flirting!

Why? You are not doing anything wrong; in fact, you are reaching out in an amusing fashion – like a child playing an innocent game. The person more likely to be pleased than angry, so don't hesitate. As mentioned before, flirting is one of the essential social graces!

Strangers I flirt with will think I'm easy and will try to take advantage of me.

Flirting may be a game, but you are an adult. No one can take advantage of you unless you let him!

Is it appropriate to flirt at a business meeting?

If the mood is ripe for social interchange, then there is no problem as long as it is done tastefully and tactfully. If, however, there is strong objection to employee fraternization within the corporation, save your flirtatious side for *after* business hours!

Flirting is for kids – I'm too old to flirt!

Nonsense! Flirting is fun for everyone. It's never too late to find an interesting partner. If you want to date, go ahead and flirt . . . it's invigorating!

This is not an appropriate place to flirt.

There is no right or wrong place to flirt – except maybe during a wake or in intensive care! The point is, if you spot someone who attracts you, flirting will help her notice you!

I won't find anyone serious about commitment by flirting.

Why not? Flirting is simply a way to get someone's attention. When you've got him all to yourself, you can then judge whether he is sincere.

You need to be charismatic, outgoing and bold to flirt.

Not really. You only need to be motivated to meet people, to believe in yourself, and to let this confidence shine through!

Flirt to attract a possible love partner.
A flirtation shows your interest in becoming better acquainted with someone who attracts you. Once you have her attention, you have opened a wide range of delightful possibilities for increased intimacy!

However, keep in mind that flirting is a no-strings-attached 'present' – an interesting way of saying, 'It would be so nice to get to know you!' You certainly wouldn't expect immediate commitment in return!

Flirting is direct flattery: you have *chosen* the other person as the object of your actions because he is attractive to you. The following anecdote is a lovely example of flirting/flattery in action.

> Two lovers were casually strolling arm-in-arm down the street when one remarked, 'I have loved you my whole life.'
>
>   The other replied, 'But you have only known me since yesterday!'
>
>   'Yes, but my life *began* yesterday!' was the gallant reply!

Flirting is an exciting way to approach a potential love partner!

Flirting leads to a quick level of mutual understanding. It is almost like being in love, without all of the serious implications of a relationship. Even an idle flirtation can be quite exhilarating for both you and the 'flirtee'. Suppose you are sitting at a table at a sidewalk café. You notice a really good-looking person sitting at the next table, totally engrossed in her newspaper. How to get her attention? Flirt – with a difference: toss a small sugar cube or sachet of sugar at her paper. When she looks up, wink and say something silly like, 'Sweets to the sweet!' Such a beginning could lead to a lot of 'sweet talk'! A flirtation is definitely a thrilling way to meet someone! Be adventurous!

Practise your flirting techniques.

Practise makes perfect, so the saying goes, and in the game of flirting it is really true. If you want to master the art of flirting, begin by flirting with people you know, such as your colleagues, cousins, friends. Polish your flirting skills by rehearsing with close companions who can correct errors and offer suggestions. These 'trial runs' will build your confidence so that when you finally flirt with *the* person you have been eager to meet, your style will be smooth, sophisticated and very effective. Ready, steady, *flirt!*

The art of flirting knows no age limits.
There is a delightful story about a 73-year-old woman who
walked up to a man sitting on a park bench and said to him:
'Sir, you remind me so much of my third husband.' The man
replied: 'Really? And how many husbands have you had?' The
woman smiled coyly as she answered: 'Only two!' Flirting is for
everyone – of any age, in any season!

Self-confidence is the key to successful flirting!
Flirting requires self-confidence. It is no secret that the best flirts
have an assured manner that reflects their ability to handle a
wide range of situations. How to develop that self-confidence?
By being totally comfortable with who and what you are! You
do not have to be stunningly good-looking or brilliantly clever
to be self-confident. Being self-assured means that you can
overlook such physical imperfections as a big nose or
misshapen ears. You can keep your level of self-confidence high
by nurturing the feeling that you are a worthy person.

Every morning when you wake up, tell yourself that you are
an extraordinary person, that you have the ability to be
successful, that you *can* achieve your goals.

Write down those words that make your spirits soar and refer
to them often throughout the day. Repeat your personal
confidence-builders several times each day. Feel the power in
each word! Soon you will have all the confidence you need to
flirt like a pro!

**Be self-confident: assure yourself that you are everything
your perfect match could possibly desire!**
Your perfect match is so beautiful you are afraid to approach
him. You think that your physical appearance is not worthy of
that person's affection. It's about time you take your positive
points into consideration: your big dark eyes and long
eyelashes, your ability to make people smile – add them all up.
Now, imagine that you are everything you think your perfect

match is looking for in a partner, that you were made for each other. Use that confidence you've been building. Be positive: you are indeed the perfect partner for the one you admire!

When you see you perfect match approaching, that person who makes you weak with love with a single glance, don't freeze! This is the moment you have been waiting for! Dare to meet the challenge: smile and flirt your way into her heart!

More ways to keep your confidence level high.
To boost your confidence, stick positive, self-affirming messages everywhere in the house: on the fridge, on your mirrors, under your pillow! Put that card your best friend sent you last week in a prominent place: the card that thanked you for being such a nice, kind person who always thinks of others first. Look for other flattering notes from friends and keep them in a special box so you can reread them often. These written comments highlight your achievements and talents and are great reminders that you are of value to others. Make a list of your abilities and read it daily. Think of yourself as a terrific, *confident* person. Others do!

How to make the person you admire feel as though she is the most fascinating being on earth!
Shower your loved one with attention. Ask lots of questions, listening carefully to her answers so that she will know that her comments are important to you. Gaze lovingly at her as though you are bewitched by her presence. Let your actions and expressions show you would rather be with her at that moment than anywhere else in the world!

Flattery is sweet music to the ear!
You have undoubtedly heard the old saying that the best way to have someone's complete attention is to flatter him, so tell

your partner that he is the most wonderful person in the world
– and see what happens! Tell him that he has the most intense
eyes you have ever seen, or that his smile lights up your life, or
that he looks so great in his new outfit he gives you
goose-bumps!

Everyone loves to be spoken of in a positive way; your loved
one is no exception! Every day, make a point to compliment her
appearance, personality, talents, or accomplishments. Say
things that will lift her spirits and make her feel important! Be
prepared for a *love*ly response!

Be accessible and *visible!*
If someone asks you to dance during a social gathering or at a
club, say 'yes' even if you are not particularly attracted to that
person. You want to be out on the dance floor so others –
people more suited to you – can see you. If you refuse too many
requests, it could discourage others from asking you. They may
think you are unapproachable or arrogant. Rather than refuse
a dance with a person who does not appeal to you, say, 'OK,
I'll dance this one dance with you.' At the end of the dance,
thank him politely and return to your table or your group of
friends.

The point of social outings is to join in the fun. Be enthusiastic
and show everyone – even those people who may not be
attractive to you – that you are a fun-loving, opened-minded
person who is there to have a good time!

When flirting, be careful not to send mixed messages that the other person could take the wrong way.
Flirting is a subtle art and should never have overtly lewd,
sexual overtones or crude, offensive suggestions. A word of
warning: today's woman is not only more independent
financially and emotionally, she expects – rightly so! – to be
treated with respect. The wise flirter will win the day through
romantic flirting, not with crude approaches. Thoughtless

behaviour will only disgust and repel the person you are trying
to attract.

The following is an example of an inappropriate comment,
masquerading as a flirtation. A woman was buying a magazine
at a newsagent's when a man she knew slightly walked over
to her and said, 'Hi, Nancy! You're looking great! Neat pair of
shoes! How about parking them under my bed some night?'
Needless to say, Nancy turned on her heel and left without
replying to the man's conceited remark!

**When you are talking with a possible love interest,
inspire confidence by mentioning your 'credentials' early
in the conversation.**
Let the person you are attracted to know that you have roots.
Talk about your family or about your co-workers. Mention
clubs or organizations you belong to. Tell her why you joined –
a good conversation starter. By talking about yourself in this
way, your possible love partner will quickly get to know who
you are, what your interests are, and where you come from.

Flirting attracts attention – in a positive sense!
Flirting turns heads. People think of flirts as confident, fun-
loving individuals who are blessed with a passionate nature –
persons who attract others with their *joie de vivre* and humour.
Habitual flirts generally have a sharp wit and a great sense of
humour that brightens everyone's day. Wouldn't you like to be
known as a flirt?

Respond to those who flirt with you: flirt back!
If someone comes up to you and says, 'Haven't we met
somewhere before?', and the person is someone you would like
to know, respond with your own flirtation: 'I really don't think
so – I would never have forgotten *you!*' Now that the person

feels unforgettable, you two can have a wonderful conversation. Flirt with those who flirt with you!

What if you see someone interesting? How can you get him to start flirting with you? Simply take advantage of where you are at the time you see him. Suppose you are in the supermarket and Mr Gorgeous goes by. Quick! Try to get in the queue behind him at the checkout counter. Ask where he found a particular item in his trolley, or say something like, 'Those grapes look good. I must have missed them when I was in the fruit and vegetable section. Do you know what country they come from?' Keep eye contact as you continue talking, smile provocatively, and see what happens!

Flirting techniques are like diamonds in the rough: both need polishing to show off their real beauty and value!
A diamond becomes more valuable as it is cut and buffed. Your personality reveals its most interesting facets in much the same way. The more you work on refining your image and your flirting techniques, the more noticeable you will become to others. By now you realize that your personality is more important than your physical appearance. Keep building your confidence and perfecting your social skills and flirting techniques, and you will attract desirable people. Today, take the first step towards a more exciting life – go out and flirt with someone!

Appearing to be shy or reserved could give the wrong impression.
What is your first impression of people who are shy or reserved? Do you consider them to be snobbish or just not interested in you? As you get to know these people, do you discover that they are only bashful or timid by nature and are actually very nice individuals? People who appear anti-social because of shyness are often misunderstood and misjudged. It is a mistake to ignore someone because she appears to be indifferent: she may simply

be too shy to respond socially. Draw her out of her shell by carrying on a light, non-threatening conversation – even if you have to do most of the talking. Eventually her shyness will evaporate; she may even begin flirting with *you!*

By the same token, if you are a shy person, make an effort to approach that person who attracts you. You needn't necessarily have to say the first word, just smile or glance at her. It's really easy to talk to people once you take that first step. Forget yourself and concentrate on saying things to put the other person at ease. There's a whole world of interesting people just waiting for your smile!

Unsure of your flirting techniques? You can easily learn!
Observe others! Surely you know outgoing people who have a flirtatious character. Whether they are family members, colleagues or friends, watch them as they flirt. Notice the coquettish way they approach people. Note how they appear confident and poised. Take your study of flirting one step further by watching old films starring great seducers such as Clark Gable or Marilyn Monroe. Examine all types of flirting techniques on television, in films, and in romance novels.

The next step is to emulate these techniques. Without turning yourself into something you're not, adapt their flirting techniques to your personality. For example, you may want to try a sexy walk like Marilyn Monroe's, or imitate the piercing, intensely dramatic eyes of the old-time silent screen star, Rudolph Valentino! He was famous for gazing soulfully at his co-stars. Practise by sitting in front of a mirror and trying different seductive 'looks'. You, too, can be irresistible!

Acting classes can improve your flirting techniques.
According to Shakespeare, all the world's a stage and we are all players. Much like acting, flirting is a way of entertaining people we want to attract. You choose your own role on the social stage by portraying the way you would like others to see

you. As the 'star', the way others respond to you depends on your 'performance'. Acting classes can help you gain enough confidence to play the role you want to project. Such classes provide a springboard for your personality as well as the opportunity to practise play-acting with real people. Be a star! The world is a stage and you have top billing – as a *flirt!*

Let people know that you are available.
As a single person, you can go where you please when you please, meeting many different types of people. Whether you are in a social, professional or family situation, let it be known that you are always interested in meeting available singles. At all times, keep your ears open for any mention of singles. If you hear a friend speak of an interesting, unattached acquaintance, tell him that you would be interested in meeting that person. If possible, get that person's telephone number when you are finding out as much as you can about her from your friend. You never know – he might be the one you have been dreaming of!

Be a happy single!
Show everyone that you have a full, positive, happy life as a single person. Talk enthusiastically about your friends and mention that you have many interesting people around you, that you appreciate your family, and that you love your work. Clearly describe your life as rich and fulfilling. Avoid statements like 'I'm tired of being alone' or 'I don't think I'll take a holiday this year because I don't want to go away alone.'

People will avoid you if you whinge constantly about being alone or complain that you need someone to make your life worthwhile. Instead, make your independence attractive. Show that you enjoy life – so much so that anyone's life would be more exciting with *you* in it! Very soon you will have interested parties wanting to be a part of this stimulating, terrific life you lead!

Enjoy your life as a single – it might not last very long!
So you are single for the moment! Enjoy every minute of this period of your life! Use this precious time to broaden your intellectual, spiritual and physical horizons and to become a self-fulfilled person aware of your capability to change your destiny.

Among the myriad choices facing you, the following activities might fit in with your plans to savour and to use your 'single' time.

- Spend a fabulous week at a spa and return with an added incentive to stick to a healthy diet and to rid yourself of cravings for too many sweets, alcohol, or cigarettes.
- Make an appointment with a colour consultant and learn what colours you should have in your wardrobe to accent your personality and colouring. You could also find out what styles suit you the best.
- Often, the major cosmetics companies offer free promotional facial/complexion analyses or make-up sessions in the big department stores. You can learn how to choose the right make-up for your particular skin and colouring. What a lift to the spirits to face the world with a 'new' look!
- To help you keep on your new diet, indulge in a Shiatsu massage and learn some of the techniques to practise on your future love – particularly facial Shiatsu!
- Develop your self-confidence by taking a special course in assertiveness, positive thinking, motivation or public speaking.
- Broaden your horizons by studying the great religions of the world, such as Hinduism, Buddhism, Christianity, Islam, Judaism.
- Take classes in T'ai Chi or Egyptian belly-dancing. Great for your figure and for reducing stress!
- Now is the time to get your finances in order and streamline your home-filing system. Make sure you have the proper insurances. Start a retirement savings plan so that you can enjoy a beautiful holiday in the future. You might want to look into a major financial plan that will give you the ability to own a place of your own eventually or to be able to share in an investment property.

- Learn a new skill, like desktop publishing or computer programming. This may open up an entirely new career for you.
- Study a foreign language. If you know a bit about a language, you may want to be privately tutored or find someone – a potential perfect match, perhaps – who is willing to be involved in conversational exchange.
- Are you adventurous? Why not try hang-gliding, scuba-diving, circus acrobatics – anything that will fill your life with colour, thrills and excitement!
- Learn how to pick up subtle clues about people by studying body language, palm reading, astrology, or Chinese reflexology. Someone's handshake can reveal a lot to you – if you know what to look for!
- Read self-improvement books and try some of the techniques that appeal to you. The idea is to develop your confidence, to make you feel good about yourself.
- This is the time to write a daily journal, or a collection of poems, or to start a novel or your autobiography. You may be surprised at what your writing reveals to you about your deepest feelings.

This 'single' period in your life is a time to really get to know yourself, your dreams, your hopes, your ambitions. It is a time to choose to do those things which give *you* pleasure, not just those things that supposedly project an 'image' others expect of you. Use this time to become your own best friend. By being yourself, you will attract those who will appreciate and love you for what you are – a unique, wonderful person!

Are you talented in the arts? Put your talents to work in your flirting techniques!
Flirting should be an extension of your personality. Your techniques should be uniquely yours. By using your special talents when flirting, you are sharing your inner nature. Are you a comedian? A romantic singer? A closet poet? Give the one you admire a chance to know the talented *you!*

Don't just talk about your abilities, use them to flatter and impress the love interest in your life. Break the humdrum routine of daily life by using your talents to show that special person how ingenious, amusing, perceptive and sensitive you are. Your style of flirting should be as stimulating as you alone can be – sensational!

If you are an artist, break the ice with the one you admire by sending him a drawing of the way you feel. Everyone tells you what a good writer you are? – send a message composed just for him. Impressive! If you can play the guitar or other musical instrument, why not an evening or morning serenade of her favourite music? Be creative – sweep that special person off her feet with your uniqueness!

Do things that reflect the positive image you have of yourself.
Join professional organizations that give you a sense of worth. Become involved in volunteer work at a hospital, a convalescent home, or an orphanage. Go to charitable events as a sponsor or to help with arrangements. These events are not only worthwhile, they will increase your social skills, boost your confidence, and help you meet other people.

Participating in activities that make you feel you have accomplished something important for others will not only reveal your compassionate nature, but will help you to gain more tolerance and respect for yourself.

Be kind to yourself: it will help you realize your own value.
Spoil yourself with little self-indulgences. Dress in clothes that make you feel comfortable and at ease with yourself because you look your best. Even if you are staying at home, be prepared: you never know when you might meet someone 'special'! That person may turn out to be a bike messenger or a neighbour ringing your doorbell to ask for coffee. How would

you feel if you looked less than your best when you met the love of your life?

Learn to pamper yourself. Give yourself a facial or a special manicure or pedicure: something you feel is a gift to yourself. Going fishing? Why not! Doing something 'just for you' reflects the importance you attach to yourself and reinforces your self-image. People will notice your self-esteem and will be drawn to you.

Honesty, towards oneself as well as towards others, also reflects a positive self-image. An honourable person stands out among the crowd.

Dress for success: make each day a special occasion!
You know those clothes hanging in your closet that you keep for special occasions? The problem is that such occasions come only a few times a year. Why don't you wear one of those terrific outfits *today?* What are you waiting for – Judgement Day? You know you look really good in your nicest clothes, and since the whole idea of flirting is to attract attention by projecting a terrific image, why not wear flattering outfits often? Who knows? By wearing your best, you just might *create* a special occasion – like a dinner date in an elegant restaurant!

Dressing for success means more than slipping into your best outfit!
A major part of good grooming is being neat and wearing clean, well-pressed clothes – with all the buttons on, and matching ones, please! Check your outfit for loose seams or holes in the fabric. You can tell a lot about someone by his shoes, so make sure that your shoes or boots are well polished. Check those heels for wear! Be stylish with coordinating apparel. Choose jewellery to fit the occasion and the outfit. It is a rule of good etiquette and a mark of elegance to wear no more than one ring on each hand. A ring on every finger gives your hands a cluttered look. When you wear several rings of

different value, the most precious is hard to recognize when surrounded by those of lesser importance. Also, many rings can confuse a person if he takes a quick look at your hands to determine your marital status! One ring is dramatic and elegant – and leaves plenty of room for future romantic symbols!

Good grooming is essential to a successful look.
When you are well groomed, you show self-esteem and a respect for your health and person. Hands are highly visible, so keep your nails clean and well-manicured. Use a rich, slightly scented cream to keep hands and cuticles soft and pleasant to touch. Shaking hands when yours are rough and chapped creates a very bad first impression!

Oral hygiene is also important for obvious reasons. Your teeth and breath influence how others react to you. Our daily interactions and conversations make it impossible to conceal our teeth. So brush your teeth and use dental floss *regularly!* You can buy folding brushes and small tubes of toothpaste to carry with you so you can brush after lunch or before important meetings. You can also buy small packages of dental floss and mouth wash. See your dentist on a regular basis to keep your teeth and mouth in excellent condition.

Keep your hair shiny, soft and touchable.
The state of your hair reflects your grooming attitude. Greasy or mussed hair says you really don't care about yourself, so how could you possibly care for someone else? Experiment with different shampoos and conditioners until you find the right combination for your hair, one that leaves it shining. Your hair should be kept soft to the touch, not so stiff with hairsprays and gels that you give the message, 'Hands-off! Do not touch!' However, all the right products will not compensate for a poor diet. Your hair and skin reflect your health habits. Eating a balanced diet and getting enough rest are essential to your overall appearance.

Visit a hair salon at least once a month, if you can afford it. Guys, if you sport a beard, use a cream rinse to make it soft and enticing to the touch: your love will be sure to appreciate your thoughtfulness!

Pay attention to grooming details.
Like exotic birds, it is natural to preen yourself when you want to impress others. Peacocks fan their gorgeous tail plumage to be attractive to their mates, just as you carefully arrange your hair or smooth your clothing. Every detail is important. A person's first impression of you depends on your appearance, and you only get one chance to make a good first impression!

Acquire special everyday objects that reflect your uniqueness: a nice pen is impressive when you are signing a document or perhaps noting a love interest's telephone number! A briefcase or a personalized agenda is an elegant touch.

If you wear perfume, choose one that expresses your personality: spicy scents for flamboyant characters, or perhaps a citrus bouquet for the sports-minded. Your 'signature' fragrance can become a central part of your total surroundings when you spray the eau-de-Cologne around your home and in your car. Keep the true perfume for a light touch during the day, adding a bit more for evening enchantment. A wise woman – or man – uses scents sparingly to enhance charm, not smother it!

Your choice of clothes and how you wear them is important if you want to attract a partner.
Dressing for success is an art. Charlene learned this by accident. Nothing had been going well in Charlene's life, so she decided to take an afternoon off work and go shopping and then to the pictures to lift her spirits. She chose a very stylish red dress that had been fitted just for her and made her look gorgeous. She had her hair done in a new way at the hairdresser's. Then Charlene went for a bite to eat at the café next door to the

cinema. She looked impeccable with her hair smartly styled, her fitted red dress, and her high heels. She felt good about herself and it showed in her face and posture. A good-looking man sitting at the next table smiled several times at her, then invited her for coffee. He ended up paying her dinner tab. Needless to say, Charlene skipped the film – her admirer kept her talking until the restaurant closed. Later, the newly-discovered partners spent an enchanted, intimate hour in an elegant club sharing a special 'nightcap' of champagne and strawberries. They dated for six months after that first encounter – the day Charlene decided to improve her image! Charlene's look improved her attitude and outlook on life, and, consequently, she attracted an interesting man. You can do the same. Try a new hairstyle, a becoming outfit, a smart jacket or hat. Go where you will be seen – to a café, a restaurant, a club. You will surely be noticed, admired, and who knows?

Maintaining eye contact is essential to flirting.
They say that the eyes are the windows to the soul. And it is interesting to know that when you feel attracted to someone, your pupils immediately dilate, indicating your hidden desire for this person. This 'signal' may be subtle, but it registers with the one you want to attract. So show that good-looking stranger your intentions . . . gaze deeply into her eyes . . . you might be pleasantly surprised by the results!

Train yourself to maintain eye contact without blinking. As insignificant as it appears, rapid blinking signals shyness, nervousness, or a lack of confidence, all of which are undesirable characteristics to project. Practise by looking at a candle flame without blinking. Look at yourself in the mirror and hold your gaze as long as possible. Ask close friends to practise staring with you.

This story of a young couple's encounter illustrates just how far you can get with eye contact. Two strangers, sitting at separate tables in a café in Paris and smoking cigarettes, were staring at each other. When the girl's cigarette had expired, she drew another one out of a silver case, wrote her name and telephone number on it, and placed the cigarette in the ashtray on the boy's table as she made her way out of the café. She did this without uttering a word. Intrigued and enchanted by this temptress, the boy rang the girl that very evening. The rest is history. You can be mysterious by using only your eyes!

Always maintain your gaze a few moments longer than the other person.
Whether you have been conversing or only 'eye-talking', stare at the other person a little longer to show that you mean business. Remember, your gaze says, 'I'm interested!' Prolonged eye contact creates an air of intrigue while showing that you are determined to carry the exchange further and that you are in control of the situation.

Avoid looking away when you are talking with someone.
Speaking to people who are constantly looking around is troubling and insulting. You begin to wonder whom they are looking at, which is very distracting! Of course they may be acting that way because of shyness, but it's still rude behaviour, and gives the impression that they are not interested in what you have to say. Which makes you want to shake them and say, 'I'm talking to you.'

When you are approaching someone new, make a point of maintaining eye contact and of noticing her eye movements. It will give you a good idea of what kind of person she is. For example, someone who continually looks around the room and notices everyone who walks in could be labelled a philanderer! The eyes tell all: look into her eyes and read her like a book!

If you are shy, gaze at a person's 'third eye' and send a message.
If you are so shy that you have trouble looking people in the

eye, focus on the person's 'third eye' – the space between the eyes, precisely between the eyebrows. This is a hypnosis point. The person will not suspect a thing, but will feel as though you are looking into his eyes.

Think of the 'third eye' as a subconscious pathway. By gazing at it, you can transmit a silent message. How about something flirty? 'I am made to order for you – we should be together!' You don't believe it can work? Try it, and be happily surprised!

Never underestimate the power of a wink!
Winking is amusing, a fanciful distraction. It is definitely a fun way to flirt! A wink suggests collusion in a prank and implies that you are adventurous. Try winking – the response will give both of you a boost!

Use those eyeglasses!
You can use your sunglasses – or your regular glasses – as a flirting tool. Take them off for a moment – let the person see your beautiful eyes! Lower your glasses onto the tip of your nose and look at the other person seductively . . . gaze for a moment or two . . . then reposition your glasses, or remove them completely and sensuously manipulate them while you bewitch the other person with an intense gaze. Whoever remarked that 'Boys don't make passes at girls who wear glasses' obviously did not know how to turn them into a flirting opportunity!

Play suggestively with an object to attract attention.
There are objects other than eyeglasses that can be used to attract attention. Any ordinary object can be used. If you're at a restaurant, you can use your wine glass to simulate a small 'wave' or 'toast' to the one who pleases you.

Keys are fun because they make a little noise. Or be

mysterious – use a newspaper to eclipse your interest, letting only your eyes peek over the edge of the paper . . . quite a seductive way to attract attention. Whatever object you choose, make sure to focus on the person of interest so that she will know you are directing your flirtations only to her. You wouldn't want to attract the 8-year-old at the next table!

Try to flirt successfully three to five times a day.

You can't expect to captivate someone every time you flirt. Some flirtations will be roaring successes while others will leave the flirtee flat. Don't get discouraged by the losses – accent your successes! If you have three successes a day, you're doing well!

A flirtation that attracts attention in any way is successful! Of course, the quality of a flirtation is measured by the response. If you can make someone smile or laugh, consider yourself a winner in the game of flirting!

Be dynamic and fun-loving: show the world that you love life!

The way you act determines how people respond to you. Wouldn't you rather be a magnetic, attractive person, who makes other people laugh, than a humdrum type who is invisible in the crowd? Everyone loves a clown! People are drawn to happy, amusing people. Be silly – make someone laugh. People will flock to you because you are fun to be with. Charm them with your charisma. People will respond – and you might meet the love of your life!

Remember, laughter is a rare commodity in our fast-paced world. If you go through life with spirit and good cheer, you will be rewarded with friendship; laughter brightens everyone's day and helps relieve stress. To make people forget their troubles and insecurities, make them laugh, and soon they will join in the fun. Laughter is contagious, so much so that you can draw a crowd with your laughter! Everyone who hears you will look forward to seeing you again, and will believe that life with you would be a perpetual party. Flirting is good fun! If you want to leave a lasting impression, give the gift of your laughter!

A smile is worth a thousand words.
Just as laughter is contagious, a smile is magnetic. When you smile at someone you are projecting an image of a compassionate, tender, approachable, welcoming, sweet, courteous, and gentle person. Indeed, smiling at strangers might surprise them, but they'll usually smile back at you. Smiling elicits an automatic response. A smile is a courtesy, a silent treaty of peace and possible friendship between two people. *Smile* – it will do your heart a favour!

Each of us knows people who may not be particularly attractive, yet when they smile, they light up a room, drawing others close. You, too, can radiate warmth – all you have to do is smile!

To attract the attention of someone who appears indifferent, send mental messages.
With patience, you can learn to send subconscious messages. For example, a young woman travelling by bus is seated behind a man whom she finds very attractive. Unfortunately, the man will not turn round. She decides to try sending him a mental message. To test how receptive he is, she begins by focusing on the back of his head while scratching her ear. Within a few moments the man scratches his ear. Continuing to focus, the young woman twirls a lock of her hair. Moments later the man touches his hair. Pleased with the reception, the young woman attempts to send a silent message asking the man to turn round and look at her. It works! Smiling radiantly, she hears him say, 'Well, hello there! Let me introduce myself . . .'!

You can practise sending mental messages in the same way. It is a fun pastime when you are on public transport or in a lift. Your transmission skills will improve with practice. In the beginning, you can try sending mental messages similar to the ones described above, in the company of a group of friends. It's certainly worth a try!

Flirting improves your social skills.
Flirting is a way to make a social connection. It is a natural responsive art that you can improve through practice. Think of flirting as a basic social grace – as basic as saying hello or smiling at someone you would like to meet. The only difference is *exaggeration*. Saying *'Hello!'* with extra enthusiasm, or smiling seductively using your entire face to show your pleasure, is truly flirting!

To become adept at flirting takes practice – and doesn't that sound like fun? Just imagine how much more relaxed you will feel around people when you think of your encounters as flirting practice!

Make a smashing first impression by flirting! Picture the scene: there you are, at a party, and across the room is the most enticing person you have ever seen in your life – you get goose-bumps just looking at her! Why not get her attention by smiling seductively the next time she looks your way? If necessary, make your way through the crowd to get closer to her – so she can see you. Then be a little bolder: brush against her arm as you walk past. Turn around and say 'Excuse me' in a sultry voice! That will get her attention!

Flirting can help you get to know someone before actually dating him.
Flirting is really a social skill for putting people at ease so they will feel comfortable talking with you. Being flirtatious is using eye contact and body language to express friendliness – it's one child talking to another child. The child in you is reaching out to the child in another person. The person you are attracted to will regard you as friendly.

Flirting shows that you are uninhibited, that you are offering a fun side of yourself that is free from formal social constraints.

By speaking openly and smiling, your body relaxed and your expression pleasant, you are non-threatening. Your actions will soon encourage the other person to join you in your flirting game.

You can tell a lot about a person from the way he responds to your flirting. If he acts aloof and cold, he probably isn't fun to be with, and you can simply smile and go on to someone more receptive. If he overreacts and literally falls all over you, turn off the power! Usually, though, if you show a genuine interest in someone by complimenting him and saying how pleased you are to see him, you will have a very pleasant – even stimulating – exchange of flirtations!

Be a compulsive compliment returner

Every time someone pays you a compliment, do you have the tendency to put yourself down and ruin the effect? For example, if someone tells you, 'Your hair looks nice', do you respond with 'How could it? I haven't had a decent haircut in months!' If that remark sounds like you, try to break the habit by answering a compliment with a smile and a 'Thank you!' then adding a compliment addressed to them: 'You always have such a nice way with words!' or 'You always wear your clothes so elegantly!'

Flirting will help you express yourself more freely.

Flirting is a natural extension of your personality. Each of us is a born flirt. Have you ever watched baby charm at work? Who can resist responding to a baby's smile, hug, or kiss? The most stuffy-looking, reserved, decorous adults become syrupy-voiced, all-smiles twits as they try to get baby to smile, gurgle or laugh! All flirting of any age has the same purpose: to encourage a response in other people. Be spontaneous and impulsive. If you are a talented piano player, play a tune at a party – providing there is a piano of course. Announce the piece as a dedication to the adorable fellow in the blue suit or the seductive woman in the red dress, whom you have not yet met. He or she will undoubtedly come over to you after such a brilliant rendition!

Don't be preoccupied with how you look or how the other person will react. Play with your fellow human beings . . . soon everyone will be enjoying a wholesome game of flirting and having a wonderful time!

Get in the mood to flirt!

Pretend it's opening night and imagine you are the star of the show – an irresistible flirt. When your stomach is tied up in knots before a party or gathering, visualize yourself flirting – it will help you combat the jitters. It's normal to be nervous. Even veteran performers get anxious before a show: 'It keeps us sharp,' they say. The trick is not to panic. Visualize yourself flirting. Close your eyes and imagine being carefree, flirtatiously flitting about . . . a social butterfly!

While you are getting ready for an event or party, picture yourself as the life of the party. Rehearse in front of a mirror, if necessary! Play some lively, slightly romantic music to get yourself into a flirtatious mood. By the time you're ready to go out, you will be in the mood to give a great performance!

Feel good about yourself.

If you feel good about yourself, you will project this to others, and they, too, will feel good around you and will want to stay near you. To be liked by other people, you must first like yourself. Do you honestly think someone worthwhile will be drawn to you if you have a bad opinion of yourself?

In order to flirt successfully, you need to be in a good mood and to feel like having fun! Ever try to flirt when your day was going all wrong? Not very likely! Flirtatious behaviour is frivolous, carefree conduct – play-acting – and you can't possibly play if you are in an uptight mood!

Flirting should be enjoyable. It is a great way to boost your self-esteem and your faith in your own attractiveness. Feeling good about your self-image will raise the ratio of favourable responses you receive from others. It will also make you the object of a flirtation!

Flirt with your eyes.

Mae West was 'discovered' by Hollywood movie moguls because of the way she used her eyes when talking to men. She would look straight into a man's eyes and stare for a few seconds, then look down shyly for a moment, and then gaze once more with great passion. The silent screen of the early days of films reflected the many moods of flirtation . . . no words needed to reinforce the power of a Mae West flirtation!

The language of the eyes is the most flirtatious body language of all. It is a powerful way to get your message across! Pull a 'Mae West' during your next encounter and find out for yourself!

Watch people's eye movements as you flirt with them. You can tell whether they are interested, shy or embarrassed or . . .! Observe the old stars of the silent screen – Theda Bara, for example – who *had* to literally 'speak with their eyes'. These stars were masters of 'the language of the eyes'. Try mimicking their movements. Practise in front of a mirror. Try it on your friends . . . on your cat. Are you getting the right reactions?

Eyes are the windows to the soul, so tell the world your intentions: flirt with your eyes!

Pay close attention when your admirer is speaking to you.

The two of you are talking together at last! Show interest by your posture, the slant of your head, the widening of your eyes. Look directly at your admirer, as though mesmerized by her every word! Maintain an intense focus that says 'I think you are the most wonderful person in the world.' As far as you are concerned, there is no one else quite like this person anywhere in the universe! Show how important she is to you by showering her with attention. By being attentive you will also learn quickly your admirer's likes and dislikes – which will make your present and future relationship much smoother and more enjoyable for both of you!

Flirt and listen with your body!

When you nod your head, it shows that you are listening attentively. It is also a way of flirting passively. You needn't talk, and you are using subtle body language that clearly says, 'I'm interested in you . . . I want to get to know you better.'

Leaning slightly forward while someone is talking to you is another way of demonstrating that you find a person engaging without actually intruding on his space. It is a very polite way of flirting! You are saying 'I am very interested in what you have to say,' without pressuring the person whatsoever.

You can use body language to size someone up, too. Give him the once-over from head to toe. Be like a computer and process the data you receive from observing his eyes, facial expression, body position changes, handshake, voice, and stance.

Open gestures, such as an open jacket, open arms, stance, laughing easily, even nibbling hors d'oeuvres and drinking while conversing with you, mean that a person is comfortable and interested in you. When people are romantically interested, they tend to blink more often and faster, and they will unconsciously mimic your body gestures.

Body language is also a polite way of telling people you are *not* interested. Giving them the brush-off can be done by turning your body away and presenting your shoulder. Noticing another person's body responses to your advances will prevent you from wasting time on someone who is not interested in you. If you are greeted by a cold shoulder and pursed lips, that person is trying to tell you that you are not for her. Body language replaces the difficult job of verbalizing these feelings.

Reading and 'writing' body language is a science. Many books on the subject are available. Check a few out from the public library – it will give you a 'social edge', for if you know the language, you can communicate with people! So become a universal flirt . . . learn to talk with your body!

Be subtle when approaching a new 'interest'.

You spot a handsome stranger across a crowded room . . . the last thing you should do is go over to him and declare your admiration and undying love! You'd scare him away fast! You can get results by being subtle. Say something like, 'I couldn't help but notice you, and you looked friendly, so I thought I'd take my chances and come over and chat for a while.' An approach like this is sure to get a favourable response!

Flirt as often as you can.
Flirt with everyone, even those people who are not in the age group you are interested in. Seize every opportunity to practise your flirting strategies, even if you know it will not result in a date. Flirt with the waiter who serves you breakfast. Flirt with the petrol-station attendant. Flirt with the bank clerk. Flirt with a colleague, or even practise flirting with pets! Flirt, flirt, flirt! Practice *does* perfect your technique! Get into the habit of flirting with everyone you deal with, and you will soon become a master charmer! When you finally meet the love you have been dreaming about, you will be very much at ease as you seduce her *flirtatiously!*

You would like very much to have a conversation with someone who attracts you . . . so start one!
Take the initiative and start a conversation. You don't have to be scintillating, just talk with enthusiasm. Pretend you are a politician, and approach people in a positive way – as though you were campaigning for votes! People respond to politicians because of the interest they show in other people, not because of their speeches!

Make sure that your comments are positive. Don't be ironic or sarcastic: you will turn people off. People go to social gatherings to have fun. If you think you will get attention by acting the wet weekend, you are mistaken. Try to say something pleasant about everyone and everything. Even if you don't like the food or the punch, act as though you do. You might actually begin to enjoy yourself!

Another no-no is to talk endlessly about yourself. People are self-centred, so focus on the one you are talking to and he will feel important. Putting the spotlight on him is a way of flirting . . . but only you know it!

So push the 'on' button! Get revved up with positive thoughts as you talk and flirt your way into having a wonderful time!

Use a party favour, a game, or a conversation piece to flirt . . . or flirt silently!
Singles need to find ways of standing out from the rest of the crowd, to be noticed – particularly by other singles. You can use almost any object to help you flirt. A party favour or game can be an ice-breaker.

Next time you're out shopping, look around for some amusing little item that will make you the life of the party when you're at a social affair.

Novelty items are a great way to help you practise your social skills. They give you a way of approaching people that is non-threatening and fun – which is exactly what the game of flirting is all about! People respond well to unique items, and they will not have to make an effort to talk to you. Funny or odd trinkets naturally lead to conversation openers like 'Isn't that interesting, where did you get it?' Magically, their inhibitions will disappear because you have made them feel comfortable. Like a wizard, you have provided a diverting illusion instead of directly confronting them with a 'let's talk' demand. Flirting is meant to be light-hearted communication. Why not make use of a fun item to set the mood for flirting? Try it and watch everyone respond enthusiastically!

Have you thought about the flirting possibilities using wind-up toys? You can use them anywhere: at parties, at pubs, at restaurants, etc. Wind up the miniature gadget and send it walking towards an interesting target. Let the fun begin!

Wearing a conversation piece is another easy way to flirt. It provides you with an outlet – something to talk about, something to make people notice you. Attracting someone because of the way you look – or with something you are carrying or wearing – is a flirting technique, a silent way of flirting. People will come over to you. So pique their curiosity: wear a big brooch on your jacket or sport one on your handbag. Wear an unusual tie clip or a far-out bow tie. Jewellery, too, is always noticeable – especially unusual dangling earrings and charm bracelets. Try the dramatic look by wearing a turban made from lavishly designed material in luminous colours, or even gold or silver lamé or sequins. Twist a scarf trimmed with tassels around your waist, or use a belt brimming with antique bells to sound the alarm – flirt coming through!

Today's clothes are often outlandish in cut and colour, so in order to attract attention, you need something super-unusual. T-shirts are fun for casual affairs, and you can even have them personalized with a caricature of yourself and a saying such as 'Jim at work' or 'Sarah as per usual'. The design is up to you! Why not advertise your business on a T-shirt? With an eye-catching slogan such as 'For a swinging time, ring Mike', you could be advertising patio, porch, or garden swings, or children's gyms!

Instead of an ordinary bit of jewellery, stick a large badge proclaiming your favourite cause on your coat; you might attract the attention of someone who also wants to save the whales . . . or the hummingbirds . . . or stop pollution . . . or traffic. Be especially daring and wear a badge that has a flirty or funny message like 'Sneeze on Wednesday and you'll kiss a stranger', making it all the more fun to wear on Wednesdays!

Flirt with perfume!
Familiarize yourself with perfumes and colognes. Go to the perfume counter of a large department store and ask for samples of the most popular ones. At home, do an in-depth fragrance study. Sniff each brand and become well acquainted with its bouquet. Inhale each lingering scent and store it carefully in your mind. Study only two or three perfumes a session, or you will mix odours and become confused. The object is to become a perfume connoisseur!

Once you have become an expert on perfume, you can zero

in on those people wearing the fragrances you have come to know so well. What a terrifically unusual flirtation you can offer them: 'Oh, you are wearing one of my favourite scents.' What an impression you will make!

Flirt with sporting accessories.
Athletic equipment seems to draw men out of their shells, so don't stash your bicycle – keep it out in plain view for all to admire.

Martha found her beau because of the water bottle that clips onto her bicycle. One day she stopped at a sidewalk café to fill her bottle with juice. She decided to have a beverage there before she continued her 20-mile ride. Martha sat basking in the sun while sipping her orange juice. When she emerged from her dreamy state, she noticed that the man at the next table was mesmerized by her. Martha sent a few seductive glances at the stranger. Her message was well received. James gave in to her spell, walked over to her table and began a conversation . . . about bikes! It turned out that he, too, was a bicycle enthusiast! Martha and James have been together for eight months and enjoy a 25-mile bike ride together every Sunday afternoon . . . only now, James carries the water!

Why conceal your football kit when you stop at the pub for a drink after your weekly match? The ladies love athletic types, so you should show off your sporty side: it is a symbol of virility. Also, only health-conscious, physically-fit people practise sports. So whether you are a male or female athletic type, use your sportiness to raise your flirting score!

Flirt with a kiss!
Or at least talk about kisses! No one expects you to run up and kiss a stranger, but discussing 'kissing trivia' is an amusing way to capture someone's attention and engage in a conversation.

Set the mood for a little flirting repartee with 'kissing phrases'. Make a game out of it . . . or make it your way of flirting. Ask someone whether he knows what 'kiss the claws' means . . . or say something like 'Did you know that the expression, "kiss the maid", comes from the mid-eighteenth century and means to lose your head in a guillotine? Did you know that "kiss a cow" means to verify the truth?'

Why not be a little bolder and blow a kiss to someone who attracts you from across a crowded room? After all, there is no harm in blowing a kiss . . . it is a sweet flirtation that gives you a reason to go over and reassure her that blowing a kiss is a gesture of great respect dating back to 3,000 BC! Such a flirtatious approach is sure to result in a kiss – at least!

Katherine found the man sitting alone at the table next to her to be irresistible. She was desperate to meet him. She decided to send him a 'lip-o-gram'. She imprinted her serviette with a 'kiss' and wrote, 'Sir, you bring out the flirt in me . . . I just had to send you a lip salute!' The couple had dessert together, and more!

Dancing is a way of flirting.
In general, moving to music is flirting. This was confirmed by an American psychologist who studied how women flirted in singles' pubs. Get into the swing of things by getting up on the dance floor or simply keeping time to the music while sitting at your table sipping your drink.

Don't wait until someone asks you to dance – get out on the dance floor with your buddies. You can flirt much better from there! Target your man, get in a position where he will notice you, and show him your moves, glancing seductively at him while you dance. He's heading your way right now!

Women need to flirt.
Flirting is an innate love call. Men often wait for signals from women before making a move, especially in the nineties, as they are more reluctant to be too forward with the emancipated woman! A woman's flirting delivers a message that turns his

wondering into action. So get out there and flirt! Do it with a subtle smile, a mischievous glance, a charming laugh, by flicking your hair away from your face, or by using your own original flirting action!

Mirroring: an interesting and successful way of flirting.
The fact is that people seem to be attracted by others who are like themselves. Notice in your own life how many things you have in common with your friends. You may have similar jobs, families, backgrounds . . . it is only natural to be drawn to the familiar!

One way to get close to a person is to become like that person. Mimic her physical ways – the way she is standing or sitting, her countenance, how she is holding her drink, her tone of voice. This type of physical mirroring is a powerful flirting technique. In a sense it is indirect because when mirroring is done properly – with subtle, natural movements – it looks as though you are the follower and the other person is the initiator. The one you admire will be magnetically drawn to you and will think she is doing the chasing!

An example of mirroring in action!
You are in front of the eligible bachelor the hostess told you about. He is sipping his drink using his left hand while standing at the hors d'oeuvres table. His left foot is crossed at the ankle over his right. Walk up to the table, nibble an hors d'oeuvre for diversion, then assume the same position as your prospect. Watch him carefully and follow his manner – that's all, you don't have to say a word or introduce yourself . . . just mirror his every gesture. Of course, if he sneezes into the punch bowl, blows his nose, or kisses the hostess passionately, you should probably think about finding another candidate to imitate!

Try to move in an unobtrusive manner when 'mirroring'; avoid mechanical movements. Practise with your friends if you must, or mimic your cat's movements – it's great exercise!

Accurate mirroring is like radar: it tells us that something familiar is approaching. You have probably been mirrored many times without ever noticing. Next time you are in a clothing shop, observe the salespeople . . . the best ones mirror their customer's attitudes and movements and end up selling them clothes they don't really need!

You needn't be daring to mirror someone: it is silent and unobtrusive. All you have to do is be sensitive to the individual and observant! This is a good way of flirting for shy, reserved people.

But how can matching someone's posture attract that individual? you ask sceptically. Imitation is the sincerest form of flattery: when you act like those you admire, you are telling them that you approve, that you like them and the way they are. Mirroring is an interpersonal technique that charms without words: it is an invitation to come and flirt with you!

Flirting can be a confidence-builder.
You have to believe in yourself to be an outgoing, fun-loving individual. You may have volumes of education and knowledge, but if you cannot project your personality, no one will notice you.

Even the most rudimentary forms of flirting – like winking at someone, mirroring someone, or staring at someone – can be a confidence-booster. You will feel like a winner, as though you have conquered the world, when someone responds with even a simple smile! The more you flirt, the more daring you will become. Before you know it, you will be experimenting with all kinds of flirting techniques, growing more confident with yourself and your skills, and feeling comfortable with people. Your self-image will expand. You will react more openly to different people . . . a whole new world will unfold for *you*, a confident person who feels good about himself!

Flirting pushes you to express yourself . . . and the nice thing is that you needn't always be obvious or outgoing when you flirt. Give a co-worker a compliment . . . you'll see how good it feels. Tell the telephone operator how kind she has been!

Maintain eye contact for ten seconds with a waiter or a bank clerk! Work up your confidence in yourself – you're on your way to becoming a professional flirter!

Move closer to the person who is speaking to you.
If you are talking with someone and realize you are attracted to him, make a strategic move: get closer physically! But be subtle about it. If you are standing, take a small step nearer. If you are sitting, move your chair slightly closer to this fascinating person. In either case, lean towards him. Sharing a smaller space is a step towards greater intimacy.

The physical distance between two people is very significant. It establishes clear boundaries from the first contact. Moving away is an obvious signal that you are not available. Moving closer is clearly a sign that you are interested and would like to get to know that person more intimately. Being near a person suggests to her that you are attracted. Your body language is saying: 'You please me!' A smaller distance also allows you to touch or brush up innocently against the person, creating even more intimacy while still maintaining a safe situation. Dare to initiate close encounters in conventional situations!

A delicate touch on the arm or shoulder while speaking to someone who interests you can be very effective!
Test the grounds of closeness by delicately touching the other person's arm. If your possible love partner does not move away, continue stroking his arm, letting your fingers trail downwards slowly until you can softly cup his hand in yours. If these gentle caresses are countered with a stiffened stance and a sudden drawing apart, stop immediately, even though the reaction may simply be one of surprise. At this point, you don't want to risk offending someone you consider desirable. Continue to smile and maintain eye contact as the conversation progresses. Of course, you may have a positive reaction to your innocent gesture, in which case you know further contact would be welcomed!

Attract a stranger's attention by 'accidentally' brushing against her.

Create an initial contact by 'accidentally' touching someone – this works well in a crowded place such as in a lift or at a cocktail party. This 'accidental' encounter provides the perfect conversation opener! An 'Oh excuse me – I'm so sorry – please forgive my clumsiness!' accompanied by appropriate flirty body language – a coy smile, a flutter of eyelashes – will usually open a conversation and encourage an exchange of names.

Another good line to open with is, 'Oh I'm terribly sorry! I've been rushing around all day and I can't seem to get out of high gear.' Perhaps the attractive stranger will suggest a tea or coffee break!

Although many cultures associate touch with sexual behaviour, it is a normal part of a healthy human being's range of tactile experiences. Consider how many people spend large sums of money for massages, facials, and relaxation therapies, which are certainly not sexual in nature. Gently cupping someone's hand or lightly brushing the hair away from her face is simply a tender gesture of friendship, not a sexual proposition.

Your posture should reflect confidence.

Check your posture in the mirror. Are your shoulders held up and slightly back? Do you hold your head high, as though an invisible thread were pulling it upwards? Try projecting this same confidence when walking. Practise walking in a dignified but assured manner that shows you know exactly where you are going on your way through life. People are attracted to a person who has an air of positiveness: you will encourage others to 'walk' with you when you pay attention to the body language your posture projects. You want others to get the message: 'I am a worthwhile person – and someone desirable to know!'

Poise and dignity will carry you through the best and the worst situations.

Whether you are sitting or standing – be poised. In addition to good posture – head up and shoulders back – avoid annoying habits such as swinging or shaking your crossed leg or jiggling your foot. Practise moving in a sophisticated manner. Imagine that you are a model or someone you admire, someone whose grace and elegance is a natural extension of his character. Learn to pick up and manipulate things with grace. It is helpful to watch lavishly-costumed plays on television, taking note of facial expressions and body movements. Of course, you don't want to appear pompous or overly flirtatious, but trying out these exaggerated forms will unleash your own special blend of elegance and poise – with a dash of flirting panache!

The crossed arms taboo.

If you habitually cross your arms, break this unattractive habit as quickly as possible! Crossed arms imply that one is a dispassionate individual, unwilling to share his existence. Crossed arms are like the road sign that says: 'Do Not Enter' – a distinctively negative signal. Not the type of image you want to project when you are trying to attract that special someone!

There are ways to overcome your tendency to cross your arms over your chest.

To break this bad habit, put one hand in your pocket, on a hip, or on the arm of a chair. If necessary, hold an object, such as a pen – anything to keep your arms unfolded. Your conscious efforts to break the habit will also help you become more of an open person, projecting a far more desirable image of curiosity and friendliness. Of course, the best part of breaking the crossed arms habit is having a free arm to slip through the arm of the person next to you!

Have you developed a nervous tic? Get professional help!
Nervous tics, such as involuntary eye, facial, hand, or foot movements, are an embarrassment and a repellent. People will go out of their way to avoid someone with a nervous tic because it broadcasts the message: 'I've got problems.' No one wants to get involved with a person overwhelmed by problems! Tics are not only irritating and distracting, they become all that others see. They eclipse a person's talents and personality.

If you have a nervous tic, don't despair! Relaxation, concentration and self-hypnotic techniques may help you greatly reduce and even eliminate your nervous reactions. However, some tics have underlying medical causes and require professional attention. Don't be ashamed to ask for competent help in getting rid of these minor problems. With proper treatment, you will feel much better about yourself and soon be able to enjoy yourself more!

A firm handshake leaves a positive impression.
Have you ever shaken hands with a person whose hand was clammy or whose grip was weak? It left you with a poor impression of that person, right? Because a handshake often marks the first and therefore highly important contact with a person, you want to make a good impression. Furthermore, although a handshake is a form of greeting, it is also a symbol – when entering into a social or business agreement – to conduct oneself in an honourable manner. Shaking hands firmly also denotes inner strength of character – and that is certainly an impression you want to impart!

Even the firmest handshake can be undermined if the hands are ice cold! When you know you will be in a situation where you will be meeting new people and probably shaking hands, keep your hands warm. If you are prone to having cold fingers, exercise your fingers or rub your hands together to improve circulation.

Do your palms tend to perspire when you are faced with social situations? A damp handshake is not very pleasant, and it certainly doesn't make a good impression. Massaging a few drops of camphorated alcohol into the palms of both hands can help keep them dry by stimulating the circulation.

Another important aspect in the Western ritual of shaking hands is to look directly into the eyes of the other person. And a word to the wise: be mindful of your strength, especially when shaking hands with someone wearing rings. A bone-crushing handshake causing a ring to gouge deeply into tender flesh will be remembered – and *you* will be avoided!

Your body language speaks volumes!
There are a number of little body gestures you can use to initiate social contact. For example, shake your watch, then hold it to your ear as though it doesn't work. Politely ask the person next to you for the time. *Voilà!* Contact!

Suppose you notice a handsome, debonair man whom you'd love to meet. You have just been shopping and your arms are full of packages. What an opportunity! Pretend that your packages are heavy, perhaps even drop one . . . or ask the handsome stranger to help you. Who could resist coming to your aid?

In another scenario, imagine that you have just checked your coat out of the cloakroom of a restaurant. You notice an unaccompanied man also checking his coat out. Go into action! Get his attention by fumbling with your coat, making sure that he sees you struggling. Nine times out of ten he will come to your rescue! If he does, seize the opportunity – engage him in a flirtatious conversation by praising his thoughtfulness while thanking him. Don't forget to introduce yourself! Perhaps he will offer to share a taxi with you – or even better, he might even drive or walk you home!

Is there someone interesting sitting behind you on a bus or train? The 'watch trick' will reveal all!
Suppose you are on a bus, and you have no interest in the people in front of you. Instead of rudely turning round and

staring at the other passengers, try the watch trick. Pretend
your watch doesn't work by tapping it gently, then moving it
up to your ear. With your wrist at your ear, turn your head to
the side, tilting it backwards. This way you can get a glimpse
of the people behind you without being conspicuous. Who
knows, someone may even offer to tell you the time! You could
also watch who is behind you from the mirror of your powder
compact.

**Send a drink and a short note to that attractive person
you've noticed in a pub or restaurant.**
You see her at the other end of the pub. You are captivated by
her. You yearn to talk with her. Have the waiter take her a drink
with your compliments and write a short note on the back of
your business card. Watch for her reaction. If she smiles at you,
smile back holding her attention for a few seconds. Nod and
raise your glass to her in a silent toast. If she responds
favourably, make your move! If a woman sends a man a drink,
he can reciprocate by sending her a flower.

Use your business cards for impromptu messages!
Suppose you are on the tube – or at a bus or train station – and
you see a handsome young man sleeping. Write a short note on
the back of your business card and slip it between his fingers –
the fate of this fairy tale depends on what you write! You may
choose to be subtle and scribble a compliment such as, 'You are
as adorable as a teddy bear!' – or you might be more daring
and poetic with a suggestive message: 'I wish I were a tear born
in your eye, living to caress your cheek, and dying on your lips!'
Yes, it is an impetuous, adventurous act to leave such notes, but
you may be pleasantly surprised when the phone rings and it's
your teddy bear – wide awake and ready to meet you!

And now another scenario! While waiting for your business
flight, you see the most beautiful creature you have ever seen.
Why not send her your business card with a note saying, 'I'd
fly to the ends of the earth to meet you!' You don't go to airports

often? No problem: fit the message to your scenario. If you are in a restaurant, you could try a note something along these lines: 'My dinner is tasty, but you look delicious! Could you join me for dessert?' Be prepared for company for coffee . . . and for who knows what else besides?

If you are wearing lipstick, you could imprint your card or a paper dinner serviette with your lip-prints and accompany this flirty missive with a note saying, 'A smile comes over me every time I look at you!' You may be smiling for a long time if you take a chance on flirting!

Saying hello can lead to surprising events!
A simple greeting can work wonders! Someone to whom you haven't been introduced may want to talk to you but doesn't dare. A smile and a 'Hello!' from you can be just the invitation he needs to approach you. A simple greeting *can* initiate a conversation . . . *and more!* Dare to try it!

Develop a sultry, low-pitched voice.
When you speak slowly in a low tone, people listen more carefully. Why? Because they must be attentive to hear every word. What a delightful psychological fact that you can use to your advantage! It is important to remember that the tone of love and romance is soft and sensuous. Anyone who drones on endlessly in a loud, annoying voice is certain to be avoided! Develop a lovely voice and you will be rewarded with lovely encounters!

Tape your voice so that you can hear its normal tone. Most people are very surprised to hear how they sound to others! To train yourself to speak in a well-modulated tone, practise the same phrase in different pitches. Keep the exercise fun by choosing a friendly phrase – perhaps something like, 'Hello there! How are you? My name is ——, and I have been wanting to meet you for a *very* long time!' Try imitating someone whose voice you admire. There are a number of self-help books on voice improvement, and you can also take voice classes or even consult a speech therapist. Your voice is a valuable asset, an integral part of *you*, and a powerful ally in your flirting endeavours!

When you offer a compliment, do so with a personalized touch.
Everyone can be complimented for something. Even though you may not know a person, you can easily find something about her to compliment. The obvious choice is appearance: hair, eyes, skin, teeth, smile, apparel, or something she's wearing. Whatever strikes you as unusual or particularly nice about a person can be used as a compliment. When a kind thought about someone is verbalized, it becomes twice as endearing. Doesn't that encourage you not just to think it but to *say* it as well?

Don't limit compliments to physical appearance. For example, you may find that someone you do business with, but have never met, has a nice voice. The next time he is on the telephone, tell him: 'You have a lovely phone voice.' Perhaps go a step further and say, 'I'd like to hear it in person sometime!' That should encourage further conversation!

Compliments can be given to anyone, at any time, in any place – in a checkout line, at the bus stop, in a lift. Elaborate a little bit when you compliment someone, and be sure to give your compliment a personal touch. Don't just say, 'You have a nice tie,' as this remark puts the emphasis on the tie. It would be better to say, 'That tie really suits you,' adding, 'it brings out the gold flecks in your eyes.' This type of compliment is sure to provoke a response! When the stranger blushes shyly or smiles, you'll have the chance to get a little more personal: 'What an illuminating smile!' . . . and perhaps engage in a two-way conversation – or more!

Always make personalized compliments. Tell your hostess that she is an extraordinary cook, rather than using a tired old comment like, 'The meal was excellent, thank you.' That statement highlights the food, not the hostess, and all she can say to that remark is 'You're welcome,' whereas she might have said, 'Thank you. I love to cook,' which is a perfect introduction to a conversational exchange!

Don't confuse a compliment with flattery. A compliment is a genuine commentary about something you believe. Flattery is an exaggeration that may not be quite true. For example, telling a man he is a better dancer than John Travolta would be taken as a gross exaggeration, not as a personal compliment! Saying to a woman that she is more beautiful than Miss Universe wouldn't endear you to her, whereas telling her that being with her is a wonderful experience, could win you a crown!

A compliment can be as simple as congratulating someone for work well done, or as complex as a beautifully-composed poem. The end result is to give pleasure to the recipient – with a hint of seduction as well!

True communication involves letting the other person express himself.
There are two advantages to letting the other person talk: first, you get to know him through his conversation; second, as long as the other person is talking, you needn't divulge too much information about yourself. Above all, really listen to the other person. Don't cut him off, and don't monopolize the conversation. If someone tells you he just got back from visiting a country you have been to, why chime in with dry facts about various landmarks? Ask him whether he enjoyed the theatres, the fashion in dress, the music, etc. – it is far more interesting to hear his point of view.

If you have just met someone, don't take over the conversation. You don't want to reveal too many intimate details about yourself. How can you learn anything from or about the other person if *you* are doing all the talking?!

If someone you have just met monopolizes the conversation, never letting you get a word in edgewise, and only talks about herself before finally asking about you, answer with a note of sarcasm 'Me? Oh me, that's old news.' Ciao, baby!

Call a person by her name as often as possible in a conversation. There is no sweeter music to the ear than the sound of one's name, especially from an admirer. In conversation, say her name often. Repeat it whenever possible: sprinkle her name throughout the conversation, as if you love the sound of it. For example, you can personalize a simple invitation to the cinema by saying, 'Louise, I am sorry to have to rush off, but could you come with me to the cinema tomorrow, Louise? Would the one at the Odeon suit you, Louise? And, of course, the evening's on me, Louise!' With a little effort, you can turn your daily conversations into personalized communications!

Be an understanding and sympathetic conversationalist. If someone tells you of unfortunate moments in his life, be sympathetic rather than judgemental and accusatory. Respond with honest, caring comments like, 'You must have found it difficult to be in that situation.'

Don't tell him he is to blame for his misfortune. For example, if someone tells you he sprained his ankle running a marathon, it isn't nice to respond by telling him that he was probably not in good enough shape to enter. Be soothing with words like, 'You must have been disappointed at not being able to finish.'

If someone mentions that his girlfriend left him because he was out of work, don't criticize by telling him he should have looked harder for work. Be understanding by responding, 'You must have felt very alone at a time when you needed support.' This type of response will help the person feel better about the situation. You might try a funny, upbeat slant: 'At least now you can make a fresh, new start in every department!' Sympathy and/or levity will raise the other person's estimation of you – as well as his feelings!

In the beginning of a relationship, avoid asking very personal questions – particularly during your first encounter.

Let the other person have enough time to express herself on her own terms. Avoid asking questions about the person's former loves or her financial status – especially if you have only just met.

Discretion is best in the beginning. Probing into someone's personal life as soon as you meet is disrespectful and tactless. How would you like it? Being nosy shows lack of judgement – it's an instant turn-off. By the same token, repeating confidences is also a negative trait. You may lose your possible love partner by revealing someone else's secret, and you will be seen as an unreliable, shallow person only interested in gossip. This new person will certainly not tell you anything important for fear that it will be repeated all over town! At times like these, remember that 'silence is golden!'

Don't be on the defensive when others ask personal questions.

If someone asks you personal questions, try not to snap back defensively. Your admirer is probably not doing it on purpose, but rather lacks diplomacy and tact. An amusing retort, such as 'Did I mention that my great-grandmother wore football cleats and drove an articulated lorry?' will leave the way open for continuing the conversation on a more tactful level.

Reached a pause in conversation? Don't panic – open up a new topic of conversation.

If there is a lull in the conversation, it may be that the other person is simply not as talkative as you are, or may have nothing more to say on the topic under discussion. You can get the conversation going again by analysing what has already been said and thinking of a good topic. You might want to talk about a film you have recently seen or a mutually admired entertainer. You could begin with a personal question about what leisure activities he likes, a favourite book, or whether he participates in sports or watches them on TV. Answers to the last topic will quickly give you a good idea about whether or not you are expected to spend weekends in front of the TV watching professional football, rugby, et al. – because now is the time to find out if your interests are compatible!

When you are trying to encourage conversation, ask questions that require more than a 'yes' or 'no' as an answer. Phrase your question in such a way that the other person has to give her point of view. For example, if you ask, 'Do you like opera?', your partner will answer 'yes' or 'no'. But if you ask, 'What do you think of Pavarotti?', she must answer with a full sentence, which can lead to a string of questions, thereby prolonging the conversation – and quite possibly exploring more intimate subjects!

Master the art of telling jokes, funny stories, and anecdotes, without resorting to crude language or vulgarities.
Build a collection of amusing stories. When you hear a good joke or a humorous anecdote, write it down and memorize it. Use the library as a source of joke books, anecdotal anthologies, and books of famous quotations. Practise your delivery: a good storyteller always livens up a party, and everyone remembers the life of the party!

Collect unusual stories and seemingly incredible facts.
Listen to people's own experiences and read about unusual life stories, such as those appearing in *Reader's Digest*. Ask your friends to tell you the funniest thing that ever happened to them. Watch TV programmes that tell of incredible feats or events. Try to memorize a few fascinating facts. Build up your repertoire of interesting stories to tell at parties or during gatherings with friends. Use your facts to impress a stranger you

find attractive. You will become known as an entertaining conversationalist!

Memorize passages from famous books.
Citing passages from classical works is impressive and can demonstrate a varied education. Choose passages from works that interest you. For example, if you are a scientist and are mostly around people with scientific occupations, you may want to quote Newton or Einstein. When slipped into your general conversation, passages from any widely known work by Shakespeare, Milton, etc., not only indicate that you are well-read but that you are complimenting the other person by assuming he will recognize the source of your reference!

Spice up your conversation by asking what she would do if she won a million dollars.
Because a reply would be spontaneous, it reveals whether that person is mature or superficial, egotistical or generous, reserved or flamboyant. A word to the wise: in asking this question, be prepared to answer it yourself!

Familiarize yourself with what is going on in the world of sports so as to be able to keep a conversation going with someone who loves sports.
Learn the names of key sports figures as well as current facts about sports such as football, cricket, boxing, auto racing, tennis, and golf, in order to keep up with a 'sporty' conversation. If watching sports events on TV bores you, read the sports section of the newspaper for facts. Make use of the library for information on outstanding athletes. A little-known sports fact can be most impressive! Who knows? You may enjoy these sports so much that it will open up a whole new world for you!

Why not read this fascinating person's horoscope?
Most people like to know their horoscope even though they
don't believe in it. Horoscopes often appear in daily
newspapers, and once you know a person's sign, you can send
him a fax or read it to him over the phone. Everyone loves to
hear what others have to say about him, and particularly about
the future!

Memorize the major characteristics of each sign of the zodiac
so that the next time you meet someone interesting, you can
tease her about her sign. Although the question, 'What's your
sign?' is now an old cliché, it remains an amusing topic of
conversation. It is an excellent way to initiate an informal chat
and to get to know new people. What's *your* sign?

**Be inventive, creative, and imaginative when looking for
ways to meet a person you find interesting.**
Adapt yourself to the situation. Take into account the place you
are in, the circumstances, and the type of people who attract
you. Be outgoing and original when devising a plot for meeting
them. Try for a spontaneous first contact. If you are in a corridor
or on the street, spill the contents of your handbag or a handful
of coins right in front of him! Deliberately forget your briefcase
by her chair! Be imaginative – the rest will follow!

**Even if a situation is not a crisis, offer to assist. Conversely,
ask for help yourself.**
If you see a person you find attractive who needs help,
volunteer with enthusiasm. Lend a helping hand with
overloaded packages. Open a car door or a door to a building
or office. Reach for that object on a high shelf at the
supermarket. Both doing laundry? Offer to help separate the
clothes before washing. Coin-operated machines are always
causing trouble, and you can take such everyday opportunities
to flirt!

Encourage the people you find attractive: ask them to help

you. Feign your helplessness if necessary. Pretend your packages are too heavy, or pretend there are so many that you can't open your car door. Look at them in an imploring manner. Who could resist? Put your map away and ask for directions. With luck, the other person will take you to your destination! Now you have two more methods to keep in mind: offer help or appear to need it!

If you must leave in the middle of an interesting conversation, do so gracefully.
Suppose that you have been talking with a person whom you find attractive, but you are late for an appointment and have to leave. Be sure to explain your reasons in such a way that you do not offend the other person and at the same time convey the message that you would like to talk with him again. You could say something like, 'I must hurry off to a previous appointment, but I would very much like to continue our conversation. Could we meet for a drink on Thursday night after work?' Usually a mutually agreeable time and date can be arranged, and your new 'date' will appreciate your courtesy, politeness and thoughtfulness – as well as understand that you are interested enough to want to see him again.

Should you have to cut short a telephone conversation, you could say, 'I was just going out, but I'd love to talk to you. May I ring you back later today or tomorrow?'

In addition to being polite, you are indicating to the other person that you really want to be in touch with her again – *soon!* That message is often more important than the subject of your conversation!

Oh, no! You've been asked to go out on an evening that is already scheduled for something else! Don't despair – there is a solution!
The one person you've been dying to hear from asks you to go to the cinema on the same night that you have classes, a family

do, or whatever. Be direct: say that you are sorry, but you will be busy that particular evening. However, you really would love to go out with him, and you suggest another evening later in the week. Be sure to explain *what* is keeping you busy that evening. You will be respected for keeping your commitments, and you will be assuring the other person that, although you are legitimately occupied on the evening in question, you are interested in being with him.

It's great to be busy, but don't give the impression that you haven't a moment to spare.

Although it is tempting to impress others with accounts of your busy, full life, try not to go so far as to appear to be too busy to date. Possible love partners will be reluctant to ring you if they think that they would only be disturbing you or that you would reject them. If people think they are disrupting your schedule, they will feel like they are leaving a bad impression. So if you are a particularly busy person, let people know that your calendar is flexible and that you always have time for interesting people and events. For example, leave a cheerful message on your answer phone that includes the following line: 'Your message is very important to me . . .' And, of course, make your message sound warm, friendly and inviting!

Learn how to say 'no' tactfully.

How do you say 'no' to a person you are not interested in, without causing insult? Sometimes it is necessary to tell a little white lie in order not to hurt a person's feelings. You may say something like: 'I'm sorry, I am presently dating someone.' Or, 'My heart is occupied with another's love.' Or blame your refusal on your work: 'I have a new job that I'm devoting all my time to these days.' Whatever reason you choose, it must be believable. Saying that you have to attend a relative's funeral or that you're having an operation can lead to embarrassing moments later on!

A smooth strategy for exchanging telephone numbers – with a plus!

You are attracted to a person whom you see only occasionally, and you would really like to get to know her better. Why not ask for her phone number? Begin by giving your number, and at the same time, tell her something about your schedule: 'On Tuesday nights I take courses at the university, but the rest of the time I'm home. I'll also give you my work number in case you want to get together at lunchtime.' You have just accomplished several things through this strategy: you have given her a way to reach you, you have verbalized your interest in accepting an invitation, and you are also giving her a chance to make that date by phoning you!

If you feel uncomfortable asking for a phone number because you have just met, you might try the following approach: 'Michael, I know we have just met, and you may find that I am being too forward, but I would like to get to know you better. If I don't ask where I can reach you now, I probably won't have another chance!' How could anyone refuse such a charming request? Being warm and direct is the essence of becoming a successful flirt!

Suggest an activity you can do together.

Listen carefully to the other person's conversations. Be aware of the other person's interests and favourite pastimes. If, by chance, she mentions a film and says she has not seen it, take the opportunity and invite her on the spot! Follow up with the suggestion that the two of you go for a bite to eat after the film. Pick up on signals during a conversation and dare to turn them into a date!

If the person refuses your invitation, it could be that he is simply not interested in what you are proposing. Suggest something else: a visit to an art museum or a crafts exhibition; perhaps he will feel more comfortable with a shorter date the first time. Use your imagination, and keep the invitations flowing!

Let your love interest know that you have admired her for a long time.

Tell your possible love partner that you have admired her from afar for quite some time, but that you have never dared to approach her until now. Recap some of the occasions when the person made an impression on you. For example: 'I saw you leave the office the other night, carrying a load of work. Do you take work home often?' Show her you are observant and concerned. 'The other day I noticed you coming out of the lift – you looked so serious. Is everything going well in your life?' Let her know you are captivated by their presence: 'Every morning on the tube, I can smell your perfume as I enter the carriage, and my heart races at the prospect of seeing you.' Be flattering: 'I looked for you at the Christmas party. When I finally found you, you were leaving – before I could say how breathtakingly beautiful you looked in that blue dress!'

People are always pleased to hear that they stand out in the crowd, and it's always nice to make someone feel special. Letting the other person know you think he is *very* special is the secret heart of flirting!

Look for opportunities to meet casually.

If the one who pleases you mentions that she will be at a particular place at a particular time, mention that you may drop by, and observe her reaction. Often someone will mention an event to see if the theme interests you. Or it may be that the person is too shy to come right out and ask you to meet her at a specific place, but she would love to bump into you there. So indulge her by being forward for her. Playing her game will make you a winner – at flirting!

Pretend to recognize someone.

You see someone you are attracted to. Say, 'Hello Patrick, how are you? I haven't seen you in ages!' When the person replies that he is not Patrick, but Piers, blush coyly and introduce yourself. *Voilà!* You have successfully made the first move with an enticing stranger!

Dishonest, you say! Perhaps a little, but you are not hurting anyone, and you can admit your little white lie later on in the relationship. If you are consumed by guilt, then wait for the opportune time during your initial conversation with your new-found friend and say something like, 'You know, I really didn't think you were Patrick, but I found you so irresistible that it was the only thing I could think of to meet you.' How could anyone be angry with these sweet words of flirty flattery?

Flirt while talking on the phone.
For example, Mark goes to ring his friend Joseph but mis-dials Joseph's number, and a lady with a sultry voice answers, 'I'm sorry, but you have the wrong number.' Not one to miss an opportunity, Mark quickly replies: 'You're quite right, and I apologize for disturbing you; but someone with such a sexy voice would be great to talk to for a little longer, if I may.'

If you are in the habit of playing this little game, haphazardly dialling numbers, make sure to note the number first, in case you get lucky!

Flirting at work – particularly on the phone – is fun and breaks up the monotony of the day. You never know what might result from playing this intriguing game! But do it with class and dignity. Have fun without being disgusting! Remember that you are at work – be discreet and don't neglect your responsibilities.

If you ring someone and are greeted by an answer phone, leave a romantic message – one certain to bring a smile to the listener's lips. Make it the kind of message sure to be returned at once! Or you may want to be even more intriguing when ringing someone you know: record a few clues but don't leave your name. Let him guess who it is from your voice!

Flirt over the phone with your friends. Naomi, for example, is flirtatious by nature. She rings at least three male friends each week. Tuesday she rang Richard to ask him how his job interview went, Wednesday she rang Eric to see if he got his new car, and Friday she rang Tom to find out how he enjoyed his holiday. Remember: the more people you ring, the more experienced you will be at flirting, and the more calls *you* will receive in return!

Don't miss an opportunity to flirt while driving your car.
Naturally you will play it safe and flirt only when the car is stopped – at a red light or a stop sign, not while you are actually driving! But on a beautiful day, while you are waiting at a traffic light, you may see a pleasing person in the car next to you. Smile, wink, wave – or if you have a convertible or the windows are down, say 'Hello!'

A cellular phone is great for playing a flirting game with other drivers who also have car phones. Print your cellular phone number on a piece of white cardboard, keeping it in the car for when you need it. When you spot a person you are attracted to who has a cellular phone, honk your horn and show him your phone. Quickly hold up the cardboard – preferably at a light or a stop sign – so he can jot down your number!

Flirting 'by car' is an amusing and original way to flirt and to meet an intriguing stranger. It can also have remarkable results. For one couple, marriage resulted from this strategy! Diane and Philip were caught in a traffic jam. Diane yielded the right-of-way for Philip to cross into her lane. When he looked in his rearview mirror at Diane, he was so captivated by her beauty that he stepped out of his car and went up to her window to say thank you and introduce himself. They dated for three months and were married within six months! A true story that might entice you to become a car-flirt expert!

Buy a pair of season tickets for the theatre or for a sporting event.
These tickets are generally sold long in advance of the event. Whether you are interested in the theatre, cricket, football, or rugby, having a pair of season tickets is a great way to arrange

a date. Why not invite a different person to each event? This strategy will certainly give you a range of people – one of whom just might have all the attributes you are looking for! Don't plan all your season's dates in advance – keep some of the tickets available in case you meet someone new and interesting. The fact that you have tickets in hand gives you the perfect opening for approaching that new interest! You may well end up enjoying more than the theatre or match!

You are attracted to someone, but you don't know if the feeling is mutual.
Because you are unsure of the other person's feelings, you are reluctant to ask her for a date, but you really want to get to know her better. Try a neutral request. Ask her to help you to decide on a stereo system, or to help you choose a set of pots and pans for your mother. Such 'mini-dates' are flattering because you are, in effect, telling the other person that you value her opinion.

Observe the person's reactions towards you while you are at the non-date event. If you feel that everything is going smoothly and that the person is responding to you in a friendly, comfortable manner, take it a step further and ask for a date or to go for a bite to eat afterwards. At this point you will be able to differentiate between a friendly individual and someone who is clearly interested in you. A lecture or an exhibition is always 'safe' territory, and simply sitting or walking together gives you both a chance to get to know each other without any 'heavy date' pressures. Take that first step and arrange a low-key date – it may lead to a high-pitched romance!

Did you know that the supermarket is a great place to flirt?
The supermarket is the perfect place to practise flirting. You can ask someone for a recipe or for information on a particular kind of fish he might have in his shopping trolley. You can approach

someone in the fruit and vegetable section by asking how to pick a good avocado, pineapple, or cantaloupe. While cruising the meat department, ask how to cook a beef roast or how to grill a chicken. If you are a novice at flirting, practise with the personnel. Usually you are familiar with them from your weekly shopping trips. Compliment a stockboy or cashier; their work seldom receives public recognition, and they will respond favourably to flattery. Confidence in your flirting techniques will soar!

When you feel confident enough to try the real thing with fellow customers, here are a few hints. Suppose you are at the frozen-dessert counter when you see someone you find attractive. She is looking at the different types of apple pies. Ask her, 'Have you ever tried that brand? I often buy frozen apple pie, but I generally choose Brand X.' Gently taking the package from her hand, continue the conversation with: 'but I'm getting tired of it . . . I need something with a little more spice . . .' while glancing seductively at her. 'Have you ever tasted this brand?' Don't forget to flash a brilliant smile to charm her into answering! If the response is minimal, place the apple pie in your trolley and walk away; but if you detect the slightest interest, pump the volume to the max with a remark like: 'Why don't we have a taste test over coffee at my house?' Either way, you are a winner. If you don't get the date, you will have still practised your flirting!

Use of your daily routine to practise flirting. Say hello to as many people as you can during the course of the day. Set up a flirting contest with your friends. See who can say hello to the most people in one day. Occasionally, strangers will be surprised at your friendliness, but will also usually smile and return your greeting. In many countries, greeting strangers on the street is common practice.

Another way to flirt on the street is to pretend to be lost and to ask a stranger for directions. It helps if you ask him how to get to a place that is located in the direction in which he is walking because he may offer to take you there in person. As

extra support in this play-acting, you may want to carry a map
as an indication that you are looking for a specific place or
street. If you are successful in meeting someone this way and
a relationship develops, you can always admit later on that you
weren't really lost but simply in a hurry to make his
acquaintance – and your flirting strategy was the quickest way
to do so!

There are opportunities for flirting even in a car-park!
Did you ever realize that there are opportunities for discovering
a new love interest in the mundane act of parking your car?
Dennis found this out one morning when he was getting out
of his car in the office car-park. He noticed a lovely woman
pulling into a space not far from his. How to meet her? Quickly,
he grabbed a glove his sister had left in the car and ran over to
the young woman as she was getting out of her car. 'Good
morning, Miss. Did you just drop this glove?' he asked her. Of
course, she said she hadn't. Dennis kept the conversation going
by asking her to take it to her office to see if anyone there had
lost it. He gave her his office suite number and his telephone
number so that she could return the glove if no one claimed it.
When the young woman brought the glove back to him, Dennis
seized the opportunity to ask her for a date! Complicated? A
little, but well worth the effort! If you don't have a glove handy,
a book or an extra set of keys will do.

Car-parks offer other ways to flirt. For example, if a person
you are attracted to usually parks in the same space, put a little
note under his windshield wipers. Or you can break the ice by
showing an interest in his car or by asking advice about his car
because you are thinking of buying that make. Or leave a flower
and a charming note on his windshield. Include your phone
number, of course!

A stroll downtown can be an exciting trip – if you use it to practise flirting!
One Saturday afternoon, you decide to take a walk downtown.
Pretend you are a tourist, and take a camera along. If you don't

own a camera, borrow one or buy an inexpensive, disposable one. When you see a person you are attracted to, ask her to take your picture in front of some landmark – no impressive backdrops, please, you want the focus to be on you! Keep the momentum going: ask whether you can take *her* picture. Now you have created the opportunity for conversation! Perhaps you'll discover this person is also alone – and offering to show you around town!

The camera technique also has a practical aspect: it will inspire you to go to romantic places such as museums or public gardens where many single people spend weekend afternoons. A professional photographer claims that when he flirts with his camera he never fails to meet interesting people. With today's fully-automated cameras, you don't have to be a professional photographer: just take aim and *flirt!*

If you are taking classes at a university or just visiting the campus book shop or canteen, you will find opportunities to flirt.
Universities are ideal places to flirt, if only because of the sheer numbers of people attending day and evening classes. If you see someone who intrigues you, ask him which courses he is taking. 'Are you going for a degree or just taking courses you enjoy?' The possibilities are endless. You can suggest a tea break or a study session in the library. Perhaps mention that you have excellent reference books at home, and would he care to see them?

Flirt while you are waiting in a queue.
In this case you have an advantage. The person in front of or behind you is waiting to see the same play, film or exhibition as you are. This gives you built-in subject matter for starting a conversation without getting personal. If you are waiting to see a film, you might say something like, 'What did you think of the previews of this film?' or 'Did you hear what the director

did on opening night?' You may decide to sit together in the
theatre . . . maybe even share a bag of popcorn!

Flirt in a café.
You see her reading the paper at the next table. Ask her about
the day's headlines, or whether there is any good news in the
paper. She will probably answer 'no', to which you can
respond, 'There should be a newspaper just for good news,
don't you think?'

To use this strategy another way, you might want to mention
the highlights of a front-page human-interest story to the man
sitting alone at the next table!

Come Sunday, you may be sharing the news over brunch!

Flirt in the park.
There you are, in the middle of a lovely park, surrounded by
trees and birds, sunlight and shadow, filling in a crossword
puzzle. You glance up just as a handsome stranger pauses at the
far end of the bench. Say something aloud: 'Hmm . . . 26 Down
. . . Aztec sun god . . . seven letters.' Then address a direct
question to Mr Good-Looking: 'Would you happen to know a
seven-letter word for an Aztec sun god?' Intrigued, he
approaches you and your newspaper puzzle. Gotcha! Lovely
afternoon coming up!

Take birdseed with you on your next trip to the park. When
you spot an attractive person, toss a few handfuls of the seed
in her direction. The birds are going to flock around your
target – trust me! – and when they do, amble over innocently
and say something like 'Those birds certainly are attracted to
you . . . and I can see why!' Smile big and introduce yourself
quickly. Another successful encounter of the flirtatious kind!

Flirt at the railway station, the airport, on the tube – *now*, before he gets away!

Your train, airplane, or tube is about to leave when you suddenly see someone you are desperately attracted to. With only 30 seconds to make contact, take action and *drop something*: your money, ticket, handbag, briefcase, packages, umbrella – *anything!* Just drop it fast near the person you want attention from. A little shout – 'Oh no!' – helps. When he dashes to help you retrieve and rearrange things, smile a thank you, say who you are and where you're off to, and slip him your business/personal card before running off.

This strategy can be used in almost any public place and at any time when you have only seconds to spare. If the person you are attracted to does not respond, there's always another chance at your destination!

Be prepared for a 'quick flirt' anytime, anywhere!

Flirt in a restaurant.

You see an intriguing person sitting at the next table, eating something that looks delicious. Ask her what it is. If the person seems to be a regular customer, ask her what she can suggest from the menu. Continue the conversation on the basis of the stranger's answers. If all goes well, you could ask her to join you for coffee and dessert . . .who knows where this little flirtation will lead?!

There are other singles in your block of flats. Plan a 'meeting strategy'!

Post a 'Just For Singles' bulletin board in the foyer of your block of flats. Anything of interest to singles could be posted there: personals adverts, information on clubs or events in the community, or a poster about the party you're planning – just for the singles in the building! You will also want to place posters in the hallways, the foyer, the lift, etc. If your building is very large, you may want to restrict the party to two or three floors. This is a great way to get to know people you see every day but aren't acquainted with, *plus* no one has to drive home!

Be creative. Have special events that only singles can attend, such as wine and cheese parties or recipe swaps. Create a flat-sitting, plant-watering or pet-sitting service for singles, where you can exchange such favours with other singles in the building. Use your imagination – the possibilities are endless!

The art of flirting at a party.
You see someone intriguing at a party, but you haven't been introduced. Walk right up to him and say, 'Excuse me, but I'm trying to avoid someone who has been annoying me. Could I please talk with you for a few minutes?' A brilliant smile helps at this point. The time span you indicated wasn't long enough to be threatening, so you will probably be deep in the middle of a very interesting conversation before you remember to say, 'Oh, I guess I've lost that bothersome person! Wasn't I the lucky one! Well, I had better go now.' At which point your newly-found friend may well say, 'I'm the one who is lucky! Please, let's continue our conversation over dinner!' Try not to look too smug as you go off arm in arm!

Flirt at work.
Ever consider how many available people are right there at your place of work? Take action and send each one a valentine – it doesn't have to be 14th February to be a day for hearts and flowers and intriguing or funny little messages! Make office machines work to your advantage: send an attractive co-worker a fax just to say, 'Hello! You're looking great today!' Fax a cartoon or send a card by messenger. Unexpected communications brighten the day and say more than just the words!

Another scenario: you are with your friend in the lift of your office building. You notice an attractive man giving you the eye. Talk to your friend about work, mentioning the company and asking her to ring you at the office number in a voice loud enough for the man to overhear. If he is truly interested in meeting you, your phone will be ringing soon after you get to work!

If you're flirting with a business associate, make sure that you don't jeopardize your work. Always be professional, without overstepping those invisible barriers of office social code.

Some relationships work downhill – flirt on the ski slopes!

Flirting at a ski resort is fun and part of the relaxation. Conversation-starters are everywhere: 'Where did you get that stylish ski suit?' At the ski-lift: 'I'm supposed to sit on *what?*' On the ski-lift approaching 'Killer Mountain': 'Do you come here often?'

Later, during après-ski at the lodge, there is the whole day of adventure to talk about as you stretch your athletic body in front of a crackling fire, sip hot toddies, and *flirt!*

Most sports lend themselves well to flirting. Ask a tennis enthusiast where he learned his backhand, and could he demonstrate, please? Ask a golfer how she handles that follow-through when in the sand – more demonstration, please! You will usually end up with her arms around you at some point. The conversational gambits are endless, as well!

Your computer can help you be a super flirt!

Computers offer a number of ways to flirt. You can send someone a romantic message via modem, and it will appear mysteriously on his screen! A good graphics package will help you to design a funny love test, complete with little pictographs and answer boxes for responding to your clever flirtation!

Aficionados of computer games even have social events that are usually sent by electronic mail or special shared 'bulletin boards'. Have you an 'entertainment programme' on your computer? Check it for the flirting game.

Flirt in exercise class.
Ask your coach or someone in the class whether your position is correct – in a flirtatious way, of course! When you ask someone for advice, you are flattering him, and you can turn a simple question into a flirtation!

The gym or local sports centre is a good place to meet people who are mutually concerned with fitness and health. Go to your gym at different times on different days. Plan ahead: join a club that has many branches located in different parts of the city so that you can meet a wide variety of individuals. Some clubs even offer time-exchange in gyms in other countries! International fitness flirting coming up!

Investigate the possibilities of flirting via the post!
You have the office address or home address of someone whom you find attractive. Why not send a flirtatious message on an amusing card? Keep in mind that flirting is a subtle art; of course, you will use tact and finesse in your message – don't be too direct! You wouldn't want the postman to blush!

Have fun playing flirting 'games'.
In the middle of the week, the one you were hoping would ring finally asks you for a date on Saturday night. Tease her with a fun flirtation like, 'Saturday night? Hmmmm . . . I was planning on going away for the weekend' – pause, then continue – 'but you have just given me a good reason for staying in town!'

Another keep-them-guessing flirtation will help keep interest at a fever pitch. You know how you're always asked, 'How are you?' at the beginning of a phone conversation? Next time reply with a cagey ' Oh, *we're* fine.' Expect a long pause at the other end of the line. You will practically hear the worry wheels turning! Finally add, 'Yeah, my dog and I are doing very well!'

Flirting games are amusing for both parties. Friendly teasing or dramatic role playing – Me Tarzan, you Jane! – between love partners can be quite exhilarating!

It is not wise to flirt if you are already on the scene with someone.
Flirting with others when you are out with someone else is tactless and insensitive. Do you really crave double the attention? How would you like it if the person you were with winked conspiratorially at someone else or draped an arm around him?

The same advice holds true for flirting with someone who arrives with someone else. How would you feel if someone flirted with your love partner right in front of you?

Be intuitive and listen to your conscience when initiating a flirtation.
Intuition is an innate awareness of what is or is not good for you. You can use it to tell whether that interesting person across the room is approachable. If the timing seems right and you feel there is a tiny mutual spark, take the initiative! Be the irresistible flirt all these strategies have taught you to be!

When an opportunity to flirt arises, take advantage of it!
Even though you know that every flirtation will not spark a romantic interlude, flirt for the sake of practice. The more you flirt, the greater the chance of meeting your perfect match!

Being snobbish will get you nowhere fast – neither will acting vain or imperious.
Now that you have read this part of the book, you figure you have a 'black belt' in the art of flirting. Are you still able to be humble, modest, simple, honest, and sincere? Any other superficial attitude will only lead to disappointment. It is your originality and spontaneity that will make people respond to your flirting. Irresistible is another word for charming, and that should be your catch phrase, the ultimate assessment of your flirting!

FLIRTING AROUND THE WORLD

♥ ♥ ♥

Austria

Earn a Ph.D. in flirting at the Vienna School of Flirting and Contacts. Loneliness in Vienna has become a major social problem, resulting in the development of countless courses, seminars, and clubs for singles. Flirting is welcomed – even encouraged! Certain hobby classes – in pottery, singing, painting, and dancing, to name a few – are organized specifically for singles. You will find a relaxed, creative atmosphere in which singles can meet while learning a new hobby – and practising their flirting techniques!

Belgium

The magazine *Elan* suggested that singles try flirting in Belgium's swankiest afternoon disco, La Cave Royale, in Brussels.[1] It would seem that while the rest of the world is busy working and reserving social pleasures for evening hours, this Brussels hot-spot caters to those who prefer the sophisticated luxury of afternoon encounters. The dress code is strictly formal, and the atmosphere is decidedly festive! Dress in your fanciest, hire a limousine, and step right up to those suave, multilingual Belgians and flirt them off their feet!

Bachelors of all nationalities live in Belgium and offer a wide resource base for meeting potential partners. You can find them by joining the Friday Cocktail Group for English Speakers, the Brussels Mannekin Pis Hash House Harriers, or possibly at the Esikoislestadoilaid Seurat Suomi, a Finnish religious group. Happy hunting!

Canada

Of all the ten provinces in Canada, the province of Quebec has the most singles: over two million! More Quebecois than ever before are turning to dating services and personals columns to find their soul mate. In 1990, Quebec held its first Singles Fair, featuring speciality items, gifts, books, cassettes, and other interesting paraphernalia for the single person.

With all these unattached people wandering around, it is surprising that the only course which seems to be given for singles in search of their ideal partner is my own 'Love Strategies'. I lead people through the steps and stages of love relationships with weekend seminars, night classes and conferences attended by groups of 150 people or more. The tremendous success of these informative sessions encouraged people of all ages to attend. Surprisingly, the ratio of men to women was almost equal for each class.

People's Republic of China

Although arranged marriages are still the norm in many parts of China, the desires of young people to meet those of their own age and make their own choices has led to the opening of special social clubs where they can meet informally. Universities also arrange social gatherings that encourage young students to mingle without the barriers of status and class. Due to the limiting of family size to one child, the emphasis in a relationship has shifted from the broad influence of the extended family to the suitability of the two people in a couple to one another. The age at which many young couples marry has also undergone a change: today's young women want a better education and possibly a career which they will continue to pursue after marriage, so they are marrying later than they did in the past.

A number of matchmaking agencies have sprung up to pair the women of mainland China with the men of Taiwan. Government agencies, such as the Republic of China's Single Persons' Association, have organized Public Matchmaker Stations as a type of social awareness work. Even so, there are millions of singles throughout China who are looking for the 'right' person – when their busy schedules permit.[2]

Czechoslovakia
Although the Czechoslovakian landscape may not be sprinkled with fancy nightclubs, specialized agencies, or pubs for singles, the people are friendly and the singles in particular are quite hip – especially in Prague. So why not enliven the scenery with a dash of your original flirting techniques!

Finland
In this cold, northern climate, where winter days are short and nearly sunless, romance warms the hearts of these hospitable people – if your approach is politely subtle.

The Finnish people are known for their legendary reserve, so to counter this attitude, the government subsidizes 'tangos in the afternoon'! So try your hand at flirting with a Finn . . . but be prepared for a heady response and a lot of flirting in return!

France
Ah, Paris, the city of love . . . and a place where flirtations are the norm! And where, more than likely, you will be the *object* of a flirtation rather than the initiator!

In some parts of France, the singles scene is kept under wraps – so much so that agencies catering to singles advertise their services in a more or less disguised manner. For example, one of the major organizations, Eurofit, based in Paris, offers social opportunities and educational packages to singles – you can take every kind of course from ballroom dancing to chess – and you're sure to emerge flirting . . . with a French twist!

The agency, Reciproque, caters to high-income singles whose schedules keep them too busy to search for their ideal partner. Many of the elite dating agencies advertise in elegant periodicals like *Le Bottin Mondain* and *L'Eventail France*. The cost of being represented by one of these agencies is approximately £1000 for a predetermined period of time.

There are also a number of travel agencies that offer singles an extensive choice of holiday resorts including those to exotic destinations. Are you ready for that trip to the Riviera?

Germany

The number of singles in Germany has practically doubled over the past 20 years. In fact there are so many singles, the media concedes that being single has achieved 'in' status! The number of singles is multiplying with such momentum that over three million Germans are now turning to dating agencies and electronic media for help. This country certainly qualifies as fertile ground for flirting! Your chances of flirting successfully with a single person are definitely favourable. Perhaps you should consider Germany for your next holiday? Why go on a cruise when you can go cruising in Germany?!

Greece

Give your flirtations a Mediterranean flair by practising in the Greek sunshine. You'll find the people warm and receptive . . . and charmingly flirtatious! You can dance the night away under the stars, or listen to a traditional ballad as you sip ouzo in a taverna and flirt your way into your partner's heart!

The most important 'meeting' agency in Athens, called Elkas, has a number of members whose families have not found suitable partners for them through 'arranged' marriages. Bypass Mama and go directly to the source!

Italy

The great cities of romance: Venice, Florence, Verona – passion and moonlight on the Lido, stolen kisses in the long, arched hallways of the museums and palaces, sun-drenched afternoons wandering the countryside hand in hand with a new love. A perfect setting in which to practise the art of flirting. And you may well be the recipient of a flirtation: according to Elan, 58 per cent of Italians flirt!

Although it may be difficult to find lodging for a single person, or entertainment for singles, there is a nightclub in the heart of Rome called Hemingway that has become the favourite haunt of singles in the early nineties.

If you venture to Turin, one person in five is single! Twenty-nine per cent of the population of this city suffers on alone. Be an angel and minister to these unhappy singles!

Japan
Japan's rapid progress in every aspect of living has brought about many cultural changes in recent years. In today's Japan, many women no longer want to be subordinate. The women of Japan have become highly educated, favour postponing marriage for the opportunity to develop a career or to travel and enjoy life, and consider themselves to be emancipated. For example, women now express their frustrations about having to prepare and serve tea at the office. Although Japanese men are not really sure how to approach a woman these days, they are ready for anything . . . even flirting!

A number of single men have signed up for courses at Satoshi Noguchi's School of Marriage in Osaka, where they are instructed in the finer points of courtship and marriage. One aspect of the course focuses on changing your appearance with contact lenses, stylish haircuts and elegant Italian-style wardrobes. However, the most important subject is the art of communicating with and complimenting a prospective partner! After two years, the school has a 10 per cent success rate: 20 out of 200 participants are now married.

There are also traditional 'matchmakers', or *omiai*, as well as thousands of computer matchmaking agencies throughout Japan. One of the larger agencies, Altmann Systems International, provides at least three matches a month; another agency, OMMG, boasts of two matches per member per week. Membership costs are high and generally cover a two-year period. There is a no-fee agency, the government-operated Tokyo Marriage Bureau, but it serves only approximately 4000 singles and you have to live in the Tokyo metropolitan area. Some companies set up their own in-house matchmaking agencies for their employees, families and friends – the Mitsubishi Diamond Family Club, for example – while others sign up with major private agencies like Altmann's.[3]

When you join an agency in Japan, your information is immediately entered into their huge data base, and possible partners are identified and their particulars printed for you while you wait. Fees are due and payable when you receive the printout. Most agency fees include a periodical featuring members' profiles. Readers can select those members they would like to meet and the agency acts as a go-between, because no names, addresses, phone numbers or any other identifying information appear in the magazine listings. As you might well imagine, weekends at the agencies are very hectic when matched members converge for their rendezvous!

Men outnumber women 2 to 1 in the 25 to 39 age category. Sharpen your flirting skills . . . and head for Japan!

Malaysia

A large percentage of singles in this country can be found in the capital, Kuala Lumpur. These fast-track singles – young executives, doctors, accountants, managers and business-people – are often found in the many social clubs, posh hotel lounges, pubs and discos that dot the city. Although men are expected to make the first move in arranging a date, an increasing number of young men would like to see more equality between the sexes when it comes to asking for a date or issuing an invitation to a social event.

Because there is a much higher proportion of unmarried women as compared to men – current figures set the estimate at nine women to one man – dating agencies are mushrooming! Professional matchmaking is not only becoming acceptable in this country, it is often the main hope of educated singles who have postponed looking for a life partner because they have been studying or working so hard.

Religious background is also taken into account in programmes such as the one originated by the Muslim Youth Movement of Malaysia, ABIM. The Islamic style of courtship espoused by Abim Islamic Outreach in its Bima Ummah matchmaking programme is particularly popular with young Moslem single women who are too shy to engage in modern dating techniques. From a base in Ampang, Kuala Lumpur, Dr Ariffin Marzuki, chairman of the programme, pairs couples from his extensive files after conducting a lengthy interview with each applicant and assessing his or her concept of a suitable partner. Dr Marzuki encourages singles to be realistic about the level of education, physical appearance and financial status of prospective partners – in other words they should not expect to find a life partner who must meet unreasonable ideals!

Perhaps this charming country could be referred to as a paradise for single men! Certainly an interesting place to flirt your way into a perfect match of your own!

The Netherlands
This area has the reputation for being the flirting capital of the world. Indeed, according to Elan, a whopping 70 per cent of Dutch people admit to flirting 'passionately' on a regular basis! In Amsterdam, women can approach men without being judged as libertines. In fact, all over Holland the atmosphere is warm and friendly . . . a perfect place to flirt!

Norway
It is interesting to note that although nearly half of the population of this country are single, many unmarried couples live together.

Norwegians are open to all kinds of love strategies. If you have read any Norse legends, you know that flirting is certainly not new to them! Your flirtations will be warmly welcomed – and just as warmly returned!

Poland

You may have to keep your flirtations under wraps in Poland. Flirting is not that common among the Polish people, and their culture is strict. Although flirting as a fun and innocent interpersonal game is not widely indulged in, there are special magazines such as *Feelings* and *Erotica* which carry personals ads. These magazines are quite popular among the population in general, and particularly in the rural areas where women want to leave the drudgery of farm life and live in the city. This exodus has resulted in a scarcity of women of marriageable age for the men who are still living and working in the countryside!

Portugal

The Portuguese flirt liberally, especially in the most common meeting places in Lisbon – the bars. You may want to visit the Bairro Alto, situated in the heart of the old city, or the posh nightclub called Fragil. But a word of advice for women: don't be too daring with your flirts – the Portuguese male is still a little old-fashioned, and a bold flirtation may be misconstrued!

Russia

With the recent upheavals in Russia, you may find it slightly more difficult to try out a flirtation or two. Many clubs and older restaurants offer fine examples of distinctive architecture, and provide the perfect old-world atmosphere for your most decorous flirting strategies!

If you are looking for a highly-educated, cultured woman, you may want to contact the agency Moscow Connections, which represents 400 professional women who hold doctorates or other professional degrees.

Singapore

Due to the growing number of singles, satirized in the popular song, 'Single in Singapore/You don't know what you're in for', the Singapore government set up the Social Development Unit (SDU) in 1984 to create opportunities for singles to meet socially. The SDU's message is, 'If you wish to have a family, don't leave it until it is too late!' Recently, the organization has set up 'Just-in-Time' activities for singles who travel a lot or who work irregular hours. Members can now book an activity – a barbecue, a 'tea' dance, camping weekend, tennis or golf – on the day it is to take place. Spur-of-the moment decisions make these well-organized activities more spontaneous and fun for all concerned.

Other than hectic work schedules, the Singaporean single's high expectations for a style of living incorporating the highly desirable four Cs: cash, condominium home, car, and credit card, would make any matchmaking agency's efforts difficult to say the least! However, the SDU is obviously doing something right: their efforts have resulted in marriage for approximately 2,700 members![4]

Currently, SDU's 15,000 members are mainly higher-income university graduates and professionals, with nearly 70 per cent of the total membership drawn from the private sector. Perhaps not surprisingly, nearly 60 per cent of all members are below the age of 30.[5]

There are two other government agencies that also promote marriage: the Social Development Section (SDS) with 60,000 members drawn from the nation's 'O' and 'A' level diploma holders, and the Social Promotion Section (SPS), whose 20,000 members have achieved up to secondary school education. Mandarin Chinese is almost exclusively the spoken language of the majority of this group, and most of them speak very little English. In this last category, as in Japan, the ratio of men to women is 2:1.[6]

In early 1992 it was estimated that, out of some 270,000 singles in Singapore, approximately 95,000 were members of the above-mentioned three major governmental agencies dedicated to promoting marriage.

It might be a good idea to check out this beautiful city and manage a discreet flirt – or two or three – while you shop to your heart's content!

Spain

Flirt flamboyantly in Spain! *Olé!* The good news is that the number of singles has *increased* in the last year – but the bad news is that many of these singles speak only Spanish! The leading dating agency, Mundo Nuevo, boasts that 1990–91 was their most profitable year ever: their membership increased by a whopping 60 per cent! Another club, the 'Second-hand Club' for divorcees, has also grown in membership.

Thanks to the spirit of the post-Franco era, Spanish women are liberated to the extent that many carry condoms in their handbags! In 1978, divorce was legalized and this changed the demographics of singles around the country. By 1990, the number of divorced women had reached more than 300,000!

While in Madrid, visit the nightclubs Milford Andrews or Kinki and get to know a wide variety of lovely people looking for a flirting partner!

A visit to romantic, spirited Spain will give you the perfect setting *plus* numerous singles to practise your meeting and flirting strategies with! Count on your share of fiery passion from marvellous hot-blooded Latins!

Taiwan

According to government statistics, there are about 4.3 million singles in Taiwan – approximately one-third of the total adult population! Although most people are not single because they *want* to be, there is a tradition of social and cultural barriers making it difficult for men and women to meet. Men and women generally attend different schools and universities, and there continues to be an uneven distribution of the sexes in the workplace as well. In the cities, where service-orientated jobs predominate, there are more women than men. The opposite is the case in the high-technology orientated industrial areas: here, men outnumber women.

In addition to these hindrances to social interaction, men and women have different ideas of what they want from a marriage. Although women say they want equality of the sexes, they are looking for a husband who is better off than they are. And many well-educated men say they respect equality yet they still want to be the dominant member of the family. However, there are agencies involved in breaking down barriers and dedicated to finding ways for people to be introduced. [7]

A number of agencies now use computerized matching of singles. One of the larger organizations, Relationship Bridge Club, gives singles the opportunity to meet several 'possible' partners during one visit to the club's offices. Costs are high for a two-year membership; however, young people feel it is well worth the price to meet people they would not encounter at their place of work or be likely to meet through friends. With the pressures of demanding jobs, irregular hours and limited leisure time to look for a suitable partner, numerous singles are turning to the services of these modern 'matchmakers' whose traditional duties have been given a computerized twist. From the smallest to the largest agency, matchmaking services are in demand! [8] Perhaps now is the time to introduce yourself to the lovelorn of Taiwan!

United Kingdom

There are so many single people in Britain that over 1,000 dating services have sprung up. One agency, Dateline, was reported to have over 27,000 members in 1991! One out of every four people in Britain will use such a service at least once. Britain categorizes its singles and caters to the needs of each group: straights and gays, the disabled, golden-agers, people of different races, creeds – every group has its own 'singles' association.

Flirting is popular in Britain, and you can find a host of appropriate places to flirt. You might try your most sophisticated flirtations at the Executive Club, an elite social agency that organizes upwardly-mobile 'yuppie' events for its clientele.

United States

There are many activities and courses geared for singles in the USA, and flirting gets top billing! One course, advertised in a New York newspaper, was titled, 'How to Flirt, Court and Seduce'! Check to see if this course is still being offered before you head for the airline ticket office!

The singles scene is also commercially huge in the United States. There are clubs and associations in all the major cities, with newsletters and even magazines catering to the unattached. In the city of Los Angeles, for example, there are approximately 150 registered singles clubs catering to a wide range of tastes such as special ones for vegetarians and for particular age groups, like 'Autumn Women and Spring Men'! There is even a club in Beverly Hills called The Matchmakers. For around $10,000 (about £5,000) they will help you look for a mate. So, just pick a state: with such a wide choice of places and people, you might find your heart has run away from home!

Alaska

Alaska is the largest state in the USA, and there are many more men than women. There is even a specialty magazine devoted to features on men who are looking for companions and wives: *AlaskaMen* is rapidly gaining international status. Rush your subscription inquiries to: AlaskaMen USA, 201 Danner Street, Suite 100, Anchorage, Alaska, 99518, USA. The magazine is published six times a year, and is a real bonanza for single women. They also publish a calendar! Imagine! Twelve gorgeous men to devour with your eyes! Can't wait to see all these great people in person? A travel company, The Alaska Connection, offers special excursions for women who want to experience the thrills of the great outdoors – canoeing, salmon fishing, glacier climbing – and meeting the men, of course! Write to them at the same address as above for full details. Just think how rosy and fresh your complexion will be after all that fresh Alaskan air – and a hug or two from your gentle giant!

References
1. *Elan*, May, 1991.
2. *The Straits Times*, Singapore, January, 1992.
3. *Link*, February, 1992.
4. Ibid.
5. Ibid.
6. *Channels*, February, 1992.
7. Op. cit. *The Straits Times*.
8. Op. cit. *Link*.

♥ 3 ♥

A Million and One Love Strategies for a Terrific Relationship

CREATING YOUR SELF-PORTRAIT

♥ ♥ ♥

Before you enter into a relationship, create your self-portrait to learn more about yourself and what type of relationship you want.

Before you begin your search for your ideal partner, it is important that you first do some soul-searching and analyse who you are and what you want at this stage in your life. In order to define those qualities which you desire in someone else, you must first recognize what you have to offer in a relationship. Drafting your self-portrait will do this for you.

Your self-portrait is a summary of your likes, dislikes, faults and accomplishments, a recounting of your experiences in past relationships, and a detailed look at what you want from a relationship. The lists in this section will help you develop this summary. Because this analysis is so important in determining your criteria for a relationship, you should take time to complete it carefully, honestly and fully.

The experiences you go through in the course of a lifetime help shape your personality and influence your relationships. However, subtle changes and shifts in your outlook and your responses to life are occurring constantly: you may want to take this into account when you are designing your self-portrait. Be flexible and aware of your changes: keep the boundaries of your requirements open to change. Mark down the date when you first draw up your self-portrait and review it regularly. Your self-concept will undoubtedly undergo changes, and you will want to update your charts to reflect your new perceptions, or even design an entirely new portrait of yourself!

My Self Portrait

- My physical description
- The kind of personality I have
- My good qualities
- My moral values
- My faults and weaknesses
- My level of intelligence
- My depth of understanding
- My culture
- My education
- My talents
- My tastes
- My dislikes
- My leisure activities
- What others think of me
- The attitudes of those I respect
- The issues important to me
- My outlook on life
- What I have to offer to a love partner at this stage of my life

Now sit down, take a pen and several pieces of paper, and construct a profile of yourself. You are about to discover yourself – what you have done, where you have been, what you like or dislike, and what your dreams are.
Draw your self-portrait with honesty. Use the real colours of your personality and the shadows of your life that have given depth to your character. Start by describing your physical appearance. Go into detail.

- Are your nails always clean and manicured or are they bitten and ragged-looking?
- Do you take care of your teeth or do you only visit the dentist in an emergency?

- Do you keep your hair clean and shining?
- What does your skin look like? Dry? Oily?
- Do you have a shower every morning or once in a blue moon?
- Men with beards, do you prefer the 'natural' look to the well-groomed?
- What is your overall appearance? Do you dress casually, elegantly, stylishly modern, avant-garde?
- Do you wear bright, attractive colours or dress in dull pastels and beige?
- Do you follow fashion trends even if they don't suit you?
- Do you dress for the occasion and the place you are going to, or do you dress according to your mood no matter where you may end up?
- Are you careful about wearing clean shoes or boots? Highly polished or down-at-the-heels?
- Are you careful that there are no stains on your clothes or any buttons missing?
- Are you slim or overweight?
- Can you improve your appearance in any way – either by losing a few pounds or perhaps by changing that hair style you have had for the last decade?

Now that you have described your appearance, take a look at the intangibles – your personality.
Do you feel that your personality has strong ties to your past, your family, your children, your past and present relationships? Then you are people-orientated as opposed to someone whose personality is geared to his talents, faults and failures, personal successes, dreams and ambitions. Are you more concerned with the things you must do to attain your goals than on personal happiness?

- What distinguishes you from other people?
- Are you weak or strong-willed?
- Timid or confident?
- Flamboyant or reticent?

- Have you got a negative or a positive outlook?
- Are you a doer or a follower?
- Have you a hard time approaching people, or can you get along with everyone?

And what about your good points, your talents? This is no time to be shy. Be sincere; this entire exercise will benefit you.
List your abilities, your talents, your aptitudes and your assets.

- Are you an honest person?
- Are you faithful, dependable, ambitious, generous, warm, sympathetic, happy?
- Are you always in a good mood, or do you go through each day with a frown?
- Are you passive and prudent or high-spirited and fun-loving?
- Are you morally good; that is, do you respect yourself and others?
- Are you boastful or humble?

What about your faults? Be sincere; this is important!

- Are you lazy?
- Are you egotistical, pretentious, unfaithful?
- Are you a habitual liar or cheat?
- Have you got many weaknesses?
- Are you disorganized?
- Jealous, envious, possessive?
- Do you overeat and overindulge?
- Do you incessantly criticize others and everything?
- Are you a slave to others?
- Are you under the spell of drugs, alcohol, gambling or some other vice?

Make a list of your educational, instructional and cultural backgrounds.

- What level of education have you attained?
- Are you going to night school to improve yourself?
- Do you want to follow a particular course in order to enrich your life? If so, when do you intend to do this?
- Is there anything you can do to upgrade your education?
- How far did you go in your schooling?
- Are you familiar with current events?
- Do you read newspapers, magazines, and a wide range of books?
- Are you a member of a cultural minority?
- Do you know something about different subjects so that you can converse about a lot of things?
- Have you many interests?
- Are you intellectually curious?
- Would you consider yourself to be a cultured person?
- Have you an affinity for the theatre, the arts, sculpture, or music?
- Do you attend many artistic or cultural events?
- Do you go to museums?
- Do you go on archaeological tours during your holidays?
- Do you know or want to learn other languages?
- Are you interested in learning about other cultures?
- Are you knowledgeable about history or geography?

Review your talents. Everyone has something he or she can do well.

- Are you mechanically-minded?
- Can you draw? Are you artistic in any way – painting, sculpture, design, interior decorating, crafts?
- Do you play a musical instrument or sing?
- Are you good at sports?
- Do you jog every morning?
- Do you ski on weekends, play tennis, or golf?

- Are you a gourmet cook? Or do you make grand desserts that everyone raves about?
- Can you sew or knit?
- Are you a great strategist at parlour games, a master chess player?

What are your favourite pastimes?

- Do you enjoy playing bridge, canasta, or other card games?
- Do you like going to the cinema?
- Do you like to listen to music or go to the theatre?
- Do you enjoy camping or indoor sports like bowling?
- If you were to increase the range of your hobbies, what would you choose to do?
- Would this make you a more interesting, desirable person? Would it enrich your life?

List your likes and dislikes.

- Foods.
    Do you like spicy foods?
    Are you a vegetarian?
    Do you enjoy fine wines and gourmet dishes?
    Do you drink coffee or tea?
- Sports.
- Holidays.
    Do you like to travel?
    Are you a conventional tourist or do you like to discover new places on your own?
- Hobbies.
- Are you a morning person or a night owl?
- Have you many friends or a few intimate buddies?
- Do you socialize with people from different backgrounds and social groups, or do you stick to those that are just like you?

Your next list will cover the things you absolutely detest!

* Do you detest housework in general?
     Cooking?
     Cleaning?
* Do you hate reading?
* Exercising?
* Do you dislike people who leave everything lying around?
* Do children drive you crazy?
* Are you allergic to anything? Cigarette smoke? Cat or dog hair?
* Are you intolerant of people who have viewpoints completely opposite to yours?
* Do you hate getting up early?

Write down all of your idiosyncrasies; they say a lot about you. Try to see yourself objectively, as though you were another person filling out your profile. This way your self-portrait will be unbiased. Make your profile an honest biography!

To finish off your self-portrait, make a list of things you like to do alone.
List at least 40 activities that you can do by yourself that cost nothing or under £10. By setting this amount as a 'just-for-me' budget, you won't have the excuse that you can't afford things on your list!

   Was it difficult to think of things you like to do by yourself? How many were you able to account for? Did you record any at all? If your list falls short, it's time you started to develop diversions you can appreciate alone. An important part of attracting your love partner is to be self-fulfilled.

♥ ♥ ♥

Did you know that there are six aspects to your life?
They are:

- physical (your health and appearance)
- spiritual (your beliefs)
- effective (your impact on the world around you)
- social (activities you enjoy with other people)
- professional (your work and business-related activities)
- financial (the money you earn and how you manage it)

Now that you have evaluated the global aspect of your life, assign a grade to each of the six aspects listed above. What are you going to do to improve each of those aspects you have given a poor grade?

Assigning a grade to your overall happiness.
If you had to assign a grade between 1 and 100 for your overall happiness, what would it be? Are you satisfied with your grade, or will you aim for a higher mark? Keep in mind that there is no rehearsal in life. Life is *it!* You don't get a second chance at being happy in this moment of time. *Now* is the time to hurry onto the road of happiness!

Are you happy with your self-portrait? Are you projecting the image you want others to see? How can you improve this projection?
The way in which you use each of your senses contributes to the image you are projecting to others, because what you see, hear, think, say and feel affects, as well as forms the basis for, your attitude about yourself. And this attitude is what the world sees as *you!*

What – or whom – you are looking for, finds you.
Not only do your senses contribute to the projection of your image, they also influence what – or whom – you attract. If

you constantly bombard your inner mind with negativity, you will increase the likelihood of 'bad luck' in your life. The wrong people, unlucky events, even accidents can enter your life because a negative attitude has paved the way for these adverse happenings. You must be careful of what you think, say, hear and feel, because all your senses affect the experiences you will have in your lifetime. Happy, positive thoughts and attitudes will bring good things into your life. If you want caring, loving, happy people to surround you, you need to condition your inner 'eye' to 'see' people with these attitudes. What you are 'looking' for will find you: look carefully!

You are what you see.
The way you perceive the world will be reflected in what you show to others. If you see yourself as an ugly person, you will inevitably send this image to others because the way you see yourself becomes a reflection of you!

The more you learn to like your image as reflected in a mirror, the more you are bound to draw to you a person who will like that image of you as well.

By surrounding yourself with beautiful things, you are certain to attract a love who will also see their beauty, and yours!

Look for the beauty in everything you see. Notice smiling faces. Fill your life with grace and splendour through joyful, energizing, radiant images. Turn away from grotesque reflections of hate and frustration.

The portrait of your life depends on what you 'choose' to see. Keep in mind that everything you take in with your eyes gives life to your dreams and your spirit, so you should try to treat yourself well by looking at as many lovely, beautiful sights as you possible can. This includes visits to museums and galleries as well as watching gorgeous sunrises and sunsets. Also, use your gift of 'inner' sight to imagine exquisite things for yourself.

Visualize the way you want your life to unfold. Use your mind as a mental screen to create the motion picture of your dream life. Envision every aspect in beautifully minute detail. The more frequently you project this film in your mind's eye, the sooner your dreams will become a reality.

You are what you hear.
You have the choice of listening to good or to bad messages. If you wish to enrich your life, do not listen to gossip, arguments, and negative or critical comments. Turn a deaf ear to those who repeatedly reprimand or denigrate you or complain to you, and never pay attention to words that aim to scare or to hurt you. Listen to encouraging speeches, uplifting lectures, and messages of hope, goodwill and love, and your innermost soul will respond with gladness and joy!

Music is not only a universal language, it is the language that speaks to the mind, heart and soul. When you listen to beautiful music, to a song associated with special, pleasant memories, you are tuning in to the highest level of your being. Everything you hear leaves its mark on your inner self and will influence your thoughts and actions. By allowing only soul-enriching sounds mingled with words of cheer, confidence and self-worth to reach your 'heart's ear', you can drown out the pessimistic, negative clamour that threatens your peace and harmony.

Furthermore, you will be more likely to attract a love partner who will talk to you in a way that will make you feel wonderful about yourself! You will thrill to the silvery notes of the sound of his words of love, and you will grow in love by his side.

You are what you speak!
When someone asks you how you are, do you answer 'not bad' or 'so so'? Why don't you tell her, 'I'm feeling fine . . .never better!' Just by saying these words, you will feel cheered up! Listen to the way you talk to other people and to the words you choose: they reflect the image you have of yourself.

Speak in the affirmative. Instead of a weak 'I should like to' or 'I wish I could,' declare your self-assurance with a strong *'I will'*, and indeed you will!

Are you in the habit of using negative terms in your everyday language? 'I had an *awfully* good lunch.' '*Unbelievable* what a great time I had.' 'She's *terribly* talented.' Do you hear what you are saying? Your subconscious mind does, and it is registering every pessimistic word! The meaning coming out of these mixed messages is that you don't think she deserves to have an amazing talent, you thought lunch was *awful*, and you *can't believe* you had a good time. You are actually neutralizing all of the good things that happen to you by expressing them in negative terms.

Even when talking about mundane, everyday things like a pint of milk, saying 'It's half-empty' is negative, while, 'It's half-full' sounds much better.

Your words influence how you perform. If you use the expression, 'I'll try', you will fail 90 per cent of the tasks you take on because you have not committed yourself. You have set yourself up for failure by what you actually said, which was to *try*, and not really *do*. The same thing applies to the term, 'I must'. You are implying that whatever you are going to do is an obligation and sheer drudgery. No wonder your life is such a struggle! Replace those negatively charged, 'I must' statements with an 'I will do . . . with pleasure!'

If you say, 'I can't,' you probably won't! Why don't you give yourself the chance to prove you can? You might be surprised at how much you can achieve!

The words you speak should inspire you and charge you with positive energy that will transform your life. Get into the habit of using positive statements. Use the word 'love' in as many sentences as you can throughout the day – particularly when talking with your family, your friends, even your boss – 'I just love my work!' – as well as with prospective 'loves'. Just saying it many times will give you a more 'loving' attitude – and possibly attract a 'love' partner!

Tell yourself and the people around you – especially your loved one – how happy you are and how beautiful and capable he is. Create passion in your world with refreshing, cheery words. Throw in a smile and boost the power of that positive bulletin!

Make every one of your sentences a pleasant incantation that will weave love's magic into your life and your relationships.

Laughter is more than an expression of happy inner feelings. It can cure the blues in a flash, and is even used as a therapy for illness. Laughter is a marvellous gift that you should cherish.

Life should be a party, not a tense melodrama! Laugh your troubles away and all your cares will evaporate.

If you find it difficult to laugh, practise! Develop your sense of humour by surrounding yourself with funny people, pictures, paintings, and sounds. Watch comical films and television programmes; read mirth-provoking books. Start your day off by reading the cartoons in the newspaper. Share your laughter – pin up those side-splitting cartoons in your office. Play a practical joke on a mate and laugh about it together. Just a chuckle raises the spirits: a real belly-laugh is good for your health and it will bring great pleasure to your life and relationships.

In times of troubles, the expression 'Years from now you'll laugh about this!' is often true. If you observe your life from the outside, as though you were hovering overhead, things are much more humorous than when you are actually experiencing them. As the old saying goes, 'Laugh and the world laughs with you! Cry and you cry alone.'

Another way to raise your spirits with the use of your voice is to *sing!* In the shower, in your car, around the house – even to your friends! Expressing yourself in song will put you in a joyful mood and project a happy picture of yourself!

A positive attitude expressed in all your conversations will make it all the more likely that you will draw to you a love partner who will speak in the same enthusiastic, lively way, and with whom you can share a most joyful relationship!

You are what you think!
You emit vibrations into your surroundings with your every thought. If your thoughts are nurtured with compassion, generosity, kindness and love, you will attract people of this very nature. Instead of thinking about everything you haven't got and worrying about everything and everyone, *cultivate the habit of thinking positively!* You will transform your life. Negative thoughts provoke disaster. Even the process of ageing is speeded up if you think you are getting old. If you think your boyfriend is cheating on you, he probably will, eventually – you have

spent so much energy diffusing these thoughts, someone is bound to pick them up!

To be your best and reflect your true loving nature, concentrate on the bright side of things. Shake off negative thoughts. Get into the habit of being optimistic. Keep your good thoughts in mind all day long and you will see your life change for the better. Your relationship will be transformed into romance on a grand scale!

Nurture yourself with wonderful, affirmative thoughts, especially before going to sleep, because your subconscious never rests. It will mull over these splendid musings all night long, turning them into miracles the next day!

Your thoughts shape your life and will influence the outcome of your relationship, so think wisely, think *big*, think *magical!*

You are what you feel!
Your feelings release such incredible amounts of energy that they are like magnets. The vibes you send out will boomerang, creating a life shaped by your attitudes.

Feelings have the power to be manifested in reality. If you are afraid of falling, you probably will fall. If you are afraid of losing your love partner, you will! If you feel guilty – when in reality you have nothing to feel guilty about – you will denigrate yourself and be seen as a loser. Your fear and negative emotions are destructive forces affecting your life adversely. You must not harbour these bad feelings: they are detrimental to your personal progress and to the evolution of your love relationship.

You must feel good about yourself and about life to project this positive attitude around you. By doing so, you will draw to you a love partner who is very likely to feel good about herself and definitely about you! Your convictions and beliefs create the patterns and texture of your life. Create a love life that is luxuriously passionate with delightful images of love!

Decide what kind of relationship you want at this time in your life.
What point have your reached in your life? Are you prepared to enter into a relationship? Take a moment to reflect on your past relationships. Do you see a pattern? Are you always falling into the same kind of relationship with the same kind of person? In all fairness to yourself and to the other person, now is the time to identify what you expect from a relationship.

What were your previous relationships like?
In determining the type of relationship you want, take a good look at your previous relationships and analyse them carefully. Use the list below as an example and draw up a similar one to use in your comparison.

   Write the names of your former partners in parallel columns at the top of the chart and fill in the answers to the following questions.

My Patterns in Love

• What qualities did each of my past partners have in common?
• What were the positive aspects of the relationship? What aspects encouraged me to stay in the relationship?
• What were the faults and weaknesses common to my past partners?
• What were the negative aspects of the relationship that caused it to deteriorate?
• What was my ability to commit to the relationship?
• What was my partner's ability to commit to the relationship?
• What aspects of my personality made me stay in a relationship even though it was a difficult one?:
     dependence
     co-dependence
     insecurity
     guilt
     financial embarrassment

    a sense of responsibility
- What was the length of each relationship?
- Who broke up the relationship?
- What were the reasons for the break-up?
- How long did I mourn the break-up?
- What did I accuse my partner of?
- Did my partners have any dependencies?
- Were my partners unfaithful, violent, egocentric?
- Did I want to change them?
- Did they want to change me?
- Who controlled whom?
- Were my relationships valuable to me?
- Did I play games?

Analyse your chart to determine whether you have developed a 'relationship pattern.' Do you see a negative or a positive pattern emerging? If your pattern appears to be positive, and your relationships have been relatively happy, then by all means, continue along the same lines. But if your pattern feels wrong, if you are unfulfilled in your relationships and with the type of person you usually date, then it is high time to start dating different kinds of people, people who want the same sort of relationship as you do and who show the same warm feelings towards you as you have for them.

Now, take a look back at your most recent love relationship

- How long has it been since the relationship was stopped?
- Am I over it 100 per cent?
- If not, what stage of my 'healing process' have I reached?
- Am I capable of starting a new relationship at this time?

Some more questions to answer about your past relationships so you can establish clearly what type of relationship you are looking for.

- Do you want a casual friendship or a serious commitment?
- How far are you willing to go?
- Do you want a torrid love affair?
- Do you want a long and meaningful relationship?
- Do you simply want friendship?

Be precise! Furthermore, you need to choose someone who wants the *same kind of relationship* that you do. The foundation of success for your next relationship is based on your honesty to yourself and to him in stating what you are looking for and expecting from a love partner.

The Strategies

♥ ♥ ♥

Paint the portrait of your ideal love partner!
Now that you know yourself inside out, you should have formed some ideas about your ideal partner. You would be surprised how many people conscientiously looking for their 'ideal partner' haven't a clue about what they really want!

You should also have a good idea of what kind of person would fit the type of relationship you are looking for. Do you want a good friend for sharing fun times, a lover, someone to become engaged to and eventually marry, or someone to date occasionally but not necessarily exclusively?

Take a pen and a large piece of paper, and start your description of the partner of your dreams. You can follow the same points you used in preparing your self-portrait. Take your time . . . take a week or more, or even longer. Don't rush this important process! Each day add some details to your description. You don't want a carbon copy of yourself but someone who will complement your talents and frailties. For example, if you have trouble budgeting or balancing your chequebook, you might add 'must be able to handle money' to your list.

Another important point to consider is that you want to enrich *your* life by being associated with this person, so look for someone who is a bit more educated than you, someone who travels in a higher or wider social circle, someone who can broaden your horizons. If you are knowledgeable about art and want to know more about another area – music, for example –

you might add 'musical talent' to your list. Of course, you should be realistic and keep in mind what you yourself have to offer in a romantic relationship! Remind yourself also that your strengths should also complement the other person's weaknesses. You may be a fabulous cook and he can't boil water, or you may be an excellent public speaker while she functions better in small, casual groups.

To further delineate your ideal love, place yourself in several question/answer roles – play *detective, interviewer, psychologist, barrister* – and ask questions you would want to know the answers to. For example:

Detective: Have you ever gone 'steady' before?
Interviewer: What do you enjoy the most about your new career?
Psychologist: How would you describe your family's relationships with each other?
Barrister: Have you ever been married?

You can no doubt think of a lot of questions you would want to ask about someone. Use your list once you have met a 'possible' love. Naturally you wouldn't ask all the questions the first time you meet or go out together, but you might want to refer to the list from time to time and see if you can live with the answers!

At the end of this section of the book, there are additional questions to discover the answers to over time, and to help in your assessment of your love interest.

From this 'master portrait,' make a new list of points, dividing them into two sections: 'essential criteria' – those points that you are not willing to negotiate – and 'desirable' – those points that are not absolutely necessary but would be nice to have.
By now you should have a nice long list. However, it is not set in stone! Every day there are changes in our lives that affect our wishes, desires and attitudes. You want to remain flexible and

modify the 'master portrait' of your ideal partner from time to time as your needs change.

From your list of desired traits, pick out the essential criteria – those points that are absolutely crucial and that you will not compromise on. Identify them by drawing a heart (♥) next to each point. Then choose the features that you would like that are nonessential. Identify these with the plus symbol (+).

You are now ready for the next step.

Here are a few 'essential' criteria you may be looking for in a love partner.

'Essential' criteria are not the same for everyone. While certain moral qualities and personality aspects are absolutely non-negotiable for some, they might not be so important for others.

However, to inspire you into making up your list, here are a few examples of 'essential' criteria that many people say they are looking for in a perfect match. For many people their perfect match must be:

- Honest
- Faithful
- Hygiene-conscious
- Health-conscious
- Thoughtful
- Ambitious
- Successful
- Able to express emotions
- Generous
- Good-hearted
- Self-confident
- Good-tempered
- Respectful
- Understanding
- Very feminine/masculine

You may eliminate from the above suggested character traits those that are not essential for you. You may also add some that are important to you that do not appear here.

♥ ♥ ♥

Once your list of 'criteria' for an ideal partner is complete, identify the 'essential' prerequisites for a love partner, and *never* settle for less!

Go over your list of essential criteria, which by now probably has at least 20 to 35 points, and pick out five to ten of the most essential criteria (those that you marked with a heart). Now choose, in order of priority, those you simply *must have* in a relationship for it to be fulfilling for *you!* This list will determine the basis for your relationship, the points you won't compromise on – or would only agree to change very slightly. The old adage 'love is blind' does not apply to a meaningful relationship. If you begin a courtship with a person who does not fit your essential criteria description, you will build a relationship with a faulty foundation, and the relationship will eventually crumble.

Suppose you find someone who seems all right, but he only meets two or four of your 'essentials'? Would you sit on a chair that was missing a leg? Or stay underneath a temple that is missing some pillars? Of course not! Time to move on to the next candidate!

Even though you may be committed to choosing a particular type of person according to the description of your ideal partner, you must also make sure that the person you find wants the same kind of relationship as you do. If you are dating someone whom you think is your perfect person, but she wants to have a casual affair and is not interested in the meaningful relationship that you have planned, you are wasting your time. Making sure that the person you are interested in wants the same kind of relationship that you want, *and loves you in the same way you love him or her,* should be your top essential criteria!

Make sure that your partner has also made an outline of his ideal love partner, listing *all his essential criteria.*

Ask a potential partner if she has made up a list of her essential criteria of things she wants in a partner. When she has done so, evaluate her 'ideal partner portrait' carefully by comparing it to your self-portrait. If you realize that you do not correspond to her concept of an ideal partner, you might anticipate that, sooner or later, she will leave you and begin her search anew for someone who better suits her needs.

Don't make the mistake of thinking you can change someone or his fundamental ideas. If he doesn't correspond to your essential criteria, or you to his, it is best for you to leave him immediately.

At the beginning of a new relationship, after each rendezvous with a potential partner, go through your list of important criteria and look closely. Compare and evaluate whether this person satisfies *all* of your fundamental needs. If you find he does not, don't continue simply because you are afraid of being alone again. You will be making a grave mistake if you put off your decision until a later date.

Keep in mind that the most important of all your criteria is that you and your partner are looking for the same type of relationship and that both of you have *the same feelings for each other!*

Don't waste the best years of your life trying to salvage a losing relationship!
If you are not compatible or if the other person does not live up to your standards, how do you expect to spend a lifetime cultivating love with this person? You can't. Sooner or later there will be an explosion of emotions! Your love partner must contribute as much to the relationship as you do! Each person must consider the other's feelings and emotions – is that not part of loving someone? Each member must be able to show her love. Words are only words, but they become love through actions! Your love partner's values must suit yours; you must complement each other. That is the key to a successful relationship!

Be discriminating from the very beginning. Pay attention to the little things: is your new partner thoughtful? Does he leave his napkin unfolded when he comes for dinner? Does she use the last drop of milk for her coffee? You would be surprised how these little annoyances can become a source of major aggravation when constantly repeated over the years! Why put up with these problems when you can, with a little patience and effort, meet the right person for you?! It will save your health and your love: a difficult relationship can wear you down and make you bitter.

Make sure that your new partner has all of the essential criteria that you listed on your 'ideal partner outline'. If your new acquaintance does not have these essential traits, consider your relationship lacking a very important factor and *don't compromise on your essential criteria*! If you start doing so now, you'll end up yielding to your partner for the rest of your life! Listen to your 'little voice' – it's your heart talking! If your intuition tells you that something is not right, pay attention: it's trying to make you face reality. Don't be afraid of being alone. You *will* find someone special, and he will be just right for you. Patience and perseverance will win the race!

Keep in mind that breaking up a relationship today will be infinitely less painful than doing it tomorrow or the next day! If you feel bad every time you are with the other person, but you just can't put your finger on why, listen to reason. If you give far more to the relationship than the other person, then something is wrong, and you might want to consider leaving!

In the early stages of a relationship, make a two-column list of what your partner gives to the relationship and what you contribute. The results might be very surprising!
At the beginning of a new relationship, writing down how you feel after a date may also help you determine the status of the relationship. After a few dates, read your notes; you may be shocked to find that you are not having as much fun as you thought!

Don't worry, be positive: your ideal partner *does* exist. There is no need to put up with an over-compromised relationship! If you feel emotionally bound to your present interest, ask yourself if you can live with your less-than-ideal partner's shortcomings for the rest of your life!

Once you decide you are ready for a relationship, give yourself enough time to find the ideal person to share it with!

You will be setting yourself an unreasonable task if you promise yourself you will find the love of your life by St Valentine's Day – if it is already December! You could get lucky, but chances are you'll need a little more time. Set a reasonable time frame and give yourself ample opportunity to meet as many people as possible. Read the first part of this book on A Million and One Love Strategies for Meeting Your Perfect Match if you have not already done so: it will help you meet the maximum number of people in the shortest length of time. Happy hunting!

In the meantime, live life to the full!

This is not the time to be upset about what may or may not happen in your life. Appreciate what is happening *now* in your life: yesterday is gone forever and tomorrow may never arrive! Live each day as it comes, marvelling at its wonders, as though it were the first day of your life – but with intensity, as though it were the last. Tell yourself, 'Today is a whole brand-new day, which never existed before; I will make it the happiest day it can be!' Why waste time on anxieties and worries that only make you miserable? Life can't always go smoothly: it's full of hurdles and puddles you have to leap across. Even the best athletes have off days . . . even the greatest romances have their dull days! So live each day with joyous intensity. Be active, but take some time just for yourself – to relax, to reflect, and to make a point of renewing your bright, golden spirit!

Treat yourself as you would wish a partner to do!

Pamper yourself the way you would someone who is very special, as you would act towards your best friend or a VIP guest. Treat yourself with kindness. For example, if you live alone, prepare a lovely dinner – one you would be proud to serve to an important visitor. Set the table with a beautiful

cloth, and your best china, crystal and silver. Candles and
flowers would be a nice touch. Put on your favourite music and
open a bottle of wine for yourself, if your heart desires it, and
finish off with a luscious dessert. Dress up – just as though you
were attending an elegant affair! Enjoy your own company as
if you were your own best friend!

Think of other gestures that would give you pleasure. Send
flowers to yourself – every week, or a single rose each day. Treat
yourself for having lost weight by going to a fancy, lean
'nouvelle cuisine' restaurant or by buying clothing in the size
you will be *next* month!

Treat yourself as though you were the most important person in the world – because you are!

Valuing yourself, and keeping a strong self-image, will help you
not to become involved in a relationship with someone who
does not appreciate your good qualities or who tries to turn
them into faults. If you do not hold yourself in high esteem, you
will have difficulty finding a partner who will appreciate your
true value. By knowing and feeling that you are unique and
desirable, by feeling positive about yourself, you will recognize
this same treatment from a prospective partner. *'Court yourself'*
with kindness and respect – it will help you find the right
partner with whom to share a loving, positive, strong
relationship! To find a great love, first love yourself!

Before you can be happy with someone else, you must learn to be happy with yourself.

You can accomplish many wonderful things alone! There is no
need to rely constantly on the company of a partner to do all
of the things you like to do. You are your own person. You still
retain your identity when you are in love. Even when you are
part of a 'couple', you are still an individual. Never compromise
your identity to please someone else! Your personal
development within the relationship is crucial! Keep your

individuality. Your love partner was attracted to *you*, she fell in love with *you* – why would you want to change now?

Your love partner should not be your sole reason for living, just as your relationship should not alter your nature. A healthy relationship will nurture the heart, not snatch it away! As an independent person, you won't fall prey to the agonies of waiting for the phone to ring . . . or the loneliness of waiting for your love partner to arrive.

Know exactly what you want! What satisfies you? What impassions you? And go for it! Establish yourself in the lifestyle you choose; don't depend on someone else to do it for you.

Always give yourself priority treatment! If you are psychologically, emotionally and financially independent, you will never become a prisoner of love! Keep in mind that you are a 'whole' person, able to think, act, and live a full life. Never become someone else's 'better half'! Picture your life as beautiful and exciting – even without a partner. The more autonomous you become, the better your chances are of attracting – and experiencing – a spectacular love affair!

Are you easily moved to jealousy? Then it's time to realize that a jealous nature is a syndrome, not a minor fault. This problem is the result of a serious lack of self-confidence, and when jealousy invades a relationship, the situation can become very nasty – even violent!

Each time you are haunted by the fear that your love partner is unfaithful to you, you transmit strong vibes suggesting to him that he should be unfaithful. Sooner or later he is bound to pick up your negative vibes and cheat on you. Be aware of the power of your negative thoughts, and overcome them! Counteract those feelings of insecurity by cultivating your self-confidence. When you think of yourself as a 'somebody,' you will realize that *you* are the best thing in your life! You will have no need to think that other people are superior, or that you will lose your loved one unless you keep her strictly under your control.

The way you perceive yourself is the image you project to others. Your negative feelings about yourself will attract losers. Answering some important questions will help your self-definition, so you might ask yourself: Who am I? What do I like? What upsets me? What abilities have I got? What are the good things in my life? What are my goals and how can I reach them? What should I improve about myself? Why am I always falling into these self-destructive patterns? How can I alter my behaviour?

If your partner is the only important aspect of your life, or if you feel he has become your 'whole life', sooner or later he will take over your soul, leaving you as a mere shell without an identity! Remember the words of Eleanor Roosevelt: 'No one can make me feel inferior unless I consent to it first.' And the wisdom of Mahatma Gandhi tells us, 'No one can hinder you except yourself!' Happiness doesn't fall from the heavens, it comes from within!

Don't be afraid of rejection!

Fear of rejection is a pervasive anxiety that can wreak havoc in a relationship. This fear stems from negative thinking and painful experiences of the past, and it will paralyse you and prevent you from being happy with your love partner. You can overcome this fear by understanding the basis for it and by resolving your false feelings of inadequacy, which are at the root of this whirlpool of anxiety.

Keep in mind that your fear of rejection is all in your head. After all, you don't know for sure the real reasons why you were rejected. When someone discontinues a relationship with you, don't fall apart. If the other person made the decision based on her feelings at the time, it is no reflection on you. She may have discovered that she was not ready for a serious relationship. Perhaps she is afraid of love. In any case, if she did not love you as much as you loved her, she did you a favour by leaving you and making space for someone new, who will better reciprocate your affection. Also keep in mind that her reasons for breaking up probably had nothing to do with you. If you did not correspond to that person's entire list of criteria, you may very well be the next person's perfect match!

Just think of rejection as a delayed success with someone else!

You may have many things in common – likes, dislikes, interests – and the earth may move every time you see each other, but if the timing is wrong, there's not much chance that this particular relationship will work. *The right person at the wrong time is not the right person for you!* If your mutual desires for the future do not coincide, it is best just to be friends and not enter into a relationship. Taking a mature look at yourself and your partner is not a rejection of all relationships; you just have to have the patience and courage to wait, to persevere and ultimately to find the right partner at the right time. It's well worth it!

There is no need to feel self-doubt or unworthiness if someone breaks up with you. Just because you don't fit his idea of the right partner doesn't mean that you are not a great person – and someone else's future love! Everyone has his own idea of the right one for him, just as you have your own set of essential criteria. There are undoubtedly times in your life when you, too, have rejected love prospects because they didn't fit the ideas you have about love and relationships. Think about those times when a near-love says 'goodbye'. Take this episode in your stride and go on with your life, secure in the belief that your ideal partner is out there somewhere!

Think of your bad times as experience – and carry on!

Don't let rejection get you down! If you get the brush-off, persevere! You'll see that these unfortunate experiences will help you grow as a person: you will become more aware and sensitive.

You can learn a lesson in persistence from a former Miss Canada, Dominique Dufour, who for two consecutive years did not win the Miss Montreal title. But during her third year of pageant participation, she not only became Miss Laval, but Miss Canada and first runner-up in the Miss Universe Pageant! How's that for tenacity! Miss Dufour's setbacks did not make her bitter; on the contrary, they gave her practice and experience, plus they taught her perseverance and how to become a winner!

It's normal to be anxious at the beginning of a relationship!
Everybody experiences 'beginnings' anxiety and fears of rejection. The important thing is not to let fear run your life. You can't be sure about a person until you know where the relationship is going, and even then there are no guarantees! Seize the chance to enjoy the relationship. Live each moment with your new partner passionately and romantically! Just think: when you're old and grey you'll be happy that you had the courage to live life to its fullest!

You're afraid of meeting people? Are the sources of your fears internal or external?
Are you timid? Afraid of commitment? Afraid that love will bring you sorrows and sadness? If you have answered 'yes' to any of these questions, you are suffering from thought-processes that will seriously interfere with your quest for your ideal love partner!

Are you afraid of going out to meet people? Are you a social misfit who coughs and sputters every time you meet someone new? Then your anxieties stem from external fears of being around people and having to interact with them.

The first thing to do is to identify the causes of your anxieties. Are they internal or external? Now the hard work begins. Change your attitude. Use positive reinforcement to replace negative thoughts. Believe you are a worthwhile person – because you are! Force yourself to confront your fears. Get out of the house and meet people – improve your social skills! Slowly you will notice an improvement. Count on your friends for encouragement when you are trying to improve yourself. They will cheer you on when the going gets tough!

If you are having a great deal of difficulty confronting your fears, you can always seek professional advice. A therapist might help you deal with your phobias more quickly than you could on your own. If you need help, ask your family doctor for references. The important thing is to get help – *now!*

Your first date with that wonderful new person! Keep it short!

It is tempting to make that first date a grand affair, but an invitation for a quick lunch can be a lot less intimidating than an elaborate dinner at a fancy restaurant. It's easier to ask someone to go out for a snack one afternoon next week than to escort you to the Admiral's ball next month! The first date should be considered a casual getting-acquainted time, not a high-pressure social affair or a long evening.

Also, if it does not turn out to be the exciting rendezvous you anticipated, another advantage of a short first date is that you will not be 'stuck' being bored for very long.

Short, sweet, and low-cost are the keys to a successful 'first date'!

Keep the conversation light on the first date.

When you are on your first date with a new flame, it isn't appropriate to reveal your personal problems or fears. Why would you want to tell that gorgeous creature sitting across from you that your last partner left saying that you were as exciting as a hibernating bear? And please, don't be too serious or formal; you're not at a job interview! Keep the conversation simple but entertaining. This is not the time to scare your date with grandiose ideas and serious life-altering propositions – the way Luke did:

Luke was one of those people who was so engrossed with his goal of getting married that, during the evening of his first dinner date with Monique, he said, 'I want to get married in a church. I know you are divorced, Monique, but do you think you could get an annulment?' Can you guess what Monique

said? Well, the date was short all right, and Monique never
dated Luke again! Luke is still single!

**It's fine to talk about yourself on a first date, but
conversation isn't one-sided!**
You have so much you want to tell this new person in your life
. . . but give him time to talk, too! Say something encouraging
like, 'Enough about me, tell me about *you!*' Listen attentively
to what he has to say. Getting to know each other takes time –
and two-sided conversations.

Talk about everything and nothing in particular.
Keep the discussion simple. For example, if you have recently
seen a play, give your opinion and ask your partner what she
thought of it. It's surprising how much information you can
learn about the other person from talk – if you listen carefully!

You have a lifetime to talk about serious matters. The
conversation on the first date should be frivolous and
entertaining. Talk about your travels, or the funny things that
have happened to you. Talk about current events, art, or
culture. It is wise to avoid prickly subjects like politics!

Your objective on your first date is to become acquainted.
Comments like, 'I'd like to have four children . . . what about
you?' are not exactly 'get acquainted' conversation! You will
probably scare the person off if you talk this way. Even though
your date may want the same things, he will certainly think you
are taking events too far too fast! Relax and enjoy chatting
with – not 'grilling' – your date. What you really need to
establish on a first date is whether or not you want to see this
person again. In fact, your first *four* dates should be times for
finding out if the two of you are compatible or not. Don't rush
the fun!

On the first date, don't order the most expensive thing on the menu ... even if you are out with American billionaire Donald Trump or the Sultan of Brunei!

You are on your first date and your partner has chosen a nice restaurant. The menu is presented. What to order? Choose something moderately priced: you don't know what the other person's financial status is yet. The Mercedes and clothes could be hired! Even if you are aware, you certainly don't want your date to think you are a gold-digger!

You only get one chance to make a good first impression!

You want to look your best for that important first meeting. Remember, there is no rehearsal! You won't get a second chance to create a good first impression. It is generally during the first three minutes of a meeting that a person will make up her mind about how she feels and what she thinks of you. There is a 95 per cent chance that the first impression will stay with her for the rest of her life. It is indeed extremely difficult to change the poor opinion someone has about you once he has decided that you are not up to his expectations.

Do everything you can to create the best first impression possible. Be realistic and accept the fact that the first impression you make on people, before you even open your mouth, is visual! So it is absolutely crucial that you take special care over your physical appearance.

Wearing your favourite clothes – ones you feel comfortable and look really terrific in – is not enough. You must pay attention to details like the condition of your hair, nails, shoes and your overall appearance. Are your clothes clean and neatly pressed? Is your hair shiny and attractively styled? Is your breath fresh? Did you brush your teeth and use a mouthwash? Take a close look at your nails. Are they well-trimmed and clean? Shine those shoes! Plan every detail of your appearance carefully.

However, your image is not only projected by your clothes: the way you walk and your overall posture are important, too. Slouching is out. Walk and sit *tall!* Keep your shoulders back in a 'royal' position, and your body gracefully balanced. Be relaxed. Smile and be pleasant and confident: you are expecting to have a nice time!

When you are speaking, keep your voice well-modulated and low-pitched. Be as graceful in your speech and gestures as you are in the way you walk. 'Charming' and 'pleasant to be around' are phrases that will spring to people's minds when you take the time and effort to make a good impression.

It is difficult to shake a bad first impression. Chances are you will have a difficult time changing your date's opinion about you the next time you see her – if there is a next time! So be vibrant, charming, pleasant, and entertaining on your first date. Second date coming up!

Are you looking for your ideal partner? Be one yourself!
Don't just ask what the relationship can do for you, ask what *you* can do for that relationship! Be generous and do for your partner what you would like him to do for you. Wouldn't you like some help if you had to address 200 envelopes? Offer your assistance: it will be more than appreciated, and you might even have fun! Your new beau needs a lift to his mother's house? Drive him there. He might be so appreciative he will introduce you to her!

Your new love needs time to confide in you . . . give her it!
You're probably not going to hear very many intimate details about the person you are with on the first date. People need time to open up, so give your date a chance to establish confidence in you; respect her rhythm. Don't expect that you will learn too many of her private-life secrets on the first few dates. Act as naturally as possible. Don't be too inquisitive. You should do everything possible to make your new partner feel more at ease with you each time she sees you. Give the person the time she needs to feel comfortable enough with you to reveal personal or intimate details about herself. Everyone is

different; some people take longer to open up than others. But with time, the person will gain more and more confidence in you and eventually you will have the kind of information you need to judge whether this is the right partner for you!

Don't be too impatient!

Love is like a beautiful melody: it flows gently into your life and fills your spirits with grace. In today's fast-paced world, people are used to instant gratification – fast food, microwave cooking, insta-banks, satellite television, cellular phones, fax machines – but you can't hurry affairs of the heart! Why should you look for shortcuts and miss all the wonderful steps in the evolution of a loving relationship? Like fine wine, it must age with time, and needs the right climate!

So many people make the mistake of being too busy to take time out for people who are important in their lives, like the business executive who says he is too occupied to spend time on love! To err may be human, but in love, a blunder may mean wasting part of life hurting someone and grieving over something that could have been avoided with patience and a little time to get acquainted!

Should you re-invite a person who has refused you once?

If you really like this person, why not? But change your approach. Let some time pass, then propose a simpler, shorter date – such as going to a market on a Saturday morning. Why not casually invite him for breakfast at a neighbourhood café? That is certainly informal! A first rejection is not a permanent refusal: she may not have wanted to see the film you suggested, or perhaps she was intimidated by you and unnerved by the prospect of a potential relationship with you. Keep in mind that people often regret having refused an invitation. Think about that possibility and give yourself and that enticing person a second chance!

Try a gentle, indirect approach when a possible 'date' seems shy!

Be subtle. Say something like, 'I really enjoyed talking to you and I hope to see you again. Here's my telephone number. I truly would love to hear from you!' You might even suggest a date: 'It's no fun going to the cinema alone. Would you like to come with me sometime? I'm flexible – you can choose the one you want to see!'

You never know where an impromptu meeting might lead!

You have just met an attractive someone and you have been talking for the past ten minutes, but now he must be off to work. He hands you his business card and writes his home phone number on the back. How delightfully discreet of him! This is an invitation! This man is saying, 'I'd love for you to ring me at your convenience.' This considerate man is a rare jewel! This is no time to play hard to get!

   Call him the next evening!

Timing is an important factor when approaching a potential partner.

Have you ever heard the expression, 'I was in the right place at the right time'? This can be true of arranging to meet a possible love partner. Approaching the right person at the wrong time could be hazardous to the potential relationship, so keep this in mind when you are thinking about asking someone for a date!

Don't become smitten by someone who is not available.

Maybe the person you are attracted to is your 'ideal,' but if she is 'taken', then she is not suitable! Don't get your hopes wrapped up in illusions or in an infatuation. You deserve better than spending Christmas, New Year, your birthday, weekends, and holidays alone while your loved one is probably having a ball with someone else. Listen to your head and not your heart -- unless, of course, the person is going through divorce proceedings! Be careful: there is the possibility that you might end up as the object of a short-term 'rebound romance', or as this person's part-time lover for many months or even years. Is this really what you want? You deserve someone whose mind and heart are 100 per cent yours!

You are looking for an honest, loving relationship, and that means not getting involved with someone else's love partner!

If a person is not free, leave him your card anyway!

Who knows? His status might change in three or four months! If he is free at that future time, he will already have your phone number! In the meantime, don't pine away hoping for a call – put him out of your mind and get on with living!

Be prepared to answer questions about your last relationship.

You can expect to be asked about your last partner. If the relationship is over, let the inquirer know. And remember that it will only put you in an unfavourable light if you talk bitterly about the relationship or about the other person! Be positive and cheerful; keep your chin up. If the other person's questions become too personal, skirt the issue by changing the subject or by cutting the conversation short.

Decide who is paying for what in advance.

You will avoid many an uncomfortable situation this way. If you suggest going to the cinema, tell your partner in advance that you plan on paying! If you are in a financial bind, you might suggest going Dutch! Say something like, 'I'd love to invite you for a nice dinner, but I'm financially strapped this week, so would you mind if we each paid our own way?' Throw in a little something such as, 'I will take care of the wine.' At least this way you have a chance to be with him and have shown that this is important to you. Also inherent in your request is a compliment: you trust him enough to reveal *why* you aren't able to splurge on a big night on the town!

You have been invited out, and you know the evening is going to be an expensive one for your date.
Why not offer to pay for something like parking, a cocktail, dessert, digestifs, or perhaps the hat-checking tip! The gesture – whether it is accepted or not – will certainly be appreciated!

Show the other person just how much you can enrich her life!
Use your charm and delicacy to bring new dimensions to your partner's life: show her that life with you is like a wonderful adventure, full of interesting diversions. Share your knowledge. Introduce her to new pastimes . . . new foods . . . new places! Show her how her life would be so much more fascinating if she spent more of it with you! Display your qualities like a peacock does its magnificent feathers! Amuse her with your sense of humour, impress her with your flair for elegance, and pamper her with your generosity, your caring manner, and your undivided attention! Offer her the innocence of your inner child by encouraging laughter and play . . . and she will see that life with you is a many-splendoured dream come true!

Be punctual!
Punctuality is a question of respect towards someone. If you are going to be late, *telephone!* Don't offend the other person by being inconsiderate, especially if he is meeting you somewhere.

If you ring to apologize for being late and he has already left, leave a message at the place where you are to meet. Otherwise, you may find an irate date waiting when you finally get there! Being punctual is an expression of politeness, of your good manners and of your consideration of the other person's time.

Please respect your telephone engagements!
You promised to ring someone back on Tuesday night . . . so why are you ringing her on Wednesday afternoon? If you are swamped with work and haven't time to chat, ring her when you said you would and simply say, 'Hi, I'm ringing as I promised to do, but unfortunately I haven't time to talk just right now. Would you hate me if we postponed this conversation? I should be free this afternoon around four. I really am looking forward to having time to chat with you!' Now how can anyone be angry at you after that?

Know when to end the date!
Respect the time-span you set for the date: an afternoon picnic, an evening concert, a morning's shopping. Choose an appropriate moment to end the outing. Tell your partner that you enjoyed yourself immensely. Then, if you are still interested in seeing him again, suggest another meeting. When arrangements have been made, say your goodbyes. Be the one to initiate the end of your date. The idea is to leave the other person with an appetite for you and to keep the other person's interest so he will yearn to see you again!

Dare to express your opinion . . . even if it differs from your partner's.
The world would be a very boring place if everyone thought alike! Show that you have a mind of your own and that yours is not a 'shadow' personality! You have a right to your own

opinion, and you should express it – in a carefully thought out way that won't offend your loved one. If your date is offended by your candidness, she is probably looking for a 'yes' person, not a meaningful relationship with someone who can think for himself!

Don't compete with your love partner.
You're on a date, not at a tennis match! If your partner is talking about his successes, listen attentively and show your admiration. This is not the time to elaborate on your own accomplishments. Instead of telling your date how talented you are, why not let him have the pleasure of discovering your every virtue for himself!

Don't blow your own trumpet!
There is nothing more annoying than a know-it-all who is constantly talking about her talent! You're not being interviewed for a job, so why brag about what you can do? Let your partner discover all of your attributes for himself as your relationship develops!

Complaining endlessly or talking about your troubles is a definite *no-no!*
What a turn-off: someone who is continually moaning about his miserable life. Have a positive attitude and don't complain about every little thing, particularly if it is your first date. You will only antagonize your date by saying things like, 'The food at this restaurant is always cold! And this salad is tasteless. We should have gone to that little bistro down the street.' Your complaints ruin the evening for both of you. How much more enjoyable a happy attitude and pleasant conversation would be! Let your date know how delighted you are to be with her, and *smile!* Even poor food will taste better!

The 'waiting game' is not for you!
Never put yourself in a situation where you are waiting for the other person to make a decision or to telephone you. Tell him to give you a ring, or invite him to go somewhere, but if he doesn't get back to you quickly, make other plans or invite someone else. Some people have so much trouble committing themselves to the simplest engagements that you could be waiting until doomsday for a reply! Make it a point of pride in yourself to wait for no one. You have a life to live, so go ahead and enjoy it – with or without that person!

Stringing people along will only cause trouble later.
It is not a good idea to be going with more than one person at a time when you are 'serious' about someone. Everyone will be confused – including yourself! No matter how careful you may try to be in keeping several people interested at one time, the world is really a small village, and sooner or later you'll get caught in your own game! The only loser will be you!

Don't blame your partner for her misfortunes.
Your partner is feeling miserably sick with the flu. Why make her feel worse by scolding her for not wearing her scarf and hat? Isn't it much more romantic to say, 'Don't worry, love, I'll take care of you. I'll bring you homemade chicken soup every day. Your cold will be gone in no time!' You can be sure she will feel much better!

It isn't wise to criticize.
How can you expect your relationship to blossom if you are constantly criticizing your partner? Do your partner's idiosyncrasies drive you crazy? Tell him so, but do it tactfully! Instead of saying: 'You never go shopping with me. Don't you like to be with me?' why not try this: 'I'd love your company

while I'm shopping. It could be fun! I would like to have your opinion on an item I've been looking at. We could stop for a coffee or tea and a bite to eat while we're out – *my* treat!' Criticism invites a negative attitude: you'll have much more success with compliments and affection!

Nagging won't get you anywhere in a relationship.
Henpecking your partner is not a sign of love; it is more likely a sign that you are frustrated about a problem that the two of you have to resolve. Why take your failures out on your partner? Presumably you are together to support each other's emotional needs, to complement one another, and to enjoy each other's company. Nagging takes the fun and pleasure out of life, and it kills love gradually with its insidiously poisonous cruelty.

Courtship is not a time to force your partner into your idea of what she should be. It is a time for discovering whether you are suited to each other, if you could live together. Why try to change your partner? Compromise is the spice of life – and infinitely more fun than nagging!

Keep in mind that a relationship exists when two partners are equal; nagging, scolding and being bossy have no place in a loving relationship. One is not the parent and the other a child! Why attempt to stifle the personality of your partner? Isn't she supposed to be the love of your life? Switch out of 'nag gear' and into 'loving-high' instead!

If something is bothering you, tell your partner as soon as possible. Be gentle and don't criticize directly – use finesse.
At the beginning of a relationship everything is rosy. You are so wrapped up in each other with the newness and the excitement of love, that you overlook each other's habits . . . until the dreaded day when you notice he inhales his food like a caveman or she slurps her coffee and it drives you round the bend! Unfortunately, no time is the perfect time to criticize, but

you can sprinkle your criticism with sugar.

Instead of lashing out at your love about his table manners, count to ten and say something sweet like, 'You know, darling, it's better for your digestion if you eat slowly, and taking your time keeps us together at the table longer!' Instead of openly criticizing Ms Slurpy, do it nicely: 'Be careful, darling, that coffee is hot. Try letting it cool before you sip it.'

Remember when you were a kid and your parents yelled at you about something? What did you do? You tuned out, mostly because of the tone of their criticism. Think about those times when you want to air gripes about your partner. If you tell him nicely, he will listen; use nasty sarcasm and you'll lose him.

Never criticize on impulse. Prepare yourself. Work out a pleasant way of saying what bothers you – write it down if you must – but make your comments short and sweet! Substitute the malicious word you have in mind for a kind or comical one, and say it with love. You are speaking to your love partner; some of his actions may irritate you, but you love him and you care about his self-respect, so watch what you say. Add 'I love you' or 'darling' or 'sweetheart' to your speech so as not to hurt his feelings. For example, the next time you simply have to show your irritation about the way your partner drives, say something on the order of, 'Darling, I love you, and I would feel more relaxed in your company if you would drive more carefully.'

There are enough authority figures in your love's world without you!
Trying to control your partner with an authoritative manner will only bring grief to the relationship. When you want your partner to do something, be subtle: make her think it is *her* idea. Avoid using phrases like 'I want you to . . .,' 'You ought to . . .,' or 'Listen, you really must . . .' Substitute gently suggestive expressions like 'Dear, if you could . . .,' 'I'd love it if you had time to . . .,' or 'If you could manage to . . .' Being dictatorial leads to no-win situations. Remember the old saying, 'You attract more flies with honey than with vinegar!'

Treat a hesitant partner with delicacy!

Often after a first date, one of the partners remains unsure about pursuing the relationship. If you feel that your partner needs a little time to think about things, give him room and time. While you're waiting you can always send an amusing card with a zippy comment such as 'When I saw this card it reminded me of you . . . and your great smile.'

It isn't a good idea to put pressure on the other person when he seems to lack interest in seeing you again. By being insistent you might just drive him away for good – which is certainly not what you really want!

Sometimes people hesitate because they are uncertain of their feelings. Perhaps they are interested in someone else. Give them time and room to think about you. They might just realize how much they want you in their life!

Take the initiative.

Dare to take the first step! Make the first call! The one you admire will undoubtedly be happy to hear from you! She may have been too busy to phone you, or perhaps she hasn't had a free moment since she last spoke to you. She may even have lost your telephone number! Go ahead, invite her out – it's a great way to start a relationship on the right foot!

Dress for the occasion.

If your new someone invites you for a day of sailing on his new 45-foot yacht, don't wear high heels and lace stockings! You'll be uncomfortable and he will be mortified by the thought of those spiked heels on his customized deck! By the same token, if you are invited out to a fund-raising dinner and dance, don't wear your T-shirt and sandals!

It is a mistake to idolize your new love interest.
It is easy to get caught up in the infatuation of a new relationship, but do try to refrain from treating the other person like a perfect superhero, idolizing her and putting her up on a pedestal! You will soon see her for what she really is . . . a normal person of flesh and blood. Instead of playing the 'love is blind' game, do yourself a favour and regard her as typically human, with flaws and imperfections like anyone else. Your relationship will be all the better for it. And don't let your partner idolize you! It's lonely up there on a pedestal – and very stressful trying constantly to keep up with the image of perfection your admirer has conferred on you! Besides, if and when you tumble from the heights, it's a long fall back down to earth!

If you want an enduring relationship, start by being a friend!
Love often blossoms from a casual friendship! If you are not sure how to act with the person you are seeing, you might ask, 'Have you room in your life for a new friend?' What a charming and non-threatening approach to a reluctant candidate! Slowly, through friendship, you can enter his life . . . and his heart. If by chance this companionship does not bloom into a romance, you are not losing a love partner, you are gaining a good friend!

Take it easy!
Don't scare your new love interest with ardent declarations of love! You may have been struck by love at first sight, but maybe she wasn't! Let your romance unfold like a rose: proclaiming your undying passion too soon will most likely nip it in the bud!

Show that you have a rich, full life!
Talk about the passions in your life, your favourite pastimes,

and your friends. Are you a 'film fan'? Talk about the great film
you recently watched. Tell how fulfilling your work is, but how
important your weekends are to you because you have so many
hobbies you enjoy! Remember to hint that you always have
time to spend with someone special!

**When you begin a new relationship, stay in touch with
your friends.**
People in love often seem to drop out of sight. They lose touch
with old friends. Whose shoulder will they find to cry on when
their relationship is troubled? It is important to keep
friendships – particularly long-standing ones. Keep in touch
with your close friends, phone them, remember their birthdays,
go to lunch with them, confide in them, send them notes about
your latest romance! Loves may come and go, but true friends
are friends forever!

**You needn't fish for answers . . . you can tell by your
partner's conduct how he feels about you.**
There's no need to question your partner incessantly about how
he feels about you. You can tell from the way he acts around
you. If your partner is always late, shows no consideration for
you, and never phones or shows up when he is supposed to,
or if you do not hear from him for weeks, his feelings for you
are quite clearly indifferent! You can draw your own
conclusions!

**Look at your early meetings as a necessity rather than as
a waste of time.**
Better to lose several evenings at the beginning of a relationship
than three or four years of your life later on! Be a detective on
your first few first dates. Find out what makes this person tick!
Keep your eyes and ears open: is this the type of person you

want to become further involved with? Does what you know about her fit in with your concept of your ideal partner? If not, then have the courage to drop the relationship before it ruins your life.

Be sympathetic and understanding about the other person's problems.
Be encouraging. Give your partner your support when he confides in you. Above all, do not judge! No one likes to be criticized or blamed – particularly when he is going through a rough time. You are not a stand-in for his parents, so why go on about what he should or should not do? Offer him your understanding and empathy; a sympathetic ear will be rewarded with gratitude and affection!

Share experiences you may have in common.
It's always fun to talk about places you have been or occasions you can relate to, even if you did them alone, before you ever met your partner. You may have gone on holiday to the same little island; why not talk about your similar experiences? You may have both seen the same film at separate times before you met; wouldn't it be interesting to know what your partner thought of it! Imagine how much fun it would be to go back and do all of those things now – together!

Try to be on the same wavelength as your partner and respect the rhythm with which she chooses to get involved.
You might have fallen head over heels in love with your partner at first sight, but you can't force her to be so quick to react! For Dylan, it was love at first sight when he saw Sylvie. According to Sylvie, Dylan was her 'ideal' partner, but she wanted to go slowly; she had been deeply hurt by her last relationship. She

told Dylan to take it easy, that she needed time, but he wouldn't listen. He hassled Sylvie to show as much love to him as he had for her immediately, until, no longer able to take the pressure, she broke it off with him! Perhaps Dylan could have lived a fairy-tale life with Sylvie, if only he had been more patient. He lost it all because he was in such a rush to have Sylvie's commitment to love! Don't let the same thing happen to you!

Be enticing and mysteriously intriguing!

A good mystery is hard to put down, so tempt your partner with *your* intriguing self! Reveal yourself, little by little, through your opinions, discussions, and actions. Make his mouth water with desire! Never give yourself totally to anyone. Human beings are predators at heart, and once they possess their prey, they become bored and disinterested.

Keep passion alive and burning brightly with subtle seductive moves! Give your partner an appetite for you and an intense desire for your company by making him discover you slowly, conquering a little more of you each day. Never give your partner 100 per cent of yourself: always keep him occupied with conquering that part of you he has not explored. Be independent – it is very attractive! Keep your partner's curiosity at a peak and you will build a solid and passionate relationship!

Take turns spoiling each other!

In the world of today there are women in all cultures who are independent, financially secure, and able to offer invitations and presents just as easily as men! Keep in mind that it is the thought that counts, not the cost of the gift: you can't measure love in pounds and pence!

You needn't reciprocate with an invitation or a gift of equal value. Furthermore, gifts are not the only way to pamper your partner. Be thoughtful, kind, and considerate. Offer her tenderness and understanding. Give the gift of laughter and happiness! But remember, giving is a two-way street! If you are the only one nurturing the relationship, it is probably time to distance yourself a little, to let the other person see what she is missing!

Forget the past! Live in the magic of the present!
It is normal and healthy to go through a period of mourning after a break-up. Some people take three months while others require six months or even two years. The length of time all depends on how deeply the relationship touched you. However, there is a limit to suffering! After a while you have to get right back in the saddle! You have to think about your future and build yourself a happy life. Your ex may have already started to do so! You are the only person who can bring yourself out of the doldrums.

Indulge in life. Take advantage of every magical moment that comes your way! Chase those blues away by living in the delights of the present. Be constructive and think positively! Tell yourself that you have gained experience, that the experience was not *all* bad, and that you are ready once again to face life head-on!

Forget about all of the bad things that went on during the break-up. Sweep away those cobwebs before they smother your spirit. Don't dilute your positive thoughts and the new wonders in your life with fatalistic thoughts from the past. Yesterday is gone and it has taken all the tears and worries and sorrows with it. Think of each new day as a beautiful gift from life. Today is a completely brand-new, sunny day full of unexpected surprises for you. Open your eyes to it, smile and liven up!

You'll exhaust yourself emotionally by remembering past grievances constantly. Stirring up your anger is no way to live. Breathe in the sunshine, feel the peace of a new day, and be assured that your chances at true love are just around the corner!

Motivate yourself!
Work in front of a mirror if you must! Talk to yourself,
encourage yourself. Make an effort not to wallow in self-pity.
Your life is yours, and only you can decide to make it grand or
sad! If you imagine that you are successful, you can be! The
choice is yours! Take the challenge of making your life a
grandiose adventure, and take the first step towards realizing
your newest, brightest hopes and dreams!

Ask your partner for help.
Asking someone for help makes him feel important and
necessary to you. Asking for help is much like giving a
compliment: the other person feels good about himself.
However, you don't want to overdo this technique, or you risk
going too far and appearing helpless and dependent.
Moderation is the key!

There is an art to saying 'thank you.'
Humour is an attention-getter! Send your love interest an
amusing card the day after your date, or leave a cute message
on her answer phone while she is on her way home from the
date. Use your imagination. You may want to buy a silly trinket,
or a sweet gift like chocolate delivered with a short note
thanking her for an enjoyable time. If you are handy in the
kitchen you could bake biscuits or cakes; what about a jar of
your famous marmalade? Send some little thing to say thanks
and to remind her of how 'special' you are!

Of course, you always thank your partner for the little things
she does. Show your appreciation for the compliments and the
encouragement that your partner gives. Tell her often how
much her attention means to you and how she motivates you.
Your loved one will be inspired to shower you with more!

Express your genuine admiration for your love partner.
Don't be shy about showing your admiration for your partner;
everyone loves honest flattery! A very wise Frenchman once
said, 'We always love those who admire us!' Let your partner
see the delight in your eyes and hear the love in your voice
whenever he does something.

Show him that you are enthused about all of his exploits –
great or small! Value his judgement, his wisdom, his spaghetti
bolognaise! Be his fan! Motivate him and show him how great
you think he is, and he will surprise you by being even better
the next time! Compliments and loving support are twin paths
to the heart!

**Good communication, honesty, and genuine caring for
the other person are 'musts' to develop and maintain a
successful relationship.**
Be flexible and adaptable, show your concern for the other
person – your relationship depends on it! If you have a
stubborn streak, keep it under wraps – you can't always have
everything going your way. Make it a point to be frank without
being critical, loyal without being clinging. If your partner is
going through a rough time emotionally or financially and
needs your understanding, be sensitive enough to notice. It is
vital to your relationship that you be there for her and surround
her with support and tenderness.

**No relationship can survive without good com-
munication.**
Many elements are important for a successful, healthy
relationship: affection, compassion, forgiveness, honesty,
acceptance, confidence, a sense of humour, romance, patience,
and respect. But communication is certainly at the top of the
list! If you don't talk about your desires and your fears, if you
don't exchange ideas or really listen to each other, how will you
ever grow as a couple?

Talk about your concerns, tell him you love him, tell him you think he's great, say how much you appreciate his presence in your life. *Talk to each other!* You are partners in love and in life. Share your experiences and reveal your dreams and goals to each other. Live your love!

Did you know that 85 per cent of all relationships break up because of a lack of communication? This statistic is particularly distressing when you consider that nothing could be simpler than talking to the one you love!

Showing affection is important to your relationship.

Hugging your partner is important! A big hug will breathe life into a weary body. Physical tenderness is a human need: touching, hugging and kissing will bring you closer together and develop the emotional, mental and physical dimensions of your relationship. Closeness is vital to the depth of a relationship.

Loving embraces are just that: the warmth of a gentle touch or a loving hug is meant to lift the spirits of your love partner – not to arouse physical feelings. In a strong relationship, closeness enhances all levels of the relationship for both partners. Time to give a hug – *now!*

Respect your love partner.

You can't expect to agree on everything, but you do need to respect your love partner's values and opinions, even if these opinions don't correspond with your own. If your loved one has strong feelings about a particular topic, re-examine your viewpoint and see where you *can* agree; at least, consider your partner's ideas, too!

Give your love partner room to breathe. Don't be jealous!

You can so restrict your loved one with jealousy that you

extinguish her love for you. Possessiveness is the greatest enemy of love! It will consume your life and make life intolerable for your partner, who will feel 'suffocated' and see you as an ogre, an enemy, and as someone who has very little confidence in himself. This is not exactly the image you want her to have!

If your love partner goes to visit family or friends without you, don't automatically assume that she wants to exclude you. Everyone needs time alone . . . even you!

Cherish the time you spend with your love partner.
Live each moment with your love partner as though it were the first . . . or the last. Put all of your passion into the relationship. True love deserves and will thrive on your energy and imagination!

Have you ever spent a wonderful evening with someone, and at the end of the evening, he asked you for your phone number and asked whether he could ring you 'sometime,' but 'sometime' never came?!
You answered yes! And you still can't figure out why you never heard from that handsome stranger you spent a fairy-tale evening with? Well, *Cosmopolitan* magazine published an article in 1990 about the way some men think! According to this article, the simple sentence 'May I ring you sometime?' often means, to these men, 'May I marry you?' Of course, to you, 'May I ring you sometime?' means just that! But apparently many men interpret a 'yes' as a signal that they must marry you on the second date! Obviously, such an absurdity is hilarious! You might use this explanation to console yourself the next time something like this happens! Or pick up that phone and make the first call yourself!

Before beginning a relationship, ask yourself these questions:

- Have I any ulterior motives in my desire for this relationship?
- Am I imposing conditions on my love?
- Am I running away from something?
- Do I want to change my partner?
- Do I need this partner for my personal growth?

If you have answered 'yes' to any of these questions, then let the person follow her own destiny – alone! She will be better off without you, and you without her!

Be wary of those afraid of commitment.
Many people are afflicted with 'commitment-phobia'! They contradict themselves and confuse you by passionately creating an intimate relationship in the beginning. They can look you straight in the eye and tell you how much they want to be with you and how much they want to develop a deep and lasting relationship. They will make you believe that life without you is not worth living and that they want to spend the rest of their life with you – yes, even marry you! But as soon as a solid bond begins to form, they suddenly need 'space'! People afraid of commitment will send you mixed messages: 'Stay with me . . . go away . . . don't smother me . . . don't abandon me!' They can cause much anxiety and suffering for people who date them.

People with commitment-phobia will avoid the intimacy they promised by accusing you of all kinds of things, blaming you for everything, and making you feel responsible for their desertion. Keep in mind that these people are masters of contradiction. Their speech and actions will drive you crazy with wondering what is going on. Be wary: watch for signs of this behaviour from the start of a relationship. Your head will spin with their inconsistencies! For example, you can spend a perfectly marvellous day together, yet the next day or even by the next week he won't even ring you to find out how you are!

Keep your eyes and senses alert for this type of person, and avoid him like the plague! He could cause you much grief and heartache.

Is your partner afraid of love?
It is not easy being with someone who is afraid of love. Serious courtship is almost impossible. Sooner or later the fear will manifest itself into 'commitment-phobia'.

In the beginning of a relationship there are sometimes no obvious signs of commitment-phobia. People who are afraid of love often act like hopeless romantics. They want desperately to be loved and to love, but the minute a courtship leads to a relationship, they flounder – mentally or emotionally – or they disappear from your life, never to be seen or heard from again!

Love may conquer all, but chances are it will not triumph over the commitment-phobic partner. But your independence might! Giving some space to a partner who is afraid of love is the best thing you can do for her. Throwing yourself at her is a guarantee that she will run . . . the other way! Go about your business; get on with your life. Showing her that you are self-possessed and self-fulfilled is what will impress her. If she comes back into your life looking lost and forlorn, don't fall for her line. Pity is not what she needs, and she craves mothering even less.

Do your best to keep away from a commitment-phobic person. Devoting yourself and your time to a problem person drains your energy and keeps you away from other potential partners. Put yourself first in any relationship; only if you love yourself can you love someone else honestly. Why should you endure a relationship that is troubled from the beginning? There may be reasons why your partner is afraid of love, but do you really want to be her therapist? Should you be the one to suffer the consequences? Is it up to you to forgive her thoughtless acts? To forget? Don't let yourself get swept away by a tormented soul! Be your own person, your own centre on which to build your accomplishments. You don't need anyone else to feel and be fulfilled.

A person afraid of love will charm you with romantic prose and promises that she will never deliver. Nice try, but don't fall for her line and get talked into keeping up the relationship. A commitment-phobic person is all talk and no concrete, positive action. Judge the relationship by what she does, *not* by what she says!

Don't be a hero: you cannot change a person who is afraid of commitment!

It is difficult to understand people who are so deathly afraid of commitment. You can't possibly explain to them that their fears control their lives, so don't bother! If you are currently in – or have had – a relationship with a person with commitment-phobia, don't let his accusations and criticism affect your self-confidence. He uses these tactics for his own gain: dominance in the relationship without the need to develop deeply caring love. Rather than become trapped in his games, leave him as quickly as you can to search for a person more worthy of your affection! You cannot change a person's deepest emotional fears – not even with patience and love. Do you really want to waste your valuable life in trying?

What to do if you have ignored the last point.

If you choose to commit to a relationship with a partner who is afraid of love, you should at least enter it prepared. Your independence, strong self-confidence and clearheadedness will be your greatest assets. If you can keep from drowning in a sea of inconsistencies and meaningless words, you will remain the master of your own destiny and inspire your partner to work out her fear – maybe! Good luck!

Listen to yourself. If you are often disturbed by your partner's faults or by what is happening in your relationship, it might be time to call it quits!

Don't go along with the saying 'love is blind', overlooking or denying your partner's faults. Make sure you are aware of his defects as well as his good qualities.

About his mannerisms that get on your nerves, ask yourself: 'Can I live with this person's idiosyncrasies for the rest of my life?' If your answer is no, you would be wise to leave him straight away – before he drives you crazy.

If for any reason you recognize your relationship as an unhealthy one, you had better act quickly before 'catching the ills' and accepting compromises simply to keep the situation dragging along. If the negatives outweigh the joys, it's time to *go!* You can either stay with what you know or go into the unknown: leaving a decaying relationship is the lesser of these two evils. Why live with unhappiness when you can free yourself to search productively for your ideal partner and enjoy life again?!

Use gentleness and tact when disengaging yourself from someone who does not enchant you.

The person you have been dating occasionally is no longer attractive to you. How can you tell her, politely? You could say, 'Although I think you are a nice person, I have met someone else.' Or, 'I am not ready for a relationship right now.'

If someone monopolizes you at a party, you can exit graciously with the following: 'I promised myself that I would circulate and meet as many people as possible tonight, so if you don't mind, I am going to respect that promise. So goodnight. There are lots of other people you can meet, too!'

Be diplomatic. No one likes to be humiliated. Use your charm and grace when dismissing those you find unappealing. You will be remembered as a kind, gentle, caring person!

♥ ♥ ♥

Why live through a bad relationship for fear of staying alone?

Fear of facing the unknown or coping with broken dreams is no reason to endure an unsatisfactory relationship. A bad relationship will leave you empty; staying in one will not give you assurance of continuing love but an 'illusion' of security. You are infinitely more deserving!

A faulty relationship will only drag you down until you feel dead and numb inside, and will accentuate your weaknesses. Why should you tolerate grief? Wouldn't a harmonious relationship suit you better, one that will boost your confidence in yourself as well as your self-image? Why continue a harmful relationship instead of severing those ties and going on to a worthwhile romance that is compatible with your priorities? Stop wasting your time in a destructive relationship. You can find happiness in love – *if* you are strong enough to keep looking!

A violent partner is unacceptable in any relationship.

Violence, whether it's physical or mental cruelty, must never be tolerated. In many countries, conjugal violence is considered a criminal act. If you remain in a relationship after being a victim of your partner's violent act, you are condoning your partner's brutality, and giving him permission to repeat his actions.

It is a fact that people who have been violent with a love partner will undoubtedly do so again, with added force, if given the chance. Violence is volatile. You don't know at what moment it will cause a person to strike out, or how far he will go. Why put yourself in a dangerous situation? No relationship is worth that!

There are professional therapists who work with people who have a tendency to react violently to certain situations. By no means should you play the therapist with a violent partner! Psychological problems require professional counselling; love will not conquer brutality! Your bruises may heal, but your heart will never forget!

Mental anguish is another kind of violence. Although there may be no physical trauma, mental badgering is as damaging. Constant emotional torment by a partner will destroy your self-esteem and kill your love. Psychological harassment can have effects that are just as long-lasting as the effects of physical violence, because your self-image is scarred forever.

If you are breaking up with someone, be considerate and do it in the least painful way possible – in the same manner you would appreciate someone breaking up with you.
Breaking up a relationship is always difficult, especially if your reasons are your partner's shortcomings. Generally, what is said during a break-up depends on the time length of the relationship or on the number of dates you've shared together. If you have not been dating very long, but you have realized that this is not your ideal person or that you cannot stand her idiosyncrasies, be vague about your reasons for splitting up. Leave your partner with her dignity; there is no need to humiliate her or yourself! You will be remembered fondly if you do not criticize every little thing she did. Highlight her good points, saying that you appreciate all the nice things about her. What is the point of making the other person feel sad? Be diplomatic!

Be discreet about breaking up. Choose a neutral place to tell your partner. Why tell her at the end of a date or when it's late in the evening, leaving her to agonize over your decision through a sleepless night? Have the courtesy to tell her during the day, when she can turn to friends or family for comfort.

You want to end a relationship but you can't face the other person.
You want to tell your partner that the romance is over and that you want out of the relationship, but you can't tell him face to face? Write a letter that explains your feelings. Be honest and

direct without leaving room for the other person to linger in self-doubt or to harbour false hopes about the relationship. With some people, there is really no way to let them down gently!

You want to leave someone who is desperately in love with you.

It is a big mistake to say that you'll remain friends or that you'll get together for the occasional lunch! Get out of her life as fast as possible and let her deal with her grief in the company of her friends. Don't ring, and *don't* ask her friends how she is doing. She will find out and think that you still care. Cut all ties to her life immediately and leave her alone!

Don't be afraid to show your vulnerability.

You are only human! It is absolutely normal to have moments of weakness; after all, you're not perfect! So why try to hide your frailties? It takes strength of character to reveal the vulnerable side of your nature. You will be surprised at how many people will appreciate your sensitivity!

Do you cry during sad films? You're not alone! The difficult part is not concealing your feelings in the swirl and bustle of daily activities. If you occasionally feel depressed, anxious or vulnerable, tell your partner. Don't camouflage your emotions. If things are not going well at work, why should you keep your concerns and worry to yourself? You are supposedly sharing your life – the good times and the bad – in this relationship with another person.

A love partnership requires each partner to 'be there' for the other. For example, you may feel somewhat helpless doing certain tasks, especially those requiring more brute strength than you can muster; you should ask for assistance! Or you may find that you are all thumbs when it comes to sewing on a button; why not ask your love to come to your rescue? Help and support in the small things, as well as during times of major trauma – such as the loss of a family member or a bad accident – strengthen a relationship. Love is *'being there'* for each other!

You and your love partner should be on the same wavelength!
Are both of you in love? Have you the same ideas of what constitutes love and affection? Do both of you feel the exhilaration of being together? Or are you the only one declaring your love, the only one who says 'I love you . . . I miss you . . . I need you'? Both partners should show their affection regularly and equally. Do you both talk about how your relationship is coming along? You should be able to discuss things pleasantly! Being on the same wavelength is feeling the same way about the basic relationship and being able to express those feelings!

A truly loving relationship is fulfilling for each partner.
Your partnership should be based on equality and fairness. Desires, confidences, honesty, admiration, devotion, happiness, tenderness, warmth and security are to be shared! You should complete each other so that each feels whole. Your relationship should be a healthy exchange of ideas, affection and attention, with mutual respect and consideration for each other. Your ultimate goal should be true compatibility!

Be on the lookout for defensive behaviour!
Do you feel as though your partner's affections for you are dwindling? Is he acting distant and uneasy in your presence? Do you feel him slipping away? Is he defensive with you? Perhaps the present state of the relationship no longer satisfies him. If this is the case, it is best to question the viability of your love partnership. If you are not certain of the other person's intentions, it is best to face him directly and ask: you are entitled

to know. Your partner may be paralysed with the fear of ending up alone or may simply be anxious about telling you 'something is wrong' or 'it's over.' But it's your future, too, so find out if there is something you can do to rekindle your partner's interest. If all seems hopeless, bow out gracefully! Better to get on with your life than spend months or years fighting a lost cause!

You deserve someone who loves you as much as you love him or her!

Get out of a troubled relationship as fast as possible! When all is said and done in a bad relationship, the only thing left to do is to say, 'So long and good luck!' You can't make someone love you. No matter how long you drag out the relationship with cunning ways, sooner or later she will leave. Why should you belittle yourself? Why would you want someone who doesn't love you? There is no need to humiliate yourself, you are entitled to dignity and respect! Now is the time to make a clean break and continue your search for a suitable partner who will return your love!

Don't isolate yourself after a break-up!

Seek solace from your friends, from your family, and from your colleagues. Find someone to confide in. You will get rid of your pain more quickly if you talk about it! Your good friends will encourage you, and their compassion will help you through this difficult period in your life. Sitting at home alone is only going to make you feel more miserable. Get out and talk to friends. Time and friendship will mend your broken heart!

A well-balanced relationship will allow each partner to show his true colours!

You can laugh *with* your partner but never *at* him; cry with him but not because of him! A harmonious relationship rests on mutual respect. Jealousy will destroy love, but appreciation will nurture it!

A stable relationship is a relaxed partnership where each member can find comfort and encouragement in the presence of the other, with constantly renewed energies! It is one where the love is so real that it grants complete security and allows you to reveal your emotions with candidness, as well as share in successes and failures. It is one that fosters the expression of feelings with the innocence and spontaneity of a child. The ideal relationship is a communion of spirit, love and honesty that heightens the identity of each partner!

Being cared for is lovely, but don't become dependent on the other person!
Keep your independence! Don't think that if someone takes charge of your life, you will be free of responsibilities. You will end up losing your identity just to please another!

Be your own person: this means not being guided by someone else's authority. Learn to be a self-sufficient, positive person who can make her own decisions. Be secure emotionally, financially and professionally. Even though you share life and goals as a couple, run your own life, set your own personal goals; then you will have something worthwhile to contribute to the enrichment of a relationship.

Have you given up your right to equal decision-making?
One way to determine if you have an authoritarian partner is to ask questions. Ask about his past relationships. Does it sound as though he acted like a parent with his past partners? Try to find out how he treats other people close to him. Observe the way he acts around his family members and the reactions of his family. Is his mother a passive woman without motivation? Is she totally dependent on her husband, always depressed and negative? Is his father overbearing, argumentative? The context

of a person's family influences his adult behaviour and how he will react in a relationship.

If you feel that your partner is acting out inter-family roles instead of a sharing, co-operative role with you, then you might be successful in pointing out this behaviour to him and in working together to bring about a change.

Be wary of being 'hooked' by an addict.
There are many types of addictions: alcohol, cigarettes, food, neatness, gambling, and a wide range of drugs. Very often one addiction leads to another: cigarettes and alcohol, for example. If you are with an addict, be very careful: you could easily become drug-dependent yourself, simply by trying to help.

An addict is often immature in judgement, and you, as co-dependent, will start to feel responsible for that person. In trying to save her from her habit, you become part of her 'game', and before long, the need to continually 'rescue' her locks you into a vicious circle that results in an inability to leave. Often a co-dependent is the child of an addicted parent and has experienced a dysfunctional family syndrome. There is also evidence that co-dependent people often suffer from eating disorders and kleptomania – shoplifting – in their adult lives. These 'minor afflictions' are 'rebellion addictions' that rise from a need to cope with the overwhelming burden of being with an addict.

If you are 'in love' with an addict, you can easily become her co-dependent in an obsessive relationship that will become a life of torment! It will become as difficult for you to leave your addict as it is for her to quit her habit! You may even develop toxic habits of your own in this destructive relationship. Remember, an addict cannot love you the way you deserve to be loved, for she cannot love herself!

Other forms of addiction that also require counselling.
Addiction comes in many forms; you can even be addicted to

someone physically! There are also workaholics – people who are so addicted to their work that it becomes such an obsession they have no time for the pleasures of life. Partners of workaholics are alone and lonely most of the time. Whatever the addiction, even though it may seem harmless or non-toxic, as the partner you will suffer the consequences. Leave this addict as quickly as you can, before you are consumed in a self-destructive whirlpool of confused emotions and the loss of self-esteem!

It is a mistake to think that you can 'save' an alcoholic. If you are in a relationship with an alcoholic, keep in mind that alcoholism is a disease and not one that you can cure with love and devotion. An alcoholic must want to stop drinking. You cannot make him do so, nor can all the love you give him.

You cannot rely on an alcoholic. He will make many promises to meet you somewhere, to run an errand, to stop drinking – and he will be very remorseful when the promises are broken. Do you really want the task of becoming his keeper . . . or his therapist? Even though you may encourage someone to quit drinking, you can never relax your guard because it is impossible to predict what will start him off again – or when! And your pain will resume. Being the life partner of an alcoholic is so difficult that you can end up psychologically 'hitting rock bottom' long before he does.

Be attentive to the signs of alcoholism in all new relationships. Does your partner drink alcohol on a regular basis? Does he drink too much alcohol at celebrations or when faced with problems? Be on your guard for the vital signs; the success and happiness of your relationship depends on it!

Are you letting daily life turn you into a dull, uncaring person?
Ask yourself whether you enjoy your own company. Are you grumpy, demanding, arrogant, insensitive, authoritarian, cold,

crude – all the while imagining that you are filled with love for your partner? If you are in love, shouldn't you be warm and tender, tolerant and sincere? Most relationships fail because of minor problems that build up into a storm, not because of one major tragedy!

Love can be lost due to the 'little things' – cruel comments, procrastination, thoughtlessness! If you were to analyse failed relationships, you would see that they had failed due to minor issues such as:

- 'She always interrupts me when I'm talking! It drives me crazy!'
- 'He can't make up his mind about anything! Not even about what to wear!'
- 'She's such a neatness freak that you can't even move a magazine!'
- 'I'm less important than an ashtray.'
- 'He never shuts up and is so boring!'
- 'She gossips too much.'

Although these habits seem insignificant, in the long run, they can destroy a relationship. But you can prevent such habits from ruining your life by discussing them tactfully with your partner. It's so easy to modify annoying behaviour with a little willpower and love!

The next time problems arise in your relationship, face them head on. Consider them a challenge that will fortify your relationship and enrich your lives. Use your heart and your head to tackle problems and to find the best solution possible. If you try ignoring the problems in the hope that they will just go away, or if you pretend that everything is rosy, you'll never change anything! Work on difficult areas together, and your relationship will blossom and grow in love!

Power struggles are common in a relationship. Compromise is the key!

Often problems arise because of a struggle for power, the need of one partner to dominate the other or 'win' with his opinions. These situations take delicate negotiating. The main objective is not to let resentment take over the relationship. The solutions to your differences depend on sharing responsibility for making the relationship work.

Suppose Marcia wants to spend every Sunday afternoon visiting her parents. Larry would like to use that time to visit museums or art galleries. After much discussion, Larry agrees to visit Marcia's family the third Sunday afternoon of every month, and that she should go alone the first Sunday of every month. Marcia agrees to go to museums and galleries with Larry two Sundays a month. This solution gave them both time to themselves and times to share. To their mutual surprise, Larry learned wood-carving from Marcia's father, and Marcia got a part-time job at the local museum designing exhibition catalogues! A very happy ending to a potentially destructive power struggle!

Tradition and rituals are important!

Tradition can be a very strong bond. It is important to respect customs and even to consider them as a romantic part of your relationship. Family get-togethers are important traditions, as are annual holidays, birthday celebrations, visits to the cemetery in commemoration of the death of a mutual and dear friend, or even a symbol of tradition such as a song or a dance! Celebrate all of the significant events in your lives as a couple – whether sad or joyful. Keep a calender of memorable days: the birthday of a mutual chum, your parent's anniversary! Weave your personal web of rituals as a couple; it will give strength to your future and add significance to your lives.

Don't give in to destructive behaviour.

If you want a successful relationship, don't give in to demeaning behaviour such as:

- being possessive or jealous by manipulating, controlling and dominating your partner
- continuously criticizing your partner
- competing with the obsession of winning and always having the last word
- nagging

It is normal to encounter conflicts as a relationship progresses.
If there are clashes, be mature instead of childishly declaring 'I'm right! You're wrong!' and placing blame on each other. Listen to your partner objectively and with empathy. Keep your emotions under control, and don't fall into the roles of 'victim' and 'accuser'!

Conflicts are inevitable and often arise when the relationship has taken a sudden leap forward in emotional depth and each partner is subconsciously scared! Another cause revolves around decisions about money, control, social status, and responsibility. There is no need to confront these situations with aggressiveness; such problem areas are inescapable in an ongoing relationship. It helps to consider any problem as a challenge.

Conflicts are often an excellent opportunity for a constructive discussion. It is through your controversies that you can grow together as a couple and develop a beautifully harmonious togetherness!

If issues such as the religious or political views of your partner differ from yours, respect his opinions and beliefs. Try to avoid any discussion of those topics, and show your love by letting your partner be free to be himself.

A properly resolved conflict will bring you closer together, but don't wait until aggravations pile up and you lose control and explode! Bring problems to your partner's attention while you can still talk them over.

Be objective: try not to approach your problems emotionally. Why make things worse by bringing up old arguments or by screaming that your partner is to blame for all the trouble? Both partners are responsible for the relationship. Use your intelligence, not your vocal powers! Intimidation will get you nowhere! Discussing the problem, amicably but seriously, will help the two of you to discover and to consider each other's viewpoint. Be frank but non-threatening.

It is important to reveal your true feelings and to make sure that you are understood. There must be give-and-take throughout the discussion, as there should be throughout the relationship. By calmly discussing your points of conflict, each of you will have a heightened perception of your partner that will strengthen the bonds of love. Each partner will emerge with a new understanding of the other. Now all you need to do is *kiss and make up!*

Identify your needs and goals.
Once you have identified your needs and goals independent of your relationship, define the ones you expect from the relationship. Then have your partner write hers down. Is her relationship list compatible with yours? If not, negotiate! Can you agree on a renewed version of your relationship that will satisfy your individual goals as well? Then you are on your way to a very happy future – together!

Your basic goals are in harmony, but the magic is missing!
Are you forgetting to share your hopes and dreams? Dreams will give your goals wings and enrich your life. Dreaming together – about a future home, a wonderful holiday, an expensive art object you both adore – enhances a love relationship with an element of wonder and delight! A mutual dream is a mutual goal you can seek together! A dream is a secret place – an enchanted garden – where you and your love partner can share a magical experience.

Now that you have set your goals, plan step-by-step how you will realize them!
Give yourself every chance to succeed. Settle on a date for achieving your objectives. Ask yourself where you want to be in a year's time, then decide what you have to do on a monthly basis over the next twelve months to achieve your goals. Make a chart of your coming year with your 'success agenda' plans noted for each month. Place this where you will see it often, and keep track of how you are doing each week and each month. Don't get discouraged if you have a few setbacks, just keep working at achieving your ultimate goals! You can do it! Persevere!

Once you have applied this method to your personal goals, use it for your goals as a couple. Perhaps the two of you have a financial goal you want to reach together over the next year. Now is the time to plan your monthly savings goal. Of course you may have to adjust the plan from time to time as situations change, but you should strive to attain your goal.

Other goals could involve better communication, demonstrating more caring, or simply working on problems between the two of you. Setting up a chart and noting things you could do each day or week to improve your relationship will help remind you to keep working at your relationship as well as showing you how much you care for each other!

Observe how your partner reacts to problems, to differences of opinion, to mishaps. The following check list of questions will help you.

- Does your partner have a positive outlook?
- Is he able to make compromises?
- Does she react with poise to problems?
- Does he recognize his mistakes, or does he accuse you unjustly?
- Does she constantly remind you of old arguments?

You can tell a lot about your partner by observing how they react to problems.

- How does he handle frustrations?
- Does she ignore problems or face them with lion-hearted courage?
- Does he blame you for every little thing?
- Can she admit her wrongs and say, 'I'm sorry'?
- Is he forgiving?
- Does she communicate?
- Is he patient or does he lack tact, understanding and respect?
- Do you feel she acts apathetic?
- Has he got a negative streak?
- Is she obstinate and hostile?
- Is he authoritarian?

Watch your partner's interaction with other people.

- Has she got a sense of humour?
- Is he flexible or rigid in outlook?
- Does she always dominate the conversation?
- Does he appear friendly or on guard?

How can you know the answers to these questions?

One way of discovering your partner's true colours is to go on holiday together! There are always many little inconveniences and problems that can crop up: lost luggage, delayed flights, language barriers, or no hotel reservations! How does your partner react when the car you hired is not available and instead you are given a 'rent-a-wreck'? Do tempers fly when the food is not very good? Can she adapt to cultural differences and the change in pace of your holiday paradise?

Get to really know your partner. Look for ways to strengthen your relationship or to give weight to your decision that this is – or is not – the partner you want for the rest of your life.

If your upbringing and culture permit, you might find it a good idea actually to live together for a short period of time – a few days or weeks – to see if the two of you are really suited to being together before you commit yourself for a lifetime. What if one of you has personal habits that are too irritating for the other person to put up with? Perhaps there are personality clashes that would only show up when the two of you are together for an extended length of time. A period of time where you are undergoing the daily stresses and strains of a committed relationship will often reveal if the two of you are truly suited to becoming 'a couple'.

Ask your love partner his opinion on children, careers and money.
These are fundamental issues! You must agree on these points if you want harmony in your lives. If you want to have children someday, but your partner is dead-set against it, can you change his mind? Probably not, if his reasons are deeply entrenched.

Should you both want children, it is wise to also discuss the details of their education well in advance of planning a family. This is particularly important if the two of you come from different family, cultural, religious or ethnic backgrounds. Disagreement on such fundamental matters as well as pressure to adhere to either person's traditions can eventually tear apart even the most loving couples.

If the love of your life is frugal to the point of being stingy or miserly, he will never understand the need for a little 'mad money' or for an occasional frivolous purchase! You may soon discover that a person who is mean with his money is also mean with his love! Often he will be selfish as well, with only *his* interests at heart!

If you are a woman and have, or plan to have, a career, make sure your partner understands and appreciates your commitment to your work. If he doesn't, he is not likely to change after marriage, and you will be hounded continually by his objections and forced to live unhappily in constant discord!

If you have a job that takes you away from home often, or if the work carries risks, as in the police force or the army, you are wise to look for a strong, independent partner.

Look at your current relationship from the viewpoint of a long-term commitment. You should share similar goals if you want a harmonious, enduring partnership!

Carefully consider all the pros and cons before embarking on a relationship with someone who has children.
Are you ready for such a relationship? You will be sharing your life with an entire ready-made family, not with just one other person. What about the ex-wife or ex-husband? What role, if any, will he or she play in your life? Also, children are a constant reminder of the past relationship!

You will become attached to the children and they to you. What will happen to their emotional lives if you break up? Your sorrows will be magnified because of the attachment you have to the children; you are not leaving just one person! Weigh your options and ask yourself if this involvement is really what you want, or if you would be better off with someone who has no parental responsibilities.

Before committing yourself to a relationship where children are involved, be prepared for the role of number two!
It is inevitable that the children's needs will come first. For example, at the last minute, your partner is asked to take the children for the weekend, and there goes that romantic out-of-town weekend you have been planning! Are you ready for such radical changes? Can you adjust to these types of situations?

You bought tickets for the theatre two months ago, and the show is sold out. At five o'clock on opening night, your partner announces that the youngest child is sick with a high fever and that she can't possibly leave him. Will you throw a fit or will you be understanding? If you are incapable of adapting to unpredictable circumstances, you had better look for someone who has no family obligations and who is completely free – to be with only you!

You have been in a relationship for a long time and it means a lot to you.
You don't want to call it quits until you are certain that you have

exhausted every possible option for salvaging the relationship. The key words here are *negotiation* and *compromise*.

It helps to make a list of your problem areas. When you have written them all down on paper, go through them and put a big *X* next to those you feel you can be flexible on. Have your partner make up a similar list. Begin with the negotiable items on each list and see where the two of you can reach a compromise.

For example, suppose money is a big issue. He thinks the household allowance should meet all household needs, including cosmetics, toiletries and incidentals. She thinks there should be an extra amount set aside monthly just for clothing and small luxuries. The compromise might be a reduction in weekly household money and the setting up of a monthly 'personal allowance'. Solutions will be different for each couple.

Now go back to your list and review the items you felt were non-negotiable. Notice a change in your opinion? Having solved one or two problems, you will begin to see creative ways to work through seemingly insurmountable differences. You are on your way to a solid, strong relationship!

Take the time to talk with your partner in a mature way, amicably, using words and gestures that encourage an empathetic exchange, not a hostile one. An aggressive approach will just antagonize your partner and will not lead to the open discussion you are aiming for. Be compassionate, warm and tender. Heated arguments solve nothing!

It's a good idea to make a list of your partner's good points when everything is going smoothly. Keep this list on hand to read when the waters are rough; it may be enough to get you through a small tempest! Next time you have an argument with your partner, think about the reasons why you love him. Do they outweigh the reasons for your argument?

It is true that people who never argue may be completely indifferent, but if you contest every little thing your partner does – or vice-versa – it might be time to reassess your roles in the relationship, as well as the pattern of your lives. At other times, it is better to forget a minor annoyance than to blow it out of proportion. Next time you feel hurtful anger brewing, take time out to look at the reason for your feelings. Remember why you fell in love with your partner, and try to find another way to express your current displeasure!

An ultimatum should be your last resort!
An ultimatum can backfire if you state it too harshly. Your partner may fight back and accuse you of threatening her; or she may simply withdraw altogether, shutting down the lines of communication. If all other tactics have failed to solve your differences, then an ultimatum is a course of action open to you. However, you should mean what you say and follow it through if you want your partner to take you seriously. An ultimatum must be chosen wisely and with caution!

A relationship requires the ability to adapt to everyday aggravations.
Life is not perfect; there are always ups and downs that may not occur simultaneously in each partner's life. You must be understanding of the upsets that occur; he might lose his job, become ill, or be transferred to another city. Changes are inevitable – promotions, graduation, new employment – and you must develop adaptability and be prepared to accept those changes if you are to live harmoniously and happily in a long-term relationship. When you really care deeply for someone, being flexible is a joy!

Conventional thinking and misconceptions often attempt to present stereotyped views
How often do you still hear phrases like these?:

- 'Women are notoriously bad drivers; they can't even park a car!'
- 'Men aren't in touch with their emotions.'
- 'Men don't talk to you, so you may as well spend the evening at the library.'
- 'Men can't communicate!'

- 'Women are simply inferior to men.'
- 'Men will never understand women!'
- 'Today's women are too strong-minded and independent!'
- 'Women should marry, raise children, and stay home.'

Do these remind you of things you have said? Making remarks about assumed roles or weaknesses does not help people understand one another. How can you have a meaningful relationship without the bond of understanding?

If you let trivial things like parking and conversational skills overshadow your love for a person, how can you improve your relationship? Everyone has his or her own little quirks – even you!

Have you ever considered that men may have as many deep emotions as women do, but that they express them in a completely different way? Also, women know how to park perfectly well, they just don't do it the way men do. The next time you find yourself saying (or thinking) that a woman is not mechanically minded, ask yourself how good you are at running the washing machine, dryer, or dishwasher!

Remember how we were brought up? Women spent much more time in their childhood relating to each other, playing nicely while pretending to socialize at their tea-less tea parties. Little boys spent their time competing with each other, trying to be 'one-up' on their best friend. Women learn very early in their lives that their role should be to nurture, to care for, to make others feel comfortable. At the same time, men learn to compete and to get what they want at any cost. Although the roles are now changing, the adults of today are the children of yesterday's ideals trying to learn to adapt to the new demands for equality in the modern world. Perhaps in another decade there will be advances made in true equality in the workplace, in the home, and in relationships. Then and now, men and women will have to make an honest effort to understand each person's unique perceptions and feelings.

Today's strong, forceful and assertive woman is to be prized and is definitely not a threat to anyone's manhood. Men should value her independence because they are blessed with plenty of it themselves. A strong woman is also a passionate one who can share a love affair that rocks the world. With two such vibrant personalities harnessed as a team, you can take on the whole world – together!

Imposing stereotypes is as bad as accepting them. They do not contribute to a better life as a couple, nor do they furnish insight into what makes each other tick. Isn't it more interesting to discover the inner beauty and strengths of your partner, rather than complain about the things he is doing wrong – in your opinion? Isn't it more fun to show her how to bring out the best in you rather than to get angry with her?

Make an effort to change your attitude and really try to see the other person's point of view, instead of trying to change your partner or impose your ideas. By helping your partner to understand your feelings, you will encourage him to tell you his, too! Using these simple tactics will lead to better communication and a happier relationship!

Many women complain that men don't communicate. Maybe they just do it differently!

It is often difficult to understand why someone else has a hard time doing something that comes so easily to you. Perhaps men just have a harder time expressing themselves emotionally. Although men and women use both sides of their brains, there is scientific proof that women use the right side of the brain more often – that is, the verbal, communicative side. Therefore, for a woman, talking and revealing her feelings and emotions come naturally. Men make more use of the left side of their brain – the mathematical, analytical side. Perhaps, women have to learn how to talk to a man in his own language using his unique vocabulary in order to draw him out of his shell!

It isn't just men who often need someone to take the first step. Inside every silent individual lies a person longing to communicate, to be understood, to be liberated enough to let loose a rainbow of feelings. If your partner has a difficult time communicating, be understanding, observant and patient. Sarcastic, cutting remarks will get you nowhere and will only make the other person retreat further away.

In order to try to understand a reticent person, you have to be patient. Look for reasons in his background – even his childhood – that would make it difficult for him to reveal his feelings. Perhaps he was always criticized by a parent or an ex-lover every time he tried to explain himself. Be compassionate and don't nag your partner. If you continuously tell him to speak his mind, or ask him, 'What are you thinking about now?' or 'Why did you react that way when I asked you to run an errand?', you will not get anywhere. Your noncommunicative partner must have the desire to express himself because you kindly invited him to open up – not because you provoked him into doing so!

Jeremy and Mary were going through this sort of problem. Mary was a bubbly, outgoing, fun-loving woman who fell in love with quiet, serious-minded Jeremy. Everything was fine until Mary began to feel that Jeremy was ignoring her, that he didn't want to do things or go places together, that he didn't care for her anymore. She would ask Jeremy what was wrong and would even cry, but he would just go into another room or seem angry with her questioning. Then one day, while the two of them were watching television, a brutal scene in which a child was verbally and physically abused by the child's parents filled the screen. Jeremy got up and left the room. Puzzled, Mary followed. She found Jeremy staring out the window, tears coursing down his cheeks. Then Mary understood: Jeremy had been mistreated for much of his young life. He was really shy and lacked self-confidence, and his silence hid feelings he was unable to express. Mary was sympathetic, and also glad to discover that Jeremy was not deliberately shutting her out. From that day on, the two of them worked towards better communication: Jeremy, by more frequently revealing how he felt; Mary, by continuing to be supportive, outgoing, loving and considerate.

If you want your partner to open up or to be more thoughtful or romantic, why not show her how by doing something *for* her instead of asking her to do something for you? Send your partner flowers, tell her a secret, tell her how you feel about her – use a card if words are too difficult. Tell her what's bothering you and show her you are vulnerable. Do it with enthusiasm, and soon your partner will be responding and rewarding your efforts with similar acts of caring.

Encourage the language of love.
Intimacy is created by both people in a relationship. You can help your partner express himself by talking to him on his terms, by translating your feelings and ideas into words he will understand. Learn to speak his language so that you can communicate with him before you teach him the language of your love!

Listening to the way your partner expresses himself will give you clues to approaching him. If your mate always greets you with, 'How's it going?' don't reply with, 'Tell me what you're feeling.' Instead say, 'How did your day go?' His answer may lead you to interesting conversations and helpful hints as to the way he looks at events. Slowly, you can guide your partner towards expressing his feelings.

Read between the lines and learn to decode the body language of the partner who says little. If, every time your partner is in a bad mood, he slams doors all over the house, and you know he had an argument with his mother, you can deal with his attitude until it blows over. Accept his non-verbal communication – the bad mood – and help him get over it by non-verbal empathetic attitudes such as a pat on the shoulder, a hug, a cup of tea offered without his asking. Help him forget whatever went wrong by introducing cheerful things to discuss or suggesting a walk together. This is not the time to resort to nagging him into telling you what's wrong.

Don't take things at face value. Everyone has a different way of expressing himself. Get to know your partner's 'silent' languages before judging him too harshly – your relationship depends on it!

Be discreet about your relationship.
You have been seeing an absolutely darling person for the last month. It's almost too good to be true! You get along famously, you have a lot in common, and you're dying to tell someone what goes on every waking moment of your relationship. Don't do it!

Be discreet. Limit your revelations to generalities. You needn't tell your friends every detail. Things are rosy now, but what happens if you break up? What if you have a really serious argument? How can you tell that to your best friend, when you rang her yesterday and said your partner is 'perfection on two legs', while today you could wring perfection's neck?

Broadcasting your partner's faults is definitely not a good idea either. Each day you are with that person is your choice; nobody is forcing you to stay with her. Obviously you have accepted her the way she is, or you wouldn't be with her!

Why criticize your partner in private or in public? Such tactics only make her feel bad and lower her self-esteem. If your partner doesn't feel terrific around you, she will be drawn to others who *will* make her feel special.

It is absolutely a no-no to discuss your more intimate moments with anyone else. Besides being a breach of implicit trust, the term 'intimate' means just that: a private exchange that belongs to you and your partner only!

A successful relationship takes work and constant attention. Sometimes couples complain that their needs are not being met by their partner. Both sides must realize that their partners are not in the relationship merely to cater to their each and every want and desire. There must be give-and-take in any socially interactive situation, and that is particularly true of a loving partnership.

Courtship is a wonderfully exhilarating stage in a relationship. If ever there were a time to be nice to each other, a time *for* each other, this is it!

There is no such thing as 'guaranteed fidelity'.
People tend to wander when the relationship gets boring. You

needn't live a television romance filled with excitement and intrigue every day of the week, but there are many things you can do to keep the love flames burning brightly.

Hold hands – just like you did in the beginning. Remember how tingles ran down your spine the moment your fingers touched in the popcorn box, during the film on your first date? Relive the moment – even without the cinema! If your culture, region or society permits holding hands in public, do so while shopping, while walking along the street, or during dinner. Otherwise, hold hands often when you are in private places. A sure way to stop an argument is to cup someone's hand in yours. Holding hands is an innocent gesture that is very reassuring, warm and caring!

Leave love notes all over the place. Send one to his office, mail one to his home, or leave one on his answer phone: 'Hi, just rang to say I love you! Guess who!' After dinner, at home, put on some favourite records and dance – cheek-to-cheek would be nice!

Offer your partner a thoughtful gift as a token of your love. Do so often and at odd, surprising moments. It doesn't have to be expensive; give him something cute, like a bow tie, a poster of his favourite animal, a horoscope, or a book he has been talking about. Invite him for a cappuccino. Do something unexpected and loving. You'll keep him on his toes if he never knows what will happen next – with you!

Tell your partner how much you appreciate him. Compliment him regularly: 'I love your nose. It gives you such a great profile!' It is important to compliment him on a feature he doesn't like about himself, so that he realizes how attracted you are to him. Don't fall into the taken-for-granted 'comfortable zone', where you are so used to seeing each other that it becomes as exciting as going to the supermarket! Make a point of showing your partner that you are thrilled to see him, that you have looked forward to being with him! Say how much you have missed him; he will feel wanted and desirable. Kisses and hugs are a big help!

Suppose your relationship has been going on for a while. You both feel comfortable talking with each other, you know each other's favourite foods, you have met each other's friends, you have discussed books and films you both like, when *bam!* you find yourselves discussing work and money and parents and problems, while you are supposed to be enjoying a nice dinner on your evening out together! Sure, it's great, if you aren't arguing about those things – or if you are, you are at the same time solving problems together; but where's the romance? It's still there, in the words, looks and caresses you have shared and need to keep on sharing, if romance is to have a place in your lives. Romance doesn't just happen; you have to plan little loving gestures and take time for caring moments, if your courtship is to enrich your lives.

Always remember the reasons why your partner loved you at the beginning of your relationship, and try to keep those qualities.
Some relationships suffer because, over time, there is a tendency to forget the little things that made the two of you important to – or attracted to – each other. People do change, of course, but the following points might help you to compare your present attitudes and appearance with those of the early days of your relationship.

- Were you well groomed and careful of your appearance? Did you take good care of yourself and your health so that you looked your best at all times?
- Were you romantic? Did you bring her flowers and chocolates, take her to the cinema and occasionally have dinner at a nice restaurant? Did you prepare lovely candlelight dinners for him? Did you send affectionate cards or greetings for no special reason?
- Were you affectionate, loving, kind in manner and speech? Did you project a positive, optimistic, supportive attitude?

It is so easy to slip into a taken-for-granted, overly relaxed approach to your daily interactions with a partner. But if you feel her feelings for you are fading fast, or that she is losing interest, ask yourself if you have changed to the point that your partner is disillusioned or feels deceived. Are you still that wonderful person she first met and loved? If not, you can still regain the special magic of your relationship by becoming again the attractive, caring, considerate, loving person you once were – and still are – if you try!

Handling problems.
Are you having courtship problems or aggravations in the relationship, such as 'He's always late! It's driving me crazy!' or 'She's always talking about her mother. Next thing you know, she'll be inviting her out on our dates!' Face the situation. Set aside discussion time to talk about these annoyances. Why let them build up to boulder proportions when you can scrape them away while they are still only the rubble of two people getting to know each other? Part of courtship is to sit back and evaluate the relationship. Every once in a while you might have a 'love meeting' where the two of you get together – over dinner by candlelight perhaps – and talk about the progress of your relationship. Are you both getting everything you want out of this relationship? What could you add? What could he add? Find out if your partner is satisfied. Ask him: 'Tell me one thing I can do for you that would make you feel wonderful!'

Make a list of what each of you gives to the relationship.
Make a list in two columns with the heading 'What I Give to the Relationship' for one, and 'What My Partner Gives to the Relationship' for the other. Output should equal input! If you have had a gnawing feeling every time you are on a date, but you can't quite put your finger on it, look at your list.

If you are having ambivalent thoughts about the relationship, one way to see things more clearly is to write things down in black and white. Make another list with two columns. Title the first column 'The times I *did not* feel good in the company of my partner' and the second, 'The times I *did* feel good in her company.' Be careful not to blame your partner for attitudes she has no control over, like your ill temper, or a bad mood brought on by an unrelated event.

As a complement to this analysis, compile a list of 'Things my partner does and says that make me feel good.' These can be as elaborate as preparing a special dinner to as simple as filling your coffee mug when it's empty!

Lists are eye-openers. You might be surprised at how much your partner actually does for you! If you have been in a relationship with the same person for a long time, you might consider listing the things that you *used to do* for each other, like writing love letters, sending flowers, ringing during the day just to say, 'I love you!', or making a formal date. It is difficult to pinpoint exactly when these behaviours end, because when people settle into a relationship, they gradually take these things for granted. Be aware of these niceties; they are important to building and maintaining a solid relationship.

A career is important to both men and women today. When a person is having career difficulties, she feels uneasy or even unworthy. In order to restore her self-esteem, she may be tempted to involve herself in 'affairs', to demonstrate her ability and power to attract and seduce others. To try to keep this from happening in your relationship, be supportive in times of stress. Encourage your partner to talk about and share her career concerns. During this time, boost her moral by reassuring her that she is desirable: 'Darling, you may have been passed up for a promotion this time, but you are *my* president, the most desirable person in the world to me!' Tell her and show her that she is your heart's darling and a real star in your life!

No excitement in your 'dates' anymore? Walk and talk yourselves out of Dull City!
Do your 'dates' revolve around ordering in a pizza and watching television or videos all evening? 'Couch potato' warning! Monotony on the way! You are not married, you have no commitments in terms of debts or children, and you have no obligations – only the joy of being together and the freedom of

doing whatever you want. You needn't spend a lot of money to do things together: you can go out for a romantic walk in the park or for a picnic. Go to a museum together; have a cup of special tea or coffee at a neighbourhood café; or go *out* for pizza and a film! Spend time together relating to each other in the big world instead of perpetually sitting isolated like 'couch-potato twins' in front of the TV. Make time to explore each other's hopes, dreams, fears and ambitions. Also, see how you can share moments of silence together, where one reads or studies and the other paints, does gardening, or listens to his favourite music using stereo headphones or a Walkman. In other words, get to know each other better!

You have found the love of your life, so why bother to keep yourself looking good? Trouble coming up if you don't!

Take care of your appearance. Just because you have at last found a wonderful woman or a great man doesn't mean you can let yourself go and not care about your appearance! With someone around who cares for you, that is all the more reason to look your best – desirable, kissable, touchable, lovable – if you want to keep him or her interested. Dress nicely. Casual clothes are fine as long as you look neat and alluring. Take care of your hair and your overall health and appearance. Watch your weight! You know you should love someone for who he is, but let's face it: an attractive, svelte physique is a stunning plus! If you have this added attraction, your partner won't be distracted by someone else's!

Keep flirting with your partner regularly – because your competition will!

You and your partner have known each other for a while, and you are often seen together as a couple. One evening, at a small party at a mutual friend's house, you are surprised and shocked when another person openly flirts with *your* partner! Don't be so taken aback! You found your love attractive and enjoyed flirting with her when you first met, so of course others will try the same tactics. Simply out-flirt the competition by being seductive, alluring, and obviously *the one* for this marvellous person in your life.

For tips on how to be an irresistible flirt, read Part 2 of this book, if you haven't already done so. Keep the lovelight in your darling's eyes focused squarely on *you* – by treating her every day as though you had just met her! Weave your daily enchantment with your sweet, outrageous, comical, loving *flirting!*

Romance is the key to a memorable courtship!

Keep the romantic fires burning. A good dose of romance is essential to all healthy relationships, and it is particularly important in courtship. If you start off dull and dreary, you can only expect more of the same in the future. Be passionately romantic from the start and keep your partner continually interested. Be absolutely and scintillatingly aglow at all times with the light of romance. The next part of this book, A Million and One Love Strategies for Keeping Passion in a Romance, will give you passionate strategies for keeping your love life – and your loving courtship – bathed in the enchanted light of romantic passion. A must for anyone who wants to lift his relationship to passion's summit.

Courting with kisses.

A well-known old song goes, 'A kiss is just a kiss'; but in courtship, a kiss can change the entire atmosphere of a date! For example, suppose you haven't seen your love partner all day when you meet at the railway station after work. What do you do? Pressing your lips together for a sustained ten seconds creates a mood – certainly one preferable to simply saying, 'Hi, how are you? Hurry! We'll miss the train!' Kissing him on the lips and holding it for ten seconds as soon as you see him creates a psychological affection bond, which will attach him lovingly to you and which will last for the duration of your time spent together – a date, an evening, or the whole day!

Although you may not choose to kiss someone on your first date, you are no doubt kissing your 'steady', your 'main squeeze'! Kissing basics are a must for courtship. Once you get beyond the theoretical stage of asking questions like 'Where do the noses go?' or 'Why kiss at all?' and into practice sessions, the following 'kissing up a storm' tip promises a fun-filled erotic-shivery love time!:

Begin your 'love storm kiss' with a gentle kiss on the forehead. Then slide your mouth down your partner's cheek, neck, shoulder, arm and hand. Go up the other hand and arm to the shoulder, where you add a 'play-bite' gently with your teeth before continuing to the back of the neck with little kisses. Nibble an ear while you are in the area. Next drop your head to the lovely hollow at the front of the neck and place tender kisses there. If your love is lying down, fill the little hollow with wine or a liqueur and lap it up – slowly. This little tactic is guaranteed to drive your darling absolutely crazy! End your 'love storm' with a long, sensual kiss on the lips. Pure bliss!

In case you need an intellectual reason for initiating a kiss, you might mention these points.
Kissing and hugging are essential elements in human relations. People need tactile stimulation. Babies who are coddled with tender touching grow up more confident and curious than children who were not hugged, carried or touched. So if you want to nurture your relationship, *kiss it!* – you'll definitely make it infinitely better!

Get in the mood for spine-tingling passion. From teasing pecks to electric contacts that set sparks flying, learn all the secrets and the many combinations of the sensual art of kissing.

Can you overkiss? Perhaps. The idea is to leave your partner literally panting for more! Remember, kissing is kissing, *not* groping. Your hands should be positioned in a hug round your partner, not grabbing at body parts, particularly if you are in public or on the dance floor! Be courteous: don't kiss your partner if you have a cold or other infection.

Kissing alert! Don't break the law!

Do you know of any laws that restrict kissing? Many countries of the world have laws that forbid kissing in public at *any* time. Even in the United States, the state of Illinois has a 'no kissing zone'. Apparently, wives in Deerfield, Illinois were holding up traffic at the local railway station by kissing their partners goodbye, so the city created two traffic zones 50 feet apart: one a 'kissing' zone and the other a 'no-kissing' zone. Louisiana's New Orleans International Airport had the same problem with passengers delaying flights with their goodbye kisses. The solution? A sign reading, 'Start kissing goodbye early, so the plane can leave on time!'

Kissing is a normal way of greeting friends in many countries. 'Hello' kisses are exchanged between men and men, women and women, men and women – and everybody kisses the children! . . . People even kiss their in-laws! You can lose weight by kissing – up to 26 calories for a passionate kiss! Kissing will keep you looking young, too! Exercising 29 facial muscles every time you pucker up for an ardent kiss keeps those muscles in tone! Also, scientific research discovered that a man's pulse hits 110 while kissing, while a woman's averages 108. Not exactly aerobic exercise levels, but good for the circulation!

Although public kissing taboos may not be strictly enforced, make your kiss short and sweet when Cupid strikes you in a public place. Save the passion for a private tête-à-tête! In certain countries, even a short kiss on the lips is not permitted, so make sure you are aware of the possible consequences of kissing in public in your country.

Make your kisses personal, like your special song. Use your imagination to explore 'signature' cuddles and kisses that have a special effect on your partner and that express your feelings for each other. Why not send a smooch by telephone, or fax a lip-print?

Always have smooth and alluring kissable lips: brush them

with a toothbrush to remove dry flakes, then apply medicated balm or vitamin E oil. Your mouth should look moist, warm and tantalizing.

Have you ever tried sending your partner lip messages by blowing kisses? These special secret dispatches will quicken your loved one's pulse and showcase your affection!

Find out your partner's deepest needs!
This is a fun exercise, and important to understanding your partner. Each partner writes down all of the pleasant activities he would like to do with the other. Compare your lists and pick at least one activity you both chose in common. If many of the activities on the lists are the same, make a game out of them. Write them down on small pieces of paper – for example, play tennis, go skating, swim, talk – and place the pieces in a hat. Each partner plucks one from the hat and *voilà*! you have just filled two evenings or afternoons that week. If there are no similar activities, perhaps you can agree on choosing a film you would both like to see or on playing a board game such as draughts or *Monopoly*.

Another exercise to help you understand your partner's deepest needs.
This simple, effective exercise will help you discover the desires behind your frustrations and will reveal your partner's deepest needs. Write down what annoys you about your partner. For example, 'I don't like the way you drive.' On a second sheet of paper write down the desire that is connected to your frustration. 'I would like to feel safe and relaxed when you are driving.' Following each desire, write a specific request that would fulfil your desire: 'I would appreciate it if you would follow the speed limit and drive even slower when the road conditions are bad. If you would do that, you would make me feel safe and relaxed.'

Make sure that your requests are specific. Don't just say, 'I want you to drive more carefully'; this is too inaccurate and only says what you want, not how it could be accomplished and how it would result in making you happier.

Share your second list – the one with the desires and requests – but keep the frustrations to yourself. The desire and request lists are the nice way of mentioning your frustrations!

Review each other's lists carefully, and clarify certain points if necessary. Assign a value of between one and five to each of your requests in their order of importance. For example, driving might have a *2* rating, and one on punctuality might be assigned a *1*. It all depends on what is important to you personally.

Switch lists with your partner and assign a number between one and five indicating how difficult it would be for you to grant her desires. Perhaps changing your driving style would be easy for you, so you could give it a *1*. On the other hand, being punctual might take an entire restructuring of your lifestyle, so you might give that desire a *5*.

This exercise lets you vent your frustrations in a kind and productive fashion. It might be a good idea to save the lists and mutually promise that you will modify your behaviour, starting with one request per week.

Taking care to respond to each other's needs and to respect a partner's feelings is central to a terrific relationship. Kindness counts on the gameboard of love, so keep piling up those love points!

Let's conclude this chapter with some suggestions for more questions you can ask your love partner – gradually, as your relationship progresses.
The answers will not only help you to find out more about your partner, they will also give you more insight as to whether this person is indeed your 'perfect match'. Make sure you ask the questions little by little, subtly, so that your partner does not realize you are 'interviewing' him.

Childhood and family life

- What was your childhood like?
- What is your earliest recollection of life?
- What do you remember about your first day of school?
- What is your fondest memory of high school? Your worst?
- Did you enjoy school? What was your favourite grade? Why? Describe your favourite teacher.
- What is your fondest memory about your homelife?
- Have you many other fond memories about your homelife?
- Did you get along well with family members?
- Were your parents a loving couple? Did they show their affection to each other? Did they get along well?
- How did you picture yourself when you were younger? What is the difference now?
- Who is your favourite relative?

Social comments

- Do you think you enjoy life more than most people?
- When in your life were you the most popular?
- When and where did you meet your best friend? Describe him or her.
- What is your attitude towards minorities?
- Have you any prejudices? What are they?
- Do you believe in capital punishment?
- Would you ever run for public office?
- If you were stranded on a desert island with only one person, whom would you like it to be? What one book would you like to have with you? What music?

Leisure-time activities

- What leisure activities do you do alone?
- What are your favourite sports? Do you take part in any of them now?
- What other hobbies do you have?
- What type of films do you like best? Do you go to the theatre often? Do you prefer going to the cinema or watching films on TV?

- How often do you go on weekend excursions or on holiday? How far do you travel? What is your favourite mode of transportation?
- What would you like your next travel destination to be?

Dating

- How old were you when you began to date?
- Describe your first date.
- Describe your first 'steady'. Who broke up? Why?
- Describe your ideal love partner.
- Which physical features attract you?
- Are you easily accepted by others?
- Do you get along easily with others?
- What holidays do you consider important to celebrate, and with whom do you celebrate them? . . . with family, friends, or someone special?

Feelings

- What moment in your life was the loneliest for you?
- What moment in your life was the happiest?
- What part of your life would you like to relive?
- What usually makes you angry?
- What things about other people make you angry?
- Who are the ten most important people in your life?
- Is there anything or anyone you detest? Why?
- What characteristics in people do you respect? Dislike?
- Do you like children? Pets?
- Do you follow fashion fads?
- How did you feel when you got your first car?

House & Garden

- Do you prefer the country or the city? Why?
- Where would you like to live – what country, city? In a house or a flat?
- Describe your dream house.

Talents, abilities and ambitions

- Who would you cast to play you in a film? What role would you play?
- What about your physical appearance – would you be willing to change?
- Do you think you have any quirks? What are they?
- If you could be anything you wanted to be, what would you choose?
- Describe your talents. How do you make use of them?
- What goal have you ever achieved that made you feel the proudest?
- What do you consider your strong points? Your weak points?
- How do you picture yourself, your career and your life 10 years from now?

Money matters

- Do you habitually borrow money? What was the largest amount? Have you ever loaned money to someone? How much?
- If you won a million pounds today, what would you do with it?
- Do you see money as power?
- What is your general philosophy about money?
- What was your first job?
- Do you use credit cards often?
- How do you regard expenses-sharing when a couple lives together?

Opinions

- What are your views on equality of the sexes?
- Have you any set ideas about sex?
- About war?
- About abortion?
- About battered women?
- About the environment?
- About politics?
- About religion?

Sex and Your Health

♥ ♥ ♥

Now that you have learned the basics of a truly terrific courtship, you and your partner may have decided to enter into an 'intimate' relationship.
The two of you are comfortable in each other's company, and you are happily involved in each other's lives to the extent that you have mutually agreed to take your relationship a step further: to include sexual intimacy as part of your expression of love for each other.

A little forethought and necessary caution *must* precede this important step. Being in love is no guarantee that both partners are free of sexually transmitted diseases (STDs). Some STDs show no external symptoms, so a person may not even be aware that he has an STD when he transmits it to someone else.

Although proper diagnosis and antibiotic medication can effectively treat syphilis, gonorrhoea, chlamydia, venereal warts, and a host of minor problems, there is no known cure for other diseases, such as HIV/AIDS. Do you really want to risk your health and your partner's by engaging in intimate sexual activity without taking every precaution?

A frank and open discussion *before* initiating intimacy is the first line of defence, a physical examination is the second, and the use of condoms is *mandatory* even if tests indicate there are no infections present at the moment. HIV can prove deadly, and it may not show up in blood tests nor indicate any symptoms for some time *after* infection.

This section has been designed to give you the most up-to-date educational information about how to protect yourself and your partner against sexually-transmitted diseases. Most important, it will demystify how to use a condom.

How to talk about STDs.
Sexually-transmitted diseases (STDs) are contagious infections acquired mainly through sexual contact, or, in the case of HIV, also through shared use of hypodermic needles or exposure of open sores or cuts to body fluids. They are communicable diseases like the flu or the mumps, yet people hesitate to talk about a sexually-transmitted infection they may have or have had because they feel humiliated, embarrassed or ashamed. Also, STDs are still considered 'taboo' subjects, keeping people from admitting to any symptoms or to any infection they may currently have or have had treatment for in the past. The current worldwide epidemic of HIV/AIDS *must* put an end to this reticent behaviour, *because AIDS is fatal*.

As the world enters the 1990s, hundreds of researchers throughout the world have reached the stage of testing a vaccination for HIV, but they have found no definite cure as yet. Any sexually active person anywhere in the world is risking exposure to this deadly virus.

Of course, the best and most effective protection against STDs – HIV/AIDS in particular – is *abstinence*.
But if your personal choice is to have sexual intercourse, the following information is vital to your relationship and to both of your lives.

Safe sex. There is no other alternative to celibacy than the condom.
To begin with, you *must choose a line of personal defence* against STDs. *Your first protection against HIV and other STDs is to discuss the*

*subject openly with your love partner as early as possible in your
relationship!* And certainly when you feel a sexual attraction
developing! Once you have chosen preventive measures, you
must always stick to them – your life depends on it!

To reduce the risk of STDs, couples contemplating sexual
intimacy *must* protect themselves by using a condom – also
called a preventative or protective. There are many types on the
market, and it's not only men who buy them; women should
carry condoms in case their partner is not prepared for the
moment. A condom for women, which is otherwise known as
a 'vaginal pouch', will also be gradually available throughout
the world from 1992. Oral sex also requires a condom – called
a 'dental dam' – for men and for women. Latex condoms are
the preferred type for every use because HIV can be transmitted
through the membranes of a natural sheepskin condom.
Because the virus is transmitted by body fluids – principally
blood, semen and vaginal secretions – *condoms are absolutely
crucial to the health and welfare of anyone engaging in sexual intercourse.*

**When is the best time to discuss condoms with my
partner?**
Any couple contemplating sexual intimacy must discuss with
each other – freely and openly – the use of condoms: their
lives depend on it!

In general, this discussion should take place when a physical
yearning for each other blooms, and certainly *before* you are
ready for intimacy. If you wait until you are 'in the heat of
passion', such as at the end of an evening when you danced
closely and your willpower has become weakened by alcoholic
drinks, you will lose your chance for bringing up the subject.
Or even worse, you may be inclined to 'forget about it just for
this once!' *'Just this once' could cost you your life!* This is not
something you should discuss when you are already in bed; it
should be talked about calmly while sitting in the kitchen, for
example, over coffee or tea.

♥ ♥ ♥

What if my lover does not want to talk about condoms?
The most important aspect of sexual relations today is the maturity of both partners to realize the seriousness of HIV and to discuss protection. If you discover that your partner 'doesn't want to know', do you really want to 'know' him? Be firm: insist on protection. Take careful note of your partner's negative reactions to your desires/wishes. If he disagrees with you on such an important issue, you may gradually discover other incompatibilities that will make him an inappropriate love partner in the long run. If a partner is inconsiderate enough to deny the importance of sexual protection, he is denying not only the importance of the two of you to each other, but your right to safe sex and your right to life itself!

There are other avenues of showing your affection without engaging in sexual intercourse.
The fear of HIV should not make you paranoid or afraid of any and all sexual activity. Take your time to explore other loving aspects of your courtship before engaging in sexual acts. Discover the joys of kissing, teasing, cuddling, massaging, mutual masturbation and other tender acts that are intimate. You can enjoy all the pleasures of foreplay without necessarily engaging in sexual intercourse itself. Get into the spirit of each other! Love in the slow lane will give you time to really get to know each other well without the additional stress of sexual performance.

You *can* say 'No'!
It's perfectly all right to say, 'I'm not ready for intimacy' or 'I'm not ready for that stage of our relationship'. Celibacy – or abstinence – is not a 'condom of the mind', it is the only alternative to unprotected sex. The horror of HIV makes it imperative that you *insist on safe sex or none at all!* Believing 'it can't happen to me' can lead to the pain of having to say, 'On our one and only night of intimacy, he brought me champagne and gave me HIV.'

Don't become paranoid with your fear of HIV.
HIV exists, it is true, but there is a sure way not to catch it: use a condom.

HIV is very much a part of our lives in the nineties, it is true, but so are condoms. Thanks to them, you can still have a wonderful love life as well as an absolutely fulfilling sex life without fear of getting HIV, if you use condoms carefully and properly. So do not deprive yourself of a normal life and become a tense, irritable, and frustrated human being. Relax and enjoy life, love, sex, and the condoms!

My partner and I have been intimate for several months and neither of us has tested positive for HIV. Does that mean we no longer have to use condoms?
Scientists tell us that due to the lengthy incubation period of the virus, symptoms may not surface for seven to twelve years. Although being tested for HIV and having a negative reading after having dated for a long time in an 'exclusive' relationship may give you a relative sense of security, there have been numerous cases of negative readings turning out to be positive and vice-versa! Furthermore, how can you be absolutely positive that your partner has been faithful during that time? Or that the virus isn't currently dormant within her and that it won't flare up at any time?

Safe sex is the only way to be sure.

But I only have sex with one person. How could I be at risk?
Protected sex with only one partner is your best assurance of not contracting HIV. However, you should be aware that every time you have intercourse, it is like having sex with a multitude of partners – all of the partners you and your partner might have had (and those partners' previous partners) for the last seven to twelve years, at least – maybe longer! According to statistical information, when you have sex with *one* partner it

is estimated that you may actually be exposed to an average of *150* people!

I don't have any symptoms of any STDs. No rash, no sickness, no loss of hair – nothing!

Don't rely on appearances. Many sexually-transmitted diseases have no obvious or physical symptoms. And don't kid yourself: no one is above catching or transmitting an STD – a judge, a secretary, a doctor, a nurse, a milkman, a policeman – women as well as men and heterosexuals as well as homosexuals. Even famous people contract and die from HIV/AIDS: the list of film stars, designers and musicians known to be infected by the AIDS virus grows daily. A very high-profile case in 1991 was the declaration by 'Magic' Johnson, the famous American basketball star, recently married with an unborn child on the way, who went public on TV with the fact that he had tested HIV-positive after a routine blood test while applying for a life insurance policy. Johnson further revealed that, in spite of his very active heterosexual lifestyle prior to his marriage, he seldom used a condom.

Anyone can transmit an STD – women as well as men! Although it takes only one partner to transmit the virus, the more sexual partners you have, the higher your chances of contracting a sexually-transmitted disease.

Do not be too naïve!

Everybody has deep secrets – probably even yourself! We have seen cases of women married to drug pushers, members of the Mafia or spies without ever knowing it. We have also heard of, or perhaps have know personally, husbands or wives having multiple affairs during marriage or having an ongoing extramarital arrangement lasting two, six, or even 18 years – without their spouses even suspecting it. This means that some people can be very good at leading a double life. It has also been seen many times that one can have many years of friendship, or intimacy with another person without really knowing that person at all.

Do not become paranoid or suspicious about everything your love partner tells you; do not start checking out his every move; but do not necessarily take all he says as gospel, either, particularly as far as his sex life is concerned. You do not know for sure every detail about his past or even about his present. He may have secrets he would rather not tell you in order to not hurt you, or to prevent you judging him badly or leaving him. Think of yourself and your health. Practise safe sex!

What STDs are the most common?
The most frequently encountered diseases are chlamydia, gonorrhoea, venereal warts (condylomas), syphilis, herpes, and HIV/AIDS.

Since 1986, throughout the world, there has been a decrease in the type of gonorrhoea that is treatable with penicillin but an increase of the variety that is resistant to penicillin. Syphilis is rare, but is nevertheless still present.

Chlamydia responds to medication, but if left unchecked, it can irreparably damage a woman's reproductive system. Herpes of the genitals is also quite common. Besides extreme burning discomfort experienced during regularly recurring 'active' periods, the herpes virus has been known to cause cancer of the uterus and ovarian scarring. The virus never completely disappears and is extremely infectious, particularly during the active stages, when painful ulcerous lesions form in the genital area.

HIV has been recognized as a sexually-transmitted disease since the mid-1970s. Instead of stabilizing, HIV is spreading throughout the world at a horrifying rate. The 1991 statistics indicate that there are an estimated 11 million people with AIDS and another 10 million infected with HIV. Scientists estimate that approximately 5000 new people a day become infected with HIV.

♥ ♥ ♥

Some points to remember about STDs and you.

- Many people believe that 'it can't happen to me,' and transmit an STD to someone else without even knowing it! If you have been or are planning to be sexually active, have the appropriate medical tests.
- If you think you might have an STD, don't self-diagnose or try to treat yourself; see a doctor. Once your treatment is complete, have a test done to ensure that you are cured and no longer infectious.
- If you have contracted an STD, it is your moral responsibility to inform all of the partners you have had sexual encounters with. This is no time to be embarrassed! Should you be too shy and lack the courage to accomplish this task in person, send each of them a note suggesting he should go for a test, or ask your doctor or social worker to ring him on your behalf to inform him that he might be infected and contagious.
- Abstain from sexual practices during the treatment period for your disease/infection.

Often young people think they needn't use condoms because 'HIV/AIDS hasn't hit *my* crowd. Sex is all new to us!' This is simply not true. The number of cases of teenage infections is staggering. One 15-year-old girl, who believed she couldn't be at risk, became infected with HIV after having intercourse only twice.

How to discuss condoms with your partner.
If you can't bring yourself to discuss condoms, you are simply not mature enough yet to engage in sexual activity. Remember, it is not just a matter of health protection, it is *a matter of life and death!*

By bringing up the subject of condoms naturally and casually, you demystify the stigma about them and are using the best possible tactic to avoid acquiring any STD. Your frank talk will preserve the intimacy and love in your relationship.

Once you have had the initial discussion, whatever it takes to keep the romance and passion alive – and still be *safe* – is a go. Since you *must* use condoms, you might as well have fun using them! You could therefore turn the use of a condom into a love game, or you could try humorous phrases to introduce the topic: 'No one aboard without a uniform!' Be cute: giftwrap a box of condoms and leave this pretty parcel on your pillow!

Develop amusing ways of carrying, using and playing with condoms. Use whichever words are the most comfortable for you to introduce the subject. Be serious, honest, funny, sexy, romantic: 'I never leave home without them!' or 'Condoms? Sure, I use them: I call them my safety valves!' Another favourite: 'Little pockets of love, that's what condoms are!'

You might also refer to condoms as 'Raincoats for love storms!', 'Umbrellas for passion rain!' or 'Protection for my Fireman!' There are also humorous nicknames like, 'My little love nightcap!', 'My diving suit!', 'My mini-pyjamas!', or 'My Little Red Riding Hood!' Variations are as boundless as your imagination!

There are so many fun, amusing and seductive ways to enjoy lovemaking with a condom! The man needn't be the only one to initiate the act of putting the condom on: his partner should also do it for him as part of the foreplay while kissing him passionately at the same time, to keep him aroused without allowing him to lose his concentration! Both partners should remember not to have the condom fit tightly at the tip of the penis – enough space must be left for the sperm during ejaculation, otherwise the condom might burst. A word to the wise: you might want to practise this art on a banana before actually trying your skill on your loved one!

A sexually active couple in a new or recently formed relationship *must* count on the protection of a condom. Both people in a relationship need to be able to deal with their feelings about the necessity for safe sex. The rules of seduction have changed: champagne and caviare are still in fashion, but champagne, caviare and *condoms* are in today's smart lover's bedroom!

♥ ♥ ♥

Talking about protection and the use of a condom is part of courtship, so treat it the same way you treat your relationship.

One of the best ways to bring up the subject of condoms is to ask your partner a direct question: 'What's your brand?' Your question assumes that she is already aware of the necessity of using condoms and that her partners always use them, and it shows her that you require condoms before any kind of sexual activity. Nowadays, you should find this question no more difficult than asking about her favourite brand of tea or cigarettes. Now that you know, buy her a packet of her favourite condoms – or maybe even a carton-full!

One enterprising young woman bought a supply of condoms in a variety of colours and shapes, with flavours from peppermint to bubble gum, some even striped, fluorescent or luminous, and kept them on her nightstand in a beautifully decorated sweets box. Whenever she and her boyfriend were together for an intimate evening, she would offer him a 'treat' from her 'treasure chest'!

The following is a typical exchange between a couple about to engage in sexual intimacy. The woman isn't convinced condoms are necessary.

Josh was going out with a woman named Leslie who told him, a week after they were intimate without a condom, that she had an STD. Josh tested positive – he had been infected by her. Their relationship fell apart shortly after that. Two months later, Josh met Josie and both were soon physically attracted to each other. Josh, now well-trained by his run-in with STDs, insisted on using a condom, but Josie refused.

Josh: Do you keep any condoms at home, Josie? If you have some on hand, I won't have to go out to the car for mine.

Josie: No, I haven't got any condoms. Why should I? I'm in good health.

Josh: I insist on wearing a condom!

Josie: Have you ever been infected with something?

Josh: Yes, and it cost me 10 days of penicillin and follow-up tests.

Josie: I'll get my GP to show you my medical reports if you like!

Josh: I'd rather show you my condoms instead!

Josie: OK, if you insist!

Josh: Yes, I insist. Protecting ourselves is respecting ourselves. Don't make such a big fuss about using them. Treat it as a game and we can have lots of fun!

Every time you bring up the subject of STDs or condoms, you are helping pave the way to avoiding infection with STDs or HIV, and keeping your love relationship – and yourself – alive and *well!*

In this conversational exchange, the shoe is on the other foot, metaphorically speaking! The man doesn't want to wear a condom.

David and Donna were students in their last year at university. Over the past several months they had become more and more physically attracted to each other. Donna was aware of the necessity for protected sex, David wasn't.

Donna: Have you a condom with you?

David: Aren't you on the 'pill'?

Donna: No, I don't take any kind of contraceptive.

David: I suppose you could use spermicidal foam?

Donna: No way! The condom is the only protection I would agree to – not only for my protection, but for yours, too. We are not talking about protection against pregnancy, we are talking about our health!

David: But I haven't made love for the past two years!

Donna: But I have! And with several other people!

David: Are you going to tease me with all the adventures you had?

Donna: No, but I have always had an active life, and as I had not had a regular boyfriend in my life for three years – until you arrived on the scene – I sometimes said 'Why not?' with a few partners. Trust me! Here, I'll slide it on sensually for you. I'll be gentle. Come on, David. I assure you that it will be pleasurable for both of us.

David: OK, I see your point. 'Safe' sex it is.

Men's objections to wearing condoms.

Many men are afraid of having problems with their erection if they use a condom. They will try to seduce you into 'trusting' them by saying things like, 'Don't you trust me? If you were really in love with me, you wouldn't ask me to use a condom. In love, trust is the most important factor.' Don't fall for this trap, it could be deadly!

Other men complain that much of the sensation is lost. In fact, good-quality condoms – thin ones – feel just the same as if the man were wearing nothing, and consequently do not interfere with a 'natural' feeling. Condoms also have the advantage of prolonging an erection, which is a bonus for both partners. A condom slows down ejaculation, and can be a very useful remedy for men who ejaculate too quickly. Some men say that placing a small amount of lubricant – like KY Jelly, available from the chemist's – inside the tip of the condom before it is put on, actually increases the man's pleasure tremendously! Certainly it's worth trying!

Other couples complain that spontaneity disappears when a condom enters the picture. Actually, when you get used to using a condom, the article itself may be used to initiate the sexual act and become an integral part of your sex games. Today, you simply haven't got a choice: *you must always use a condom with a new partner.*

Using a condom prolongs foreplay, which is an advantage for both partners and for intimacy. In foreplay, the exploration of the body, the closeness, and the touching are all part of a healthy sexual relationship.

The story of the 'safe' rose.

A man sent his new woman friend one exquisite, long-stemmed rose, to which was attached a card with a condom inside of it. His message was twofold: he loved her and desired her, and he was concerned about protecting their health and preserving their love relationship.

The blood test: a passport for love?
You have been together for three months. Everything is going great, and you decide to have a test for HIV antibodies. The tests prove negative, and you are both in perfect health. That's wonderful, but don't be naïve. Have you forgotten that HIV can lie dormant for up to twelve years? Also, as previously stated, the blood test results are not definitive: the percentage of error can be quite high, particularly if the virus has been contracted recently. Furthermore, fidelity is not a guarantee. Make a pact with each other that if ever one of you has the urge to be unfaithful, or actually is, that you will use a condom to protect yourself and your relationship. Be open-minded and aware. The next time your love partner goes away alone, stick a pack of condoms in his or her suitcase, just in case!

A young woman from Montreal, who dreamed of having a sexual adventure on a business trip, fulfilled her fantasy when she met a nice, good-looking man upon her arrival in New York City. She had one night of unbridled lust, then left the next day. At the airport, this man gave her a beautifully-wrapped package as she left for home. 'Don't open it until you arrive in Montreal,' he said. When she finally unwrapped the mysterious package, there lay a card inscribed, 'I have HIV – you'd better have a test.' Today, the young woman is dying of AIDS.

This horrifying story is true and is a reminder that you must be cautious and never have unprotected sex with a stranger. It is one thing to flirt and to search for your perfect match, but quite another matter to have numerous unprotected sexual 'flings' – or even one!

You and your partner want a future together, so must you use condoms forever?
You have been together and faithful to each other for a reasonable period of time, long enough to know each other well enough to decide that you want a future together. You are also deeply in love with each other. You have been practising safe sex, exclusive sex all along, but now you want to know if you need to use condoms for the rest of your life.

When you have reached this stage of a relationship, it is suggested that you both consult a doctor and have a general check-up, to see that you are both healthy as you enter your future life together, to find out if you are both compatible to have children – if you want them – and to take the opportunity to ask for a blood text for STDs, including HIV. Because HIV may sometimes take up to twelve years before it shows in the blood cells, you will never really know for sure that one of you has not been infected with it earlier and that it will not surface eventually. You have to take a certain chance; and let's say that at this stage of your relationship, your risks of having it are rather slim; the percentage of your contracting it is quite low. It is now time to show faith in life and love. So go for it! Live it up, and be happy together!

Note: This chapter has been written in collaboration with the Director-General of the Québec Sexologists Association, Alain Garlépy, M.A.

♥ 4 ♥

A Million and One Love Strategies for keeping Passion in a Romance

Being in love is an experience like no other. All the new, spine-shivery feelings of deep caring, joy and passionate excitement are extremely exhilarating. However, like any high-intensity exchange of energies, a relationship is subject to a lessened state of excitement. This new level of 'comfort' can be very rich and satisfying, and certainly is perfectly normal, but occasionally each of us wants at least a brief return to the feelings of those initial encounters. The tips in this section will show you how to keep passion in your times together. By sprinkling the days and months of your relationship with truly romantic moments, you will keep the flame of your romance burning as brightly as the evening stars.

ROMANTIC SUGGESTIONS THAT COST LITTLE OR NOTHING

Today, being romantic is more popular than ever!
Today's busy world still offers chances to add an unusual twist
to daily routines. Be imaginative when putting a touch of
romance into the simplest acts. A single flower delivered first
thing in the morning adds a romantic glow to the entire day.
Think of thoughtful gestures that will make the person you love
feel special – and that's the nicest feeling there is!

**There are two important times to show your romantic
side: special holidays and spontaneous occasions.**
Of course you remember to give your loved one a gift on
'calendar' occasions, such as birthdays, anniversaries,
Christmas, New Year's, St Valentine's Day, and so on, but these
dates are the bare minimum! There are many occasions for
spontaneous expressions of your love. For example, a simple
walk through the park just before sunset can end with a
surprise dessert you thoughtfully prepared and packed in a
small basket. It doesn't have to be something elaborate: cakes
or biscuits and a soft drink are nectar when shared by two
people who care for each other! Keep your impromptu gifts
simple yet imaginative. Love will thrive on these impulsive
gestures!

Think of romance as the icing on the cake.
Think of your relationship as a cake. Of course, a cake can be quite delicious without icing; but a beautifully-decorated cake with luscious, sweet icing is much more appetizing! Don't you agree? Likewise, a relationship can continue to exist without romance; but wouldn't a relationship filled with expressions of caring and passion be far more delightful?!

Romance is different from love and passion.
Romance is the expression of your love. It requires skilful and creative use of your imagination, and it is sure to enrich your love relationship. Look for simple ways to show the one you love that you want to be near him, that you care deeply about him. A gentle caress on the cheek, reciting a love poem, sharing of a special treat – things you choose to do because you care. Romance is not just for special occasions: the daily routine will be far more interesting for both of you when you make room for romance!

A romantic gesture should have but one purpose – to please your loved one!
A romantic gesture should not be offered to make amends for something you have done that hurt or angered the other person. Sending flowers after an argument is not a romantic expression; it is a request for forgiveness. Using supposedly romantic acts to cover up incorrigible behaviour or problems such as alcoholism is a fruitless exercise that only serves to foster resentment. Instead of paving a magical path to greater love, it will leave a trail of bitterness.

Everyone has a different idea of romance.
Although most people enjoy romantic happenings, no one perceives these events in exactly the same way. The one to

whom you are directing your romantic advance should be the only judge of whether or not it is romantic. Be sure you know the other person's preferences before you plan a romantic outing! How often has a young man thought that going out for a drive on a bright, sunny day was a romantic adventure, only to discover that his partner finds driving on a hot afternoon tedious at best?

A romantic outlook will improve the quality of your relationship.

Since romance brings magic to a relationship, improving your romantic actions will enliven your relationship by kindling its passion and maintaining its flame. It will reinforce a relationship, making it more satisfying for both love partners. Wouldn't you rather have a vital, fun-filled life than a cool existence?

Be considerate when choosing a gift.

At times, you will have to choose between giving a gift that you like and a gift your loved one would enjoy receiving. Suppose a man chooses a perfume because he likes the scent. Unfortunately, it is not the one his partner has chosen as her 'signature'. The underlying message he is sending to her is 'my likes are more important than yours' – not exactly what anyone would consider romantic! A woman might buy an article of clothing for her partner in a colour combination she likes, without considering his preferences. The same wrong 'message' is conveyed! Keep romance in your gift-giving by choosing something you may not appreciate as much as she will, and you might be surprised at the result! For example, although you may detest opera, your lover may be crazy about it. You buy a collection of classical opera cassettes and find yourself sharing a very romantic evening! Would it surprise you if you suddenly developed a fondness for opera?

Really listen to your loved one, so that you know what the little things are, that you can do, to please him.

Actions speak louder than words. When we say we love someone, we should show that person just how much. How can we do this? Through our actions! By being polite, considerate of the other person's feelings, and truly listening with an open heart, you will keep romance fresh and new. Those who are not willing to show their true feelings or to take time to be thoughtful have no idea how to love – much less how to be romantic!

Add a few drops of romance to your relationship and keep upping the dose as the relationship progresses.

When a new love enters your life, the sheer pleasure and excitement is so all-consuming and captivating that there is little need to be concerned about romance! However, once you become more familiar with each other, there is a tendency to forget the little romantic embellishments that made your first encounters so wonderful. This is the time to add those romantic touches that will endear you to the object of your affections!

Surprise your loved one with silly anniversaries . . . a special evening planned because you met on that day of the week, for example. If your culture and religion permit public displays of affection, you could hold hands when doing something as normal as walking to the corner shops. It's exciting to slip a love note into a pocket and wait to see how long it takes for your love to find it. Plug your relationship into romance and keep increasing the voltage! Enjoy a romance-charged, electrifying love life!

Romance is a state of mind.

Develop romance radar! Everything you see, hear, touch and feel could inspire romance. When passing by that flower shop around the corner reminds you that she loves flowers, pay attention! Buy an exotic flower or a plant and enclose a card that says, 'I can't fly with you to an exotic land, so I thought I'd bring part of it home to you!'

Have you discovered a little shop that sells special chocolates? Whether it's one apiece to savour with arms entwined or a sinfully expensive boxful, chocolates are a sweet beginning to a lovely evening!

What is going on in town that would make the two of you feel romantic? Is the local cinema showing a romantic film? What a great inspiration!

Try not to be overwhelmingly romantic in the first days of a possible relationship.
It is wise to keep your romantic enthusiasm under control at the beginning of a relationship. Let your romance evolve slowly so that you can enjoy every step in getting to know the other person.

You don't really know someone well enough to be outrageously romantic until the third or fourth meeting. Although you can entice your love with chocolates, flowers, dinners and films, you might want to reserve the candle-lit procession of a 35-piece orchestra serenading him with his favourite music until a little later on in the relationship! Yes, you plan to sweep him off his feet, but such an extravagant display early in a relationship risks sweeping him away – for good!

It is difficult to judge romantic advances. Time will tell!
Your new love interest doesn't seem to act very romantic. Is she timid, shy, or unsure of herself and the impression she is making on you? Be warm, loving and accepting of her hesitant advances, and you will soon know if there is great love on the threshold or simply no interest!

On the other hand, your intriguing-at-first-meeting love possibility may have been too much to handle on subsequent encounters. Are her over-amorous advances compensating for a sense of insecurity, or is she really deliriously, impetuously in love? Cool the scene down until you have known her for a longer time, when you can evaluate her true feelings better.

If you are not the romantic type and your partner is.
Romance not your style? Try returning some of the little romantic gestures your partner seems so intent on lavishing on you. Give an impromptu gift: a funny card, a special flower, a favourite magazine . . . something that tells him that you are thinking of him and that you want to show it. Even a phone call just to say, 'Hello, how is your day going?' will be very much appreciated. Once you begin expressing your romantic side, you will both enjoy the renewed energy in your relationship. Romantic gestures are well worth your effort!

Are you a flamboyant lover and a hopeless romantic?
Would you go so far as to proclaim your love on a hoarding in the centre of town? Or have a message sky-written? Then you are really into the *big gesture!* And why not? If you are both so head-over-heels in love, you can do no wrong in your loved one's eyes! Think of the fun you'll have while planning something truly outrageous! On a smaller scale, a single perfect rose presented at midnight under a full moon is intimately romantic – until the four violinists strike up a Viennese waltz!

If you are not sure how the person who intrigues you feels about you, *orange light!* – proceed with caution!
If the other person is uncertain of her feelings for you, any romantic advances you make may scare her off! The concert tickets for a shared evening would probably be OK – as long as you don't suggest a ride home in a horse-drawn carriage! Keep your romantic notions to yourself until you are sure of the other person's feelings.

A romantic advance should be purely for the benefit of the other person.

You prepared a delicious dinner by candlelight, and all your loved one talked about was work at the office! You are doing a slow burn as the candles melt away. Relax! Smile and enjoy the other person's company. So what if he didn't respond to your romantic gesture in quite the way you expected? You have had pleasure in the planning. The gesture was for him, to show him that you care. You have done your part – no strings attached, please! There is time in the future for him to return your fervour!

Your relationship is not a financial statement!

Ever hear someone talk about her relationship using words straight out of a financial report? Words like 'negotiate', 'invest', 'assets' and 'liabilities', in phrases like, 'Let's negotiate this evening: you want to go to the cinema, and I want to go to the opera'; 'Your love is a real asset to me!'; or 'This discussion is definitely a liability to our evening!' How impersonal can you get! This is a relationship?

When a woman asks her partner to be romantic, she doesn't expect a fortune spent trying to impress her!

Don't panic if your lady love asks you to be romantic. She does not mean that she wants you to cover her with diamonds, shower her with luxurious gifts, take her to expensive restaurants, or whisk her off to exotic locations! All she wants is attention by means of little thoughtful gestures, such as giving her a kiss while she's preparing dinner, making and serving her a coffee, or telling her to relax when you both get home from work. Try suggesting, 'You look like you've had a tiring day; why don't I make dinner tonight?' If you can't cook, order in! Being thoughtful is romance in action! Be attentive to the little things – they weigh heavily on the scales of romance!

Criticizing your loved one is not the way to encourage romantic responses!

If you constantly reproach your love partner for not being romantic, you will lose your chances for romantic moments altogether! Say things like, 'You haven't a romantic bone in your body!' or 'You're about as romantic as a block of wood!' and you will *never* have a warm, responsive partner!

Sometimes people need hints as to what to do, simply because they really don't know how to be romantic. Tell them – in a romantic way of course: 'You know what I think is romantic? . . .' Plan little scenarios for getting the message across. For example, choose to go for a walk which takes you past the flower shop. Turn his attention to the shop and say, 'Look at that beautiful display! I just love flowers! You know something? When I receive flowers, I tingle all over!' He will surely want to make you tingle! Count on at least one bouquet – maybe a houseful!

If you see a romantic scene on television, point it out. Tell your loved one, 'Now *that's* romantic!'

If you are trying to instil romance, you must act romantic. Try whispering softly, 'I wish you were being romantic with me right now . . . under the stars . . . don't you feel the romance in the air?' Cuddle up to him as you are talking, and – va-va-*voom!* he's got the idea!

Call her and read her horoscope to her first thing in the morning!

What a thoughtful gesture! It says that you woke up thinking about her. How flattering! You went to the trouble to get the paper and cut out her horoscope – what a marvellous way to start the day!

Write to your loved one once a week.

Mail cartoons, messages, lottery tickets, anything that makes you think of him. Send him tickets to the theatre with a beautifully-calligraphed invitation. Send him a book of love poems. What a thrill it is to receive a gift in the post! How marvellous even the smallest bauble is when it's from the one we love. Sending something, no matter how inexpensive, shows you are thinking of him a lot – and often!

Give your love a tape of her favourite music.
You are listening to the radio when you hear her favourite song! Hurry and find your tape recorder . . . your loved one will love this! Add a brief message of your own, then either post the tape or ring and play it to her (or record it on her answer phone, if she's got one). The idea is to make her feel very special, knowing that you have taken the time to do something unusual for her.

Write a cheque for one million kisses made out to *'the love of my life'*!
Using an ordinary cheque, replace the pound symbol with a heart, and write in 'one million kisses' where you'd normally fill in the amount. Or make it for one million kisses and two hundred thousand hugs, or two million years of happiness, or . . .? Use your imagination! Send it to your love partner with a note: 'Spend this with pleasure.' You will undoubtedly receive a million pounds worth of passion in return!

There are terrific 'gift certificates' to offer the love of your life.
Everyone likes to receive thoughtful gifts, and the following list of possible 'gift certificates' are sure to make the recipient very happy! Draw up a certificate in exchange for which you will –

- clean the house
- wash and wax the car

- change the tyres
- paint or decorate
- go along to dancing classes or hobby classes
- watch a love-story video or film
- go shopping for two hours – at least!
- mow the lawn
- do all the ironing for the next three weeks
- go on a fishing weekend
- prepare a favourite meal

Use your imagination: choose something that your loved one would appreciate having done for him! Of course, you can offer other creative alternatives!

Include a personal message on your 'gift certificate'. This personal message will mean just as much as the 'service' offered on the certificate. Be passionate! Don't say something like 'I hope you enjoy this!' or 'Hope this makes you happy.' This makes your offer sound like you're doing him a big favour. Your note should show that you will enjoy doing this and that you are looking forward to it because you want to see him happy!

Be imaginative and amusingly seductive. Say, 'I will clean your house from top to bottom . . . then I will sweep you off your feet!' Or how about this: 'I offer you this service for no particular occasion, just to tell you that I love you and to show you how much I appreciate you.' This is what *romance* is all about!

A single rose presented on the first day of every month for a year has more impact than a dozen roses once a year!
What a lovely romantic gesture to look forward to each month! A rose, fresh and beautiful, a symbol of an ever-renewing love! How romantic can you get? Expect a lot of hugs and kisses for this romantic notion!

When the florist asks what roses you want to send, be aware of the secret message in the colour of each rose!
Red roses declare the giver as 'passionately in love'! Yellow ones whisper of jealousy. White roses symbolize purity, and pink ones honour friendship. Coral-toned roses offer tranquillity. Why not send a hidden message in your choice of roses, with a written message mirroring the sentiment? For example, your card might say, 'This morning you mentioned you were going to have a hectic day. I hope these little flowers bring you a sense of peace and love.' Lovely! And what message will you write with the red roses? – Really? *Wow!*

Real men shave even on weekends.
You put your best face forward every workday morning, so why wouldn't you do the same for the love of your life? Besides, by being clean-shaven, you are saying, 'Here I am, all ready for a little *kiss!*' Expect this little sacrifice to be well worth it!

Thanks to romance, you can develop a 'magical' relationship with a special person.
Romance can work magic! A humdrum relationship can become a passionate love story with a little 'romantic' imagination. The French philosopher Jean Paul Sartre remarked, 'The act of imagination is a magical act.' Work your romantic magic and charm to captivate your loved one imaginatively! A Sunday morning brunch by candlelight is entrancingly romantic. Why not a candlelight picnic under the stars?

Romance is the expression of your love.
Showing someone you cherish her is what romance is all about. A romantic gesture is a lovely way to say, 'You are in my thoughts.' A small photo of the restaurant where you met or a

love poem copied in your handwriting on beautiful paper –
these are simple but personal gestures that come from the heart.

**Learn how to dance so you can go out for a romantic
evening of dining and dancing.**
Learning how to dance is a great way to inspire romance.
Picture just the two of you on New Year's Eve . . . at your own
intimate party in a special restaurant . . . having a lovely dinner
followed by 'close' dancing and an evening of romantic
conversation! Truly a memorable beginning of a new year to fill
with romance!

Dancing is like setting loving to music. You may not need
dance lessons to hold the object of your affections in your arms
and move around a dance floor, but it is much more exciting
if the two of you can tango, mambo, samba and waltz your way
through the evening – and it's a lot more elegant!

Disco dancing is a favourite 'night out on the town' in many
parts of the world. The driving beat of the music and whirling
strobes of light will have the two of you throbbing with
excitement as you show off your latest 'moves' to each other.
Exhilarating!

Going out for an evening of dancing also encourages you to
dress up for the occasion. The glitter, fancy decorations and
orchestras of grand balls are marvellous – almost magical –
affairs that will transport you and your love to an evening of
enchantment as you float lightly through one lilting waltz after
another!

Fairy-tale evenings are not weekly occurrences, so where else
can you enjoy ballroom dancing? The restaurant and
entertainment sections in your local newspaper generally list
dining and dancing clubs. You might want to form your own
group or club of dance-lovers, hiring a hall and holding a dance
every so often.

Dancing is a romantic activity you and your partner can
enjoy throughout the years you are together. You are never too
old for dancing – or for romance!

Collect newspapers and magazines with the date of the month and year you met.
How thoughtfully romantic! A collection of magazines and newspapers from the days when you first met! What a surprise when you show them to your love partner years from now. Imagine the fun you'll have comparing the way things were – the fashions, the cars, the furnishings – during a romantic trip down memory lane! Of course, the two of you have stayed the same: romantically in love!

Cut out magazine articles of interest to your partner.
While reading a magazine, you come across an article on antiques. You know your partner loves antiques, so you cut out the article and give it to him with a little note saying, 'Something interesting about one of your passions . . . to one of mine!'

Your favourite monthly magazine is running a series of articles on Byzantine art, complete with gorgeous colour photos. Your love has taken you to special museum exhibitions on the subject; so buy a second magazine, cut out one of the best pictures, and have it laminated or decoupaged onto a small wooden box. Save the series of articles and present the whole package to your surprised and pleased art-lover.

These thoughtful gestures say, 'I'm thinking about you even when I'm absorbed in something I like.' It shows that your life revolves around your love partner . . . and that is the essence of romance!

Return to the place where you met or where you spent a memorable time together.
Relive your shared memories. Lucy and Thomas did by returning to the beach where they had met and had shared a bottle of chilled champagne. The identical brand of bubbly accompanied their return to the spot. As they poured the shimmering liquid and gazed into each other's eyes, *zingo!* the

heady sensations and romantic passions of their first meeting were reawakened! You can imagine how they celebrate the anniversaries of their first meeting: at the beach with champagne and *passion!*

You, too, can ignite the passion in your relationship by reliving your fondest romantic memories while creating an even more romantic one!

Chart your lives, highlighting the important events in each of your lives before and after you met.
When and where was he born? Which of you lost your baby teeth first? Where did she go sailing the first time? When did he say her first word? When did she graduate from college? When did he receive his degree? When did she travel alone for the first time? When did he get his first car? When did she first kiss someone?

Make a chart outlining both of your lives. It's fun! Include your first date and continue plotting the course of your lives, reliving the course of your love and celebrating the fact that you two are still romantically one!

Prepare your loved one's favourite meal.
You know she really loves a certain food prepared a special way. Practise the recipe first on a good friend, then surprise your darling with a dinner invitation *chez vous*. An attractive table setting complete with flowers and candlelight, *you* in the kitchen preparing the dish! . . . what a terrific way to heat up a romance!

Relive your first date on the anniversary of that momentous occasion!
Remember your first date? Now that a year or two – or even only a month – has passed, relive your first date. Wear the

same clothes you did then. See if you can remember what you said to each other. Re-experience the excitement! Of course, if you hated each other that first time you met, you might want to recall another episode, like the day or evening you knew you were *really* in love!

Practise sounding romantic.

No one has ever told you that you have a seductively thrilling or romantic voice? You can change your voice by listening to recordings of it. This technique is fun as well as effective! Repeat several sentences in different tones until you hear a 'romantic accent': low-pitched, rounded and slow-paced. Imagine what a sultry voice will do for your romantic phrases!

Send your love partner a love letter!

The great romances of history have one thing in common: love letters. Romancing through correspondence is an art. Pull out all the stops and use attractive writing paper, matching or contrasting envelopes, and your best handwriting.

What to write? You might begin by recounting an incident from your day, then go on to describe how much more pleasant it would have been with your loved one there. Or pretend you are living in another era by writing in an old-fashioned style. Try and work in a bit of poetry – your own or a quotation. Keep in mind that you are writing to the one you love – you can be as passionate, melodramatic and lyrical as you wish! Just keep the tone upbeat and loving! A running journal of your days apart is a real treat to present to the love of your life when he returns from a business trip. Love letters can take many forms: brief and tender-sweet, long and passionate, humorous and caring. As long as the love shines through the words, your letters will be cherished.

Of course, with today's technology, you can transmit your written feelings of love by fax! What a thrill for your loved one, to receive your romantic thoughts unexpectedly! The romantic glow your words create will linger all day, and by evening the mood will blaze with passion!

Make a friendly bet with your loved one.
Propose a friendly wager on who is going to win the soccer match or the Derby. The loser has to arrange an amusing day . . . or an interesting night in honour of the winner!

If you are the loser, be imaginative when creating your fun time. Go to a bazaar or a household-goods sale with the challenge of spending exactly £5.75 which you have previously placed in a fancy envelope and presented with a kiss! Or try winning that five-foot tall stuffed animal at the amusement-park arcade. Or visit the wax museum and imitate the poses of the figures. The idea is to go somewhere you would not ordinarily go and to give the outing an unusual twist. Be different – and amusing! Shared laughter deepens a relationship. Plan to end the day with something incredibly romantic – like a moonlight canoe ride! Win or lose, romance is always a safe bet!

Be there for the other person.
You have, no doubt, heard the old saying, 'Out of sight, out of mind.' No gift can take the place of being with the one you care for. Long absences and prolonged separation can lead to bored indifference, and the relationship will be in serious trouble. Sharing time together often is what keeps romantic passion alive!

You have to go out of town for a whole week? Remind him of your love.
If you simply must be away from your loved one for a week or more, leave a set of envelopes containing a love note for each day you are to be away – just to say you're thinking of him! Or

be more imaginative: prepare a recorded message for him to play every day – or every evening before he falls asleep! To dream of you, of course! Leave love messages in odd spots around his flat or house, or arrange for a florist to deliver a flower each day. These strategies say, 'My heart is always with you.' You will return to a loving welcome!

Your love is going on a trip? Slip thoughtful items and love notes into her luggage.

Arrange for little surprises to be slipped into your love partner's luggage, such as imaginative cards with your lip-print, or a love note, or a picture of the two of you with a note saying: 'Since I couldn't come along as a stowaway, I'm sending this along!' There are all sorts of small travel items to tuck into luggage: a special soap, travel slippers, silk pyjamas, hand lotion – anything you know your loved one would appreciate. These little tokens of affection will keep you in your loved one's thoughts.

A good way of hinting that you would like to hear from her is to include pre-addressed, stamped envelopes – addressed to you, of course! You can even add international reply coupons instead of stamps if your love partner is going overseas.

Pack a little romance in her luggage, and your travelling lover will want to pack up and come back to you – *soon!*

Serve up a special treat!

Want a surprise ending – or beginning – to an evening together? Write an especially romantic thought on a beautiful card and present it to your love partner on a silver platter! If your note is passionate enough, you may have just served a sweet dessert!

Make a collage of your souvenirs.

Whenever the two of you go to a special event or a restaurant, try to obtain a memento of the occasion. These items might include theatre ticket stubs, a poster, match boxes, a brochure, photographs, even the label from the bottle of champagne you had to celebrate your love. Keep these souvenirs in a special box, and once a year assemble them in a collage. Be artistic and imaginative: surround the tickets from that fabulous cruise with the photographs you took. Add the theatre tickets from your birthday celebration and the label from the special wine you had that night. The more souvenirs, the better. You can save your '*love*ly memories' in a large album and add a page or two each year, or have the collage mounted and framed to hang on the wall as a reminder of all the happy moments you've spent together. Did you remember to include that 'Do Not Disturb' sign from that wonderfully romantic little inn you went to last St Valentine's eve?

Send a card every day.

Send your partner a love message written on a beautifully-designed – or humorous – card every day for a week. Be mysteriously creative: send only a part of the message in each one. The suspense and romantic passion will build with each card! What a lovely Sunday you two will spend together!

Prepare a milk bath for your love partner.

You've no doubt heard of the beauty benefits of a milk bath, but what about a perfumed milk bath as a prelude to an evening of love? Simply prepare a tub of hot water, add a few pints of milk, then sprinkle fresh rose petals on the surface. Add an essential oil – lavender or sandalwood perhaps – and call sweetly to your lucky love!

Of course, you have already removed all ordinary bathroom toiletries such as deodorant, toothpaste, hair dryer and the like, and replaced them with delicate objects you have around the house. Arrange the décor to create a dreamy atmosphere. Add even more glamour with candlelight. Make sure to have thick, fresh towels ready nearby.

Let your love partner bask in the warm, scented waters and enchanting peace of the candle-lit bathroom . . . Perhaps you might offer to scrub his back!

Tired of going to the same places and seeing the same groups of people? Hire some videos for a quiet time at home.
If the weather forecast looks dreary, or if you're tired, plan a quiet weekend at home. Make it romantic: hire several videos you can watch while you cuddle. And don't forget the popcorn! Buy or make a number of varieties: sweet, spicy, caramel- or chocolate-covered – have a taste test!

Let the world whirl on without the two of you for a while!

Organize a theme evening.
Did you think the film *Dr Zhivago* was romantic? Why not use the video to create a theme evening?! Plan a typical Russian feast. Remember to chill the vodka! Go all out and dress in Russian folk costumes! Why not act out the parts – with your own twist, naturally!

There are any number of themes you can use to create your memorable night. Look for ideas in the old love stories and in the films of the forties and fifties, when romance was a way of life. Your love partner will take up where the film ends!

Your romantic inventory.
Romance is central to your relationship. Keeping the glow of romance in your everyday life is your aim, and there are things you should have on hand to help foster romantic feelings. You could call this collection of items your 'romantic inventory'. It's

fun to take stock of these items, and shopping for new ones or replacements will give you a 'loving lift'. So take a pad and pencil and start listing your romantic inventory. Have you got:

- Candles . . . not just dull, white wicks for power failures, but beautiful, tapered candles in different colours and sizes?
- What about fancy hand soaps, carved into lovely shapes and delicately scented? Potpourris to delight the eye and the nose? Scented facial creams and massage oils? Foot and nail creams to pamper her hands and feet?
- Cloud-soft blankets or afghans for you and your love to snuggle under during a chilly evening while watching television or listening to music?
- Romantic snacks like delicious chocolates?
- Crushed ice for those exotic drinks (when neither of you has to drive home!)?
- Interesting board games or crosswords you can do together? Handsome playing cards to tell fortunes or for a little game of Hearts?
- Confetti, ribbon, lace serviettes, and sparklers for special occasions like anniversaries and birthdays? Lovely crystal and china just for the two of you?

Get into the habit of picking up items that appeal to your romantic side every time you see them. Be prepared for romantic interludes. Having a romantic inventory will help you get into the habit of being romantic every day. With a 'passion pantry', you will always be ready to inspire romance!

A few good wines, champagnes and special liqueurs could be considered essential to a romantic inventory, unless you and your love partner don't drink at all.

Sweets, such as chocolates, are a *must!* Casanova always pre-sweetened his conquests with gifts of European chocolate! Why don't you try energizing your love partner with a chocolate delight? Today, chocolatiers all over the world offer extravagant chocolate bonbons, desserts and gifts. Just the packaging inspires romance! A single Belgian creation wrapped in a minuscule designer box is an enchantingly sweet way to say, 'I love you!' Keep baking and fondue chocolate on hand for special desserts, like chocolate mousse or luscious fruits dipped in a chocolate fondue.

Another item on the *must have* inventory list is perfume! Not only to dash on pulse points, but to scent the air in your home. Spritz the hallway just minutes before you expect your guest. Fragrance is a personal cachet, a scent signature, and every time your loved one smells your perfume – no matter where he is – it will conjure up sweet images of you. Does he have a favourite coat or jacket? Dab a little on the underside of the lapels – just a touch to keep you with him each time he wears it.

How is that list coming? Does your romantic inventory have enough items? Do you need to restock your favourite passion promoters? Make a list and hit the shops! Romance is waiting!

Spray your favourite 'signature' eau-de-Cologne around your house and in your car.
Have you a favourite scent, one that signals 'you' when you are in a room? It is a thrill for someone who cares for you to sense your presence through your special scent. By spraying some of your cologne throughout your flat or house – and in your car – your love partner will be reminded of you even when you are not physically present! Scent is powerfully suggestive: it is like a gentle caress touching the heart with a remembrance of love. Use your perfume to create romantic allure. You'll be a scent-sation!

Go shopping together in search of a token of your mutual affection.
Go off together, searching for a fun gift you can offer each other. As a challenge, aim to keep the total expenditure under £10. A gift needn't to be expensive to be sensuous. Heart-shaped sweets often have little messages on them that are quite suggestive. If you are fortunate enough to have a bake shop in your area that specializes in 'romantic goodies', you might be able to buy sweets and chocolates in exotic/erotic shapes!

Tubes of colourful body paint are great fun to use! Painting hearts, flowers, or love words on each other's face can lead to hilarious, exciting – and *love*ly – moments!

Give your loved one a special nickname for you to use when you are alone together.
Nicknames are charming endearments for private as well as *en famille* occasions. Among the names currently in favour are bunny, love, darling, dearest, *ma chérie, mon cher, mon amour*, poopsy, muffin, love puff, liebling, sweetie pie, sugar, heart's dearest, and angel. Choose one of these, or invent one with its own special meaning. Try it in private first so your loved one has a chance to react! Calling someone 'darling sweetie-pie' in public and having him ignore you is *not* a fun experience!

Impromptu meeting with your loved one? Keep a toothbrush, mouthwash, cologne and other appropriate toiletries in your office and car.
It is better to be prepared than to be embarrassed! Keep toiletries in your glove compartment, handbag, desk drawer, or brief case, in case you need to freshen up before an unforeseen rendezvous. You can find all kinds of miniature toiletries at the chemist's, cosmetic boutiques, or department stores. Why take a chance on ruining an opportunity to be romantic?

Romantic music at your fingertips!
You have prepared a fantastic dinner. The candles are lit, the table is set exquisitely, and all you need is some romantic music to complete the scenario. You turn on the radio and switch to your favourite station. *Oh no!* That soccer match will be on for hours! Frantically you switch from station to station, but you find no soft music, only hard rock or jazz! Now you know why you should take a rainy afternoon or a lazy Sunday to prepare

a long tape of your favourite romantic melodies!

Another time, say you are driving through the countryside, your lover by your side, and you switch on the radio. Boring speeches all over the dial! Never mind, you are all ready with a taped concert of lovely music to make your time together romantically memorable.

Collect romantic sayings and short love poems.
When you hear or read romantic messages, jot them down in a journal – you will need them for your own romantic missives. Beautiful thoughts are lovely to receive. Ellen was very impressed when she received the following tender, thoughtful note from James: 'A day without sunshine is a sad day. A sad day is a black day. But a black day with you is a day filled with sunshine!'

Light his fire with a love note for inspiration: 'Love and passion were made for each other . . .and so were we!'

If you think poetry will impress your loved one, but you freeze at the thought of writing a poem, choose an exquisite card with a special, loving message. Let the card do the talking for you by choosing one that expresses your feelings. Even a beautiful, blank card can be used if you add a small, handwritten note, such as 'My life was a blank page before you appeared . . .'

Romantic words are always appreciated!

Keep little inexpensive gifts, gift bags, wrapping paper, and all-occasion cards on hand.
Be prepared for all those occasions when you suddenly remember an anniversary or a birthday and there is no time to shop for an appropriate card or small gift. Keep gift wrappings on hand, at home and at the office. You'll be appreciated, and people will say, 'You think of everything!'

Become a member of a gardening society, or simply revitalize your love with a walk through a landscaped garden!

Do you like gardening with your love partner? Do you like to spend hours pruning and fussing over colourful blossoms that you admire together? Do you enjoy creating floral border patterns and looking for new species and shades of flowers? Why not join a gardening society? The two of you can cultivate your passion for gardening and flowers and meet others with the same interests.

The fact that you are sharing a hobby is a wonderful foundation for deepening a romance. Clip, snip and fertilize those buds, and together you will have a beautiful romantic garden to reflect the splendour of your love!

Are you daffy for daffodils? Do you delight in dahlias or go simply ga-ga over gardenias? Then share your fascination for blossoms with your loved one and turn a passion for flowers into a romantic excursion through the botanical gardens. As you admire the unusual species from far-away lands, let their exotic textures and scents touch your hearts and kindle romantic fantasies.

Flowers speak the language of romance, so 'talk' to your partner with sweet bouquets and dazzle her with a flower-bright celebration of your love!

Outrageous behaviour is contagious.

Life is tough enough without taking everything too seriously. Do something outrageous together! George and Bonnie take walks in the middle of the night . . . during a snow storm . . . and at Christmas time, they camp all night under the Christmas tree!

Break the monotony of everyday life. Be outrageous with your love partner. Become childish with joy and let your laughter inspire each other. Discover each other's sense of humour.

Lynda admits she used to be uptight, quick-tempered and moody, but Gerald's comical nature changed her. Every time

Lynda was in a bad mood about something, Gerald would draw a funny face or wear a pair of Groucho Marx glasses (complete with big nose attached) until Lynda smiled. 'It used to take a whole afternoon of my best antics to get her to change her disposition,' says Gerald. 'Now, after six months, it takes half an hour . . . and I don't have to stand on my head wearing a duck suit, either!'

Now that Lynda feels much more relaxed, she indulges in zany behaviour, too. Recently, she showed up for a date with Gerald dressed in rags. Wearing ragged clothes over her good dress as well as make-up that made her look twice her age, she greeted Gerald at the elegant restaurant where they were to meet. In front of everyone, she planted a passionate kiss on the unsuspecting Gerald's lips, then proceeded to remove her disguise right there in the restaurant! Gerald's response? 'You've come a long way, baby!'

If you and your partner want to do something different, why not plan a midnight champagne picnic on the beach for just the two of you?! Definitely romantic!

In troubled times, offer support to your loved one.
When the atmosphere in your relationship turns tense, don't get angry. Take a deep breath and support your partner through the rough spots. He *is* your special love, the person to whom you would offer the world on a silver platter. Why else are the two of you together? Don't be bitter during quarrels, troubles or mishaps; be supportive and reassuring. Your relationship will survive and grow in love.

Be supportive in all the things your love partner chooses to undertake. The next time he wants to take karate lessons or to learn to drive a truck, encourage him. After all, you would want the same encouragement from him if you decided to try something new!

Treat the love of your life as you would a dear friend.
Be friends first. You know how considerate and understanding

you can be towards your friends. Offer these same courtesies to your love partner. Never take your relationship for granted. To have a friend, you must be one, and what better person could you befriend than the love of your life? Share your feelings, secrets, desires, and troubles . . .just as real friends do!

Compromise is necessary.
In any society, compromise is necessary for peaceful interaction, and even more so in a close 'society' of two! A relationship cannot be expected to run smoothly every hour of every day. There are certain to be a few misunderstandings and disagreements from time to time. But when you hit an 'iceberg' of a problem, one partner is going to have to compromise. Every compromise has two sides, and both partners should be aware of what the solution means to the other. The following story dramatizes this point.

Ann adores alpine skiing. Her boyfriend, Bob, goes surfing every chance he gets. Ann learned how to surf so she could go along on Bob's next outing. They had a great time. But when Bob refused to go skiing with her, Ann was hurt and angry.

The problem centred around Ann's not ever mentioning to Bob that she learned how to surf as a compromise; in return, she had expected Bob to learn how to ski in order to please her. Bob assumed Ann went surfing because she really wanted to!

Hurt feelings and misunderstandings can often be avoided by simply stating what you want from your partner. Your partner may not realize that a deal was struck and that you expect the favour returned at some point. Compromising without telling your partner that you are making a concession gives her the wrong impression. The partner who is the object of a compromise must remember to show her partner that, not only is she aware of the 'compromise', but because of it, she is highly flattered, pleased, and feels *romantically* special!

Romance and springtime!
The delights of spring fever! That sweet malaise that takes our

thoughts away from drudgery and the workaday world! A time to celebrate renewal of our feelings for each other. Go on a springtime walk – hand in hand, of course. Have a picnic. Take an end-of-the-day bike ride and top it off with a cappuccino at an outdoor café. Feed the birds in the park and revel in sweet whispers as you stroll along.

Meet your favourite person at the zoo for lunch and watch all those newborn baby animals. Their endearingly clumsy antics are sure to inspire feelings of affection.

Experiencing the magic of spring as a couple can be scintillating! Springtime mystically awakens romance so that wherever you live you will feel its bubbly effervescence. Take a deep breath of fresh spring air and breathe new romance into the springtime of your loving!

Organize a love hunt.
Are you bored with going out for dinner and a film? Then do something original and zany! Remember those treasure hunts you used to have as a kid? Why not have a grown-up version?

Invite your love partner for a homemade dinner – perhaps with a theme . . . Italian, Russian, Lebanese? Plant little gifts around the flat – fragrance samples, facial masks, chocolates, flowers, stuffed animals, or treasure items you have chosen to complement your dinner theme: Russian caviare, Belgian chocolate, German champagne, French perfume!

The prizes may or may not be expensive. Why not try homemade chocolate biscuits or a jar of your famous spaghetti bolognaise sauce? Fold a 'love map' marked with clues into your partner's serviette. Use your imagination to make the clues obvious or maddeningly cryptic.

You can be elaborate and require the 'hunter' to go to different shops – the flower shop, off-licence, wherever – to pick up pre-arranged purchases like a bottle of champagne, a bouquet of red roses . . . items that spell romance!

Your love map can promise bonus prizes, too, like a kiss, a hug, or a foot massage! It's up to you to make it interesting and extraordinary. Happy hunting!

Be your love partner's personal stylist!
If you can't do hair, then give him a manicure, pedicure, facial –
or simply wash his hair and blow-dry it. The attention is the
important part. If, however, you are adept with the scissors,
brush or comb, then go ahead and fluff, tease, and spritz until
you have him looking like a star!

Indulge your love the way a real hairdresser would. Offer
magazines, bring him coffee – and don't forget to brush off the
stray hairs from his clothes. With all this attentive service you're
sure to get a tip – a little romance – in return!

Say 'I love you' with music.
Send your love partner a singing telegram with a difference: you
compose the lyrics! Many agencies cater to these
'fantasygrams'. Decide whether you want a gorilla, a clown, a
dancer or a bear to deliver your message, then send it to her
workplace during a busy day. What a declaration of love! If
such a service does not exist where you live, dress up and do
it yourself!

Dress up as the Easter Bunny, Santa Claus, or . . .?
Why wait for the actual holiday? Be impulsive! Christmas with
Santa Claus in July can be great fun! Don't forget to ask if your
love has been naughty or nice before giving him his 'present'!

A December 'bunny' can be naughty *and* nice!

Plan a theatrical evening.
Do you find the legend of Robin Hood romantic? Or do you
prefer the love story of Napoleon and Josephine? Choose a
story, legend, film or play that you and your partner both enjoy,
and make plans to act out the main characters. Go costume
hunting, or devise your own. Look for appropriate 'stage props'.
You can be as elaborate as you wish and stretch out the project –

and the romance – for weeks while preparing for opening night!

Flatter your partner by asking for her advice.
Is your love a golf pro? A racketball champion? Ask her to give you lessons. You'll not only improve your game, but the close quarters will give you plenty of opportunity to romance your sportswoman. Swing that club and flirt your best! In the game of romance there are no penalties for touching! And no rules against flirting and flattering!

Share little secrets or a conversational exchange of a shared viewpoint.
It's like having a secret that no one in the whole world knows except you and your partner. Sharing the same impressions of people or fashions is an intimate, conspiratorial exchange. Comments such as 'Isn't our waiter tall, like John Wayne? He looks a little like him, too!' or 'Did you see that dress she's wearing? Right off the Chanel runway!' are part of building common confidences.

Go people-watching with an eye for points to agree on. Sharing impressions will bring you closer together. During quiet moments at home, thumb through a fashion magazine, commenting on the bathing costumes or the return of the mini skirt. If some of the photos arouse particular interest, you may want to go on a little shopping trip and transfer that interest to you!

After watching a film or a video, discuss it over coffee and dessert. Make a point of mentioning emotional or intimate scenes. You may even end up re-enacting them!

You dreamt about your partner last night? Tell him:

'You'll never guess whom I dreamt about last night. *You!* You were Superman, and you swooped me up and awaaay! We flew off to the Bahamas, where we had banana daiquiris on a gorgeous deserted beach, danced the limbo, then flew home!'

The point is that you'll get his attention by relating your dreams, especially if he is the hero. But even if you don't dream of your love partner, it is a way of disclosing your subconscious longings to the one you love. Who knows? You might start trying to decipher those nighttime visions together!

Watch a scary film.
Even if you are not spooked, clutch her hand, cuddle close, and don't let go! Perhaps this strategy is as old as the hills, but it still works like a charm!

Learn a foreign language . . . or at least a few phrases.
How many times have you been enchanted by people who can speak other languages? Ever been bewitched by a foreigner's sexy accent? A foreign language hints of mystery, intrigue and the possibilities of a passionate romance.

Spark that passion by telling your love partner, 'I love you' in Spanish: 'Yo t'amo.' Or remind your girlfriend she's beautiful in French: 'T'es belle.' Learn the language that has always fascinated you, and surprise your love by sprinkling your conversation with delightful phrases.

Imagine the magic: one evening you're at dinner – at a French restaurant – and you order from the menu in French, then you sweet-talk your love with flowery French poetry! He'll be enchanted and under the passionate spell of the romantic 'foreign power' of the moment!

'May I have a bite?' and other shared intimacies.
Sampling your love partner's passion-fruit sorbet is like taking a giant leap in the intimacy department. It is a privilege to share the same food, and it inspires romance.

Feeding each other – preferably with your fingers – is also a way of inciting passion. It's good, clean fun, unless you start a food fight!

Serve your love partner in the kitchen.

There is something sensuous about a woman with her hands in flour . . . and something irresistible about a man who can cook. So next time you invite your loved one to dinner at your flat, let her help you in the kitchen – even if it's only to watch you stir the bolognaise while you both sip the cooking sherry!

Be a fortune-teller!

Everyone is intrigued about the future. For an amusing evening, buy a book on palmistry, on divining crystal balls, or on reading tarot cards, then spend some time getting acquainted with the main points. Invite your partner for an enchanted evening. Decorate your flat like Madame X's Fortune-telling Parlour, complete with candles and incense. Dress the part of a gypsy – man or woman – and read your darling's fortune. Since you're the fortune-teller, you can make all the suggestions you want . . . ending with, 'I see romance in your near future . . . within the next few moments!' A big kiss at this point shows him that everything you say comes true!

Romance is magic! Let it add a touch of passion to everything you and your love partner do together!

Read poetry by moonlight.

The next time the moon is full, choose a book of love poems – perhaps by Robert Browning or Elizabeth Barrett Browning – and charm your loved one by reading it aloud. Set the mood with candles, scented silks, and flowers. Now is the time for those lovely crystal glasses your aunt gave you. Add a bottle of wine or champagne to sip as you become intoxicated with verses of passion!

Neither of you can stand poetry? Then read from your favourite novel, or buy a Barbara Cartland and read it together. Adapt one of the classics to your romantic oration, or recite a mutually-adored play. The type of book is up to you: erotic, funny, fantastic . . . just find one that will appeal to and stimulate both of you.

Michelle and Jason spend at least two evenings a month reading recipes from gourmet magazines and cookbooks. They become so enthralled with the exquisite photos of sumptuous foods that their creative juices – among others – start flowing! At the height of the evening, they head for the kitchen and start cooking! They say that this activity really brings them together because they love cooking and adore eating! Quite often, when they have chosen the recipes they want to use, they need to go out shopping for special ingredients, which prolongs their fun.

Prepare an aphrodisiac!
Certain foods have an aphrodisiacal connotation. Everyone knows that oysters have this reputation, but did you know that the Basque people of northern Spain and southern France believed that lightly roasted peppers served with a dash of virgin olive oil were sensually invigorating, especially for older individuals? The French and English searched for truffles, believed to contain a volatile substance similar to the male hormone. Throughout Asia, ginger is thought to have stimulating powers!

Whether or not aphrodisiacs truly exist remains to be proven, but besides the possibility of actually adding vitality to romantic prowess, the mere thought of preparing an aphrodisiac for your love, or having one prepared for you, can be quite stimulating!

Romantic menus to delight the senses!
Although you have chosen the food because it may contain aphrodisiacs, creating a passionate, stimulating atmosphere is also important. You want to arouse your partner's romantic appetite with colours, shapes, textures, smells and tastes that delight and excite him!

The perfume of your food should not clash with your personal fragrance. Spicy foods with their exotic, heady bouquet mix well with the 'spicier' perfumes. If you plan to wear a sophisticated outfit and perfume, you might choose to serve an elegant dinner such as chicken Kiev, rice, miniature vegetables, and white wine, for example. A formal flower arrangement set between candles, and your best china, silver and glassware would make a lovely table setting.

Consider your surroundings as well as the menu and table. You might want to decorate your flat with items that fit in with your dinner theme. For example, you could hang a Mexican hat on the door if you are serving a Mexican dish. Why not put a fake fur rug under the table if you are serving Russian Borscht and blini! Imagine how much fun you'll have preparing this special dinner for your special guest!

The way food is presented is 90 per cent of its appeal. You don't have to be a Cordon Bleu cook to make a fabulous meal – even plain dishes can be spruced up with creative touches. Thoughtful attention to little garnishes on the serving plates, along with cleverly folded serviettes and delightful or whimsical place cards, will add a special flair to the table.

A lovely dinner well prepared and beautifully presented is a truly sensuous pleasure.

Good table manners are important, too!
Good etiquette and table manners are as much a part of the romantic atmosphere as the food and wine being served.

Be refined and graceful, keeping your voice soft and low as you engage in polite dinner conversation. Your sophisticated demeanour and impeccable manners will captivate that wonderful person across the table.

Take your love partner to see a sensual show.
Traditional Spanish dance troupes put on a very provocative show! The slow, languishing motion of the women and the sharp dominant moves of the men intertwined in their unparalleled dance of passion will have you and your love partner tingling with delight all evening.

There are many thrilling shows that stir romantic desires. A favourite singer can touch your hearts with passion, or a Las Vegas-type show can send your spirits soaring and your hearts racing with its tempo, colour and spectacular sets!

Plan to see a live show that will please both of you. Feel the energy enliven the two of you and suffuse your romance with new power!

Take advantage of the heat of a summer night.
Go to an outdoor concert. Stroll downtown wearing your lightest clothing. Stop for ice cream, or choose a sidewalk café where you can sip a Sangria or other cold, refreshing drinks while watching passers-by. Listen to a jazz band in the park. Feel the warm air flow over your bodies, and get into the spirit of a hot summer's night.

A hug a day will keep the blues away and romance fresh as a daisy!
Scientists have discovered that the simple act of hugging releases a hormone that makes you feel great. But you already knew that, right? And a cuddle makes you feel wonderful!

The power of touch is one of the great mysteries of the world: it is a fundamental part of human communication. A simple touch can relieve stress, mend relationships, or bind a contract. You can tell someone 'well done' with a pat on the shoulder. When you hug a friend who is sad, you are saying, 'I'll take care of you.'

In a love relationship you naturally use the friendlier gestures: an arm round the shoulder, 'bear hug' greetings, or holding hands – all leading to the more intimate touches involving kissing, caressing, cuddling, and other loving gestures that express your fondness for each other.

Touching and kissing should not be confused with sexual behaviour. Remove the erotic element altogether, and you have the perfect pleasure mechanism for 'getting in touch' romantically. Psychologists say that touch satisfies basic needs like comfort, acceptance, self-esteem, and can even transmit healing energy. Explore the powers of touch in all your relationships; you and your intimate circle of friends and family will be happier and emotionally healthier.

Touching is very important to human relationships.
Touching someone is a way of saying, 'I really like you, I enjoy your company, and I want you to be comfortable!'

We soothe babies and beloved relatives with gentle stroking, sweet kisses, and cooing, so why shouldn't we do it regularly with our love partner?

Try to set aside an hour every day just to caress each other and to hold each other in a tender hug. Gaze deeply at one another. You could begin by sliding your hands across your love partner's arms, sloping down her shoulders to rub her back. Run your fingers through her hair! Kiss her tenderly on the cheek . . . hand . . . up her arm . . . until you reach her lips.

Louise and Craig have raised snuggling to an art form. They make sure that they kiss before going out together or alone. They spend entire evenings in front of the television, not watching but cuddling and kissing. 'It's the ultimate luxury!' sighs Louise. 'When one of us is feeling terrible and hurt because something lousy happened during the day, we'll hug each other hard for a few minutes and emerge energized and relaxed . . . it's a great feeling.'

Are you a born cuddler? Or do you cringe at the thought of a hug?
Some people are naturally more touchy-feely than others, but an aversion to touching can be an emotional dysfunction. In serious cases, the person should seek professional treatment, but for those of you who are simply not used to being touched, you can learn. Touching equals power. Reluctance to touch or to return a snuggle declares, 'I am totally independent. I don't

need you – do not touch me.' On the other hand, it could also mean a low self-image and a feeling of not deserving the affection associated with a cuddle, hug, kiss, or other physical attention.

There is hope, so don't despair. Touch specialists say you can learn how to touch, but you must first develop a 'feeling' for it. If you respond to touching but feel uncomfortable and non-deserving, you will undoubtedly project a mechanical, formal response. But with an encouraging partner to initiate you into the joys of touching and kissing, you'll soon be conducting a symphony of love-touching 'music' of your own!

Kissing is part of touching.
Make a point of greeting each other with a warm handshake and a hug. It is so loving to make physical contact within the first ten seconds of seeing each other. You can add a kiss if you are meeting in private. This small contact will charge the atmosphere with a jolt of affection for the rest of the date!

You could say that kissing is part of ancient history! The earliest kiss was a kiss of greeting and signified great trust in the other person. The theory was that by allowing a person to get so close that he could easily bite you, you showed that you did not fear him. It was in India that the 'romantic kiss' was born, and to this day, in many parts of the world, it remains a symbol of affection.

If your culture and religion permit it, should you kiss in public?
Although in some societies attitudes towards kissing in public are extremely tolerant, in many areas of the world it is considered not only in poor taste, but against the law and subject to a fine. In ancient times, even royalty had to have a good excuse: King Louis XII of France kissed every woman in Normandy under the pretext of giving them his royal benediction! Although a little kiss is innocent enough in itself

and does not indicate that a couple is sexually involved, it is best to keep overt affection for private moments. Why take a chance on being embarrassed?

What is the right technique for kissing?
For those of you who are still wondering about kissing techniques, quit worrying and start practising! There are lots of ways to kiss, and you can have a great time developing your personal favourites with your love partner. To get you started, here's a little advice from expert Mae West: 'I always felt that the look *before* the kiss was more important than the kiss itself.' Practise your special 'I am about to kiss you, you adorable person!' look, and be ready for some lovely kisses coming your way!

Send your partner 'love vibrations'!
Did it ever happen that you were at work or busily involved with your daily tasks when you suddenly thought about your love partner and she seemed so close to you that a rush of warm energy flooded your body? Why not use the power of suggestion to enhance those romantic feelings and your love relationship?

Visualize your 'love energy' as a real image. Sitting quietly, picture in your mind's eye that energy enveloping your love partner. Imagine that she is glowing in the delight of your love energy. Watch this energy flow like a golden thread between you and your love partner. Hold this thought for about a minute, then snap out of your love trance and resume what you were doing!

You can do this exercise together, too, incorporating touching. Sit face to face. Hold hands or place your hands on each other's knees, or simply let the tips of your fingers touch. Close your eyes and imagine the love energy flowing between you. Hold this position for about three minutes in silence and feel the transfer of energy, as though you were pumping yourselves full of romance!

If you want to be romantic, talk the same language.
What is romantic to one person is not necessarily so to the other. Julie and Maurice had a real problem with this one because they were one of those opposites-attract couples. Julie's idea of romance was to go hiking all day and camp out under the stars. She felt this was exhilarating! Maurice, on the other hand, equated romance with opulent settings, flowers, gourmet food, and wine . . . not 'bugs and dirt of the open range'. Their relationship deteriorated quickly until they finally reached a point where they were more polite than intimate. Then Julie had a brilliant idea. One night as she sat home alone – which had become the norm – she decided to make a list of all the things that she felt inspired romantic feelings. Then she rang Maurice and asked him to do the same. The next day, the couple got together with a new spark of hope. They compared lists, and wouldn't you know it, they had more things in common than they had thought!

During the previous four months Julie and Maurice hadn't allowed themselves to explore each other's thoughts and dreams. The lists proved they were closer than they could have imagined; out of 25 points, they had seven mutual romantic interludes. Going for a walk under a starlit sky was in position number one on both lists! Receiving a thoughtful gift was second, and enjoying music together was also on both lists.

If you have trouble communicating verbally with your love partner about romance, each of you should try writing your list of what is romantic. Turn your comparisons into a game . . . into a date! Before you know it, you'll be talking about romance and living its passion!

The romantic agenda: making room for romance in your life.
Romance doesn't occur naturally in everyday life because there are too many pressing obligations that keep us preoccupied. That is why you have to make a point of fitting romance into your busy schedule.

Even mundane tasks like grocery shopping can have their

share of romance. While you are rushing round the supermarket for your weekly staples, take a minute or two to choose at least one item that will serve as a romantic prop: fancy candles, unusual fruits, or smoked oysters! The idea is to make a conscious effort to think, live and breathe romance *every single day*. Just as you would take your vitamins every day, get your daily 'dose' of romance. Exercising your passionate nature is as important as exercising your body. Letting your romantic nature falter is letting your relationship down.

If you are so busy that you find yourself continually forgetting to put some romance in your life, keep an agenda! You keep one for the errands you have to run, for the people you have to see, and for your telephone messages, so why would you neglect an important thing like romance? Write a note on your calendar: 'Today I'm going to buy my love a little fun present'; 'Today I'm going to read a romantic novel'; 'Today, remember to pick up champagne to celebrate our love!'

Making romance part of your daily routine will turn your life into a vibrant, loving experience that will benefit *both* of you – passionately!

Turn boring, nuisance errands into romantic interludes. You are stuck with shopping for groceries, doing laundry, picking up the dry cleaning, and there goes Saturday afternoon. What a waste, particularly when you were wishing to spend it with your loved one. Well, why don't you?! It's a matter of changing your perspective. You both have nuisance errands to run, so turn them into a romantic time by doing them together!

Begin by planning Saturday's course of action earlier in the week. 'We'll stop at the cleaner's first, then do groceries, and shop for your mother's birthday present after lunch.'

You're together, so no need to rush. Treat the day like an enjoyable date. Meet for a leisurely breakfast on Saturday morning . . . read the paper. Even if you use the car to do your errands, walk as much as possible – hand-in-hand if you like! Pause often for a discreet kiss or a quick hug.

Linger over romantic items displayed in shop windows, such

as paintings, lovely linens, or lingerie – his *and* hers. Pause at the perfume counter and sniff a fragrance or two, taking mental note of which one your partner is fond of! If you like books and magazines, take some time to look through the latest issues, perhaps adding your favourite magazines and newspapers to the shopping basket. Take a midday break and have lunch at a chic restaurant . . . or stop at a fast-food counter at the mall for a bite and a smooch!

The idea is to do your errands together. If you treat the day as a fun outing, you will enjoy yourselves and build romantic memories. Wouldn't you rather spend the day shopping together and then go out for the evening rather than rush round all day alone and then be in a bad mood for your date? Both quality and quantity time are possible with a little loving co-operation!

Revitalize the romance in your relationship with the 're-romanticizing' exercise!

During the first three months of your relationship, you were floating on a cloud of romance. Feelings of passion flowed effortlessly because the newness of the relationship took care of that for you. But lately you have sensed the excitement wane, and your high-flying romance has drifted to ground level. A simple, effective 're-romancing' exercise can help!

First, identify the things your partner does that please you, by completing the following sentence in as many ways as possible:

'I feel loved and romantic when you . . .'

Be specific and positive. List actions that occur on a regular basis, such as:

- fill my coffee cup
- give me the sports section of the paper
- read my horoscope
- call me just to say, 'Hi! I love you'
- massage my feet
- ask if I want a treat from the shops

- make special dinners
- compliment me

Now list the romantic things your love partner used to do at the beginning of your relationship – when you were infatuated with each other! Complete this sentence:
  'I felt loved and cared for when you used to . . .'
  Some possibilities:

- write me love letters
- buy me flowers
- talk to me all night
- hold my hand when we were at the cinema
- nuzzle my neck when I was cooking

Play fair and list real actions, not wished-fors!
  Draw a third list of the caring behaviours you always wanted but never got – or asked for. Complete this sentence:
  'I would like you to . . .'
  Avoid listing activities that are a present source of conflict, such as going shopping together – particularly if you've had a recent argument with your love about how she never accompanies you to buy clothes. You could mention how you would love to have a back rub for 20 minutes non-stop; to meet for lunch during the week once a month; or for your partner to read aloud to you instead of watching television.
  On each list, assign a value in order of importance to each and every caring behaviour. Then exchange lists with your partner and ask her to put an *X* next to each item that she is not willing even to consider, let alone do at any time!
  Now comes the fun part! For two months, fulfil one caring behaviour a day for your partner. Start with the easy ones, and as time goes on, add new ones to the list. Take time for your romantic duty every single day, no matter how you feel about your partner. The object is to find out whether you are still in love and if you can have a lasting romantic relationship.
  When your partner demonstrates a caring behaviour for you, acknowledge it by saying how much you appreciate it. This is very important – after all, you have just received a gift!

If you encounter resistance with this exercise, continue doing it anyway – you will soon overcome the opposition!

Increase your romance potential with a list of pleasure 'surprises'!

The unexpected pleasures you give to your love partner are essential to romance. They increase your caring attitude, his caring responses, and strengthen the bonds of your relationship.

You can keep tabs on your caring 'triggers' with a 'surprise' list. First write down all of the things you have done and do for your partner that he particularly enjoys. Next learn your love partner's secret desires. You can do this by dropping hints and observing his responses. For example, Ruth gave her lover a magazine describing sensuous pleasures. She left the magazine open at the page that showed how to give a relaxing back massage. Her love commented immediately: 'I would love to have a professional massage.' Ruth indulged her partner that very day!

Plan to accomplish one nice thing per week as a surprise for your partner. Record the date when you offered these indulgences as well as your partner's reactions. Keep your list secret so that your partner won't know when a surprise is coming his way!

Caring generates caring, and romantic actions create passions that lead to more romance. Keep the kindnesses and romantic overtures flowing in your relationship and you will form a lasting love bond with your partner.

Don't let fear of rejection get in the way of romance.

The beginning of the relationship was lovely! The courtship phase was delightful and exhilarating! But now you are in tears and on the verge of breaking up! What has happened? For many people it is the old fear of rejection, of 'if I am this happy, something must be wrong!' or 'What's the point of being in love? I will only be rejected later on!' Not a winning attitude.

A strong, lasting relationship takes work! Part of this work is to encourage romantic pleasures and pastimes that will sustain interest and love. If you are afraid of being rejected, you will unconsciously stifle your ability to weave romance into the tapestry of your love . . . you will be oblivious to its magic because you are too absorbed by your all-consuming fear of rejection.

You must conquer this fear of rejection, as it is rising from your anxiety over past experiences. It is a fear that truly is all in your head! Should you be paying so much attention to this destructive force? If someone said 'no' to your overtures once, there is no reason to deny romance now! Think of that someone's rejection as a delayed 'yes' . . . from the person you are with now!

Don't take previous rejections to heart. You can never be 100 per cent sure of the reasons for any rejection. Most of the time, they had nothing to do with you and everything to do with the other person. So why let such incidents rip your life apart? Remember that you, too, have rejected someone at some time or another in your life, and you certainly had your reasons, didn't you? Why pass up a chance to live a rich, scintillating life full of passion and romantic delights with your present partner? Throw your fear of rejection out the window! Literally! Write your fears on a piece of paper, tear it in pieces and throw them out the window! And keep them out there!

You don't have to re-evaluate yourself every time someone says 'no' to you. And don't get insulted if your partner's idea of romance is not the same as yours. You can work these things out with a little give-and-take and a lot of love!

Moderately-priced Romantic Suggestions

Why wait for a special occasion to open a bottle of champagne?
The bubbles in champagne have long been associated with that lovely, light, effervescent feeling of being on top of the world . . . of being in love! Celebrate your loving relationship with a surprise bottle of champagne!

Live each day with your love partner as though it were a cork-popping party affair, and your love life will bubble with romance!

Pack overnight bags and whisk your love away for a weekend of romance!
Choose a destination your love partner will appreciate: that charming inn she keeps talking about or that weekend resort by the sea he's been wanting to return to. Send your loved one a card giving only the date and time you will pick her up. What a surprise for her to find out that you have arranged everything: the packing, the accommodations, the perfect romantic interlude! Keep your weekend agenda open for impulses, spontaneity, romance, and a terrific time!

If your loved one is a practical person, choose a practical surprise present.
Your practical-minded love would probably appreciate a flowering shrub or plant for his garden, rather than a huge bouquet of cut flowers. Your gift will be all the more appreciated because you took his preferences into consideration. Expect a big smile and a hug – for you and your thoughtfulness!

Do something silly and fun to amuse your darling.
Does your love partner flip over Turkish delight or some other sweets? Why not send her a *giant* jar of her favourite sweets? A simple but effective way of showing your 'sweet' side!

Amy was crazy about kites. She came home one evening to find kites hanging all over the tree in her front yard . . . wonderfully brilliant kites in all shapes and sizes! She and Don – her kite man – spent a memorable Saturday flying kites and flying high on love!

Is the love of your life a busy career woman? Give her a special toiletries kit designed to pamper her.
Like many women of the nineties, the woman in your life is busy with her career. She doesn't have much time to shop for herself, so why not surprise her with a basket of appealing body cosmetics? She will realize how much you care when she opens the fragrant bubble bath, luxurious bath oils, milky softening lotions, and extravagantly rich, soft-scented creams. Surprise her by sending the beautifully packaged cosmetics basket to her office! When she arrives home that evening, be prepared to continue the pampering!

Send your man a hamper of food – for *two!*
Many pastry shops, greengrocers and department stores stock food hampers. Try a French wine-and-cheese sampler . . . or

maybe a Hungarian picnic complete with spicy sausages and robust red wine! The shop may be able to prepare these hampers according to your tastes. Dare to be exotic – tantalize his taste buds with your inventiveness!

Include a romantic note suggesting where the two of you will share this feast: in the park . . . on the beach at sunset . . . on a friend's yacht . . . at a scenic vista point far above the city . . . or at a cosy spot known only to the two of you!

Surprise your love partner with a box full of fun.
Send your man a box filled with fun things like a neon-orange hairbrush, red braces with whimsical designs, a polka-dot bow tie, a miniature of his favourite cologne, or a demi-bottle of wine. Wrap each item in several layers of paper, each in its own small box. Half the fun is getting to the item! Pack everything in a larger box, wrap it in gaily striped paper, and have it delivered – perhaps by a clown messenger service!

Send her purple bath salts, a box of miniature Swiss or Belgian chocolates, sexy, black lace stockings, a brightly coloured scarf, an embroidered handkerchief, the latest issue of her favourite magazine, and any other small items you think might amuse her.

Use layers of tissue paper or odd-shaped boxes, then pack all the items in a decorative box complete with lots of colourful ribbon curls! Arrange to have the box delivered to her office first thing in the morning. Imagine her delight and surprise when she finds a box full of gifts instead of an in tray full of work!

Of course, the *real* fun begins when your love partner thanks you *personally!*

Present your love with a gift of lingerie or loungewear.
If you would love your lady to wear fancy lingerie or elegant loungewear, but you are too shy to make her a present of some, offer her a gift certificate at a fine lingerie shop. To nudge her towards buying the kind of thing you have in mind, cut a

picture of something similar out of a magazine and staple the money to the picture! Enclose this in a blank card on which you have written, 'For you, so that you can pamper yourself . . . for me, because I think you would look beautiful in it!' If you are not quite sure that she will wear sexy lingerie, you might ask indirectly by mentioning something like, 'Would you wear Dior lingerie if you could afford it?' Or look through a lingerie catalogue together and see what she likes. If she picks plain cotton pyjamas, you'll have to be more direct!

There are also all kinds of sexy underwear available for men, such as silk briefs or fun boxer shorts. If you're shy, you might say, 'To your good health! These pure silk items let your skin breathe.' Look for ones that are unusual: perhaps a bold jungle design or an exotic leopard print.

One of the most 'far-out' gifts you could imagine for your loved one is naming a star after him!
Is your love partner a 'stellar' attraction in your life? Then name a star after him – officially! All you have to do is to write to the International Star Registry–Pacific giving them your love's name and address and enclosing a bank draft or money order for $70 US made out to: Giftmark Marketing (M) Sdn Bhd and send to:

The International Star Registry–Pacific
Lot 7 Jalan Pelabur (23/1) Seksyen 23,
40000 Shah Alam
Selangor Darul Ehgan, Malaysia.

The certificate will arrive in approximately eight weeks.

Your loved one will receive a beautifully calligraphed certificate designating a specific star in the heavens which has been given his name, and certifying that this name is permanently filed in The International Star Registry's vault in Switzerland.

Furthermore, the star's new name will be recorded in a book

and registered in the copyright office of the Library of Congress in the United States.

A star map showing the exact position of the star is also included in the 'star kit' that you will receive. What fun the two of you will have finding this star on a beautifully clear, star-filled night!

Are you two so much in love that your entire lives seem to revolve around each other? Then you may want to own *two* perpetually revolving stars! The price of this 'double star' package is $140 US including handling and postage. When ordering, include *both* your names and send the bank draft or money order to the address listed above. Wouldn't it be lovely to *truly* say your romance is 'star-bright'?

An old-fashioned horse-drawn carriage can add a romantic touch to your evening.
Take a bright, moonlit night, add a couple in love, mix in an old-fashioned carriage ride through quiet city streets or a tree-filled park, and *voilà*! Success! Even on a sunny day there is nothing more romantic than a ride in a horse-drawn carriage! Imagine cuddling with your love in a curtained buggy, whispering sweet nothings in her ear as your carriage meanders slowly through city streets? Romance is a breath away!

Have you ever seen a dozen long-stemmed biscuits?
Everybody loves biscuits and flowers. Marry the two in a biscuit bouquet! Instead of buying biscuits by the box, buy them by the bunch! Isn't it much more original – and romantic – to offer your love partner a dozen long-stemmed biscuits?

If you can't find a bakery to do this, you can buy some artificial flower stems from a florist and bake them yourself using flower-shaped biscuit moulds.

Hansel and Gretel and the Gingerbread House: a love story!

Did you ever dream of having a gingerbread house when you were a child? Fulfil that dream and buy or construct one with your love partner. Cookbooks and magazines often show designs and detailed instructions for making gingerbread houses. What fun to nibble on your 'house' as you dream about and plan the home you would share together!

Present your loved one with a description of his name!

What a beautiful and thoughtful gift! A numerical and astrological description of your love partner's first name, written in calligraphy on fine paper.

Finding out about his Chinese astrological symbol would also be a great idea. You can have a chart prepared for your love partner and for yourself, then you can compare the characteristics of your animal signs. Cuddle your rabbit, chase your monkey, kiss your tiger – you will find many inventive ways to please your 'little animal'!

Soft, caressable silk is always a romantic gift!

Sensuous, colourful silk lends itself to a dazzling array of lovely gifts ranging from a wisp of a scarf to elegant evening wear. Silk feels soft and light, like a lover's first kiss . . . silk is definitely the preferred fabric for setting *the mood!*

For the man in your life, you might choose a robe or a pair of pyjamas . . . with a suggestive, sinuous snake embroidered on them!

For luxury pampering, spend a day together at a spa!

Relax in a hot tub or a whirlpool with your love partner. What a great opportunity to show off that terrific new bathing costume you bought last week! Drift into a dreamy half-sleep as you are pampered with herbal wraps, creamy facials, and gentle massages. What a lovely prelude to a sensuously delightful evening together!

Make an appointment with a professional photographer to have pictures taken of you and your love partner together.

You and your love partner can become a 'cover-couple'! Today, many photographers specialize in – or at least offer – romantic photography sessions.

Props and special set designs enable you to have the background of your choice for that 'special moment' photograph. Matthew and Katie sipped champagne against the backdrop of an alpine meadow. Laura and Raoul preferred provocative shots under a moonlit sky!

A make-up artist and hairdresser are usually present to help you achieve the look you want. If the photographer has not employed these professionals, make sure that you bring your own or someone who can help you with costume, hair and make-up changes. If the studio hasn't got everything you need – lingerie, flowers, lace and ribbons, fans and other romantic accessories – bring what you need to create the ambience you think would be the ideal setting for a romantic interlude for just the two of you!

A romantic photography session is exciting and a bit like a wedding day, with both partners dressing in special costumes and preparing for the 'moment of fame'! They are indeed stars for a day. This excitement can charge a 'tired' relationship with new energy. On the day of the actual session, the two of you will be in a romantic setting, posing in a loving manner. *Bazaam!* Both of you are sparked with passion for the rest of the day and night . . . and probably many weeks to follow.

Once this flame is ignited, fan it with loving attention every day. When you get those pictures back, you will have a lovely record of your romantic episode. Keep the photos in a special album, and have your favourite pose enlarged and framed. Place the picture in a prominent spot where you are sure to be 're-inspired' into recreating the romantic atmosphere of your photography session!

Turn your dreams into reality!
You are a hopeless romantic, but your partner is not. You dream of dressing in eighteenth-century costumes and sweeping her off her feet! But you feel that this scenario would just make your darling laugh, so you haven't even dared mention it. You could be wrong. Go with your dreams and dare to set the stage for your fantasy evening.

If you want to wear the noble trappings of a knight and charm your royal lady, no one is stopping you except yourself! Any gesture of attention should be appreciated, and going to the trouble to show your love through elaborate fantasy is true admiration.

Plan your romantic diversion around a specific historical date, or one that has meaning for the two of you. You might want to send your love a flowery card inviting her to an evening of sixteenth-century romance, for example. Of course, a candle-lit décor is a must! Can you just imagine her delight and surprise when she arrives by horse-drawn carriage! Who surprised whom?

Charles had no qualms about dazzling his lady love with a bit of fantasy. One afternoon, Charles donned a suit of armour and parked himself – on his horse – in front of his lover's house. When Vanessa arrived home from work, she was overwhelmed! Her knight in shining armour had come to ask her to marry him! How could a girl refuse such an elaborate proposal? Wouldn't you have said yes?

If you have a fantasy that would make you happy, why not act out a romantic scenario complete with all the props? Your love will undoubtedly be delighted to join in the theatrics!

Give your love partner a surprise half-year birthday party!
Imagine the astonishment on your love partner's face as he

walks into a room full of people shouting 'Surprise!' What are they celebrating? A half-year birthday! And why not? A great reason to have a fun evening with a group of friends – topped off with a romantic interlude with the party-planner!

Place a romantic ad in the personals column of your local newspaper.
Be unusual! Instead of placing an ad in the paper to say 'Happy Birthday', or to sell the extra pair of football tickets you bought last week, write a love note to your darling. List her most outstanding qualities and perhaps a teasing comment about them. Write something like 'To my darling Annie, whose lovely laugh adds sunshine to my rainiest days, I just wanted to say I love you. Jack.' Good for a hug and several kisses – at least!

Flowers too conventional for your unusual sweetheart? Send a bouquet of balloons.
Balloons come in all shapes and sizes. Heart-shaped balloons, shiny balloons, polka-dotted balloons, designer balloons. Arrange a special bouquet in your lovemate's favourite colours and surprise him at the end of a long work day. Or fill his car with balloons! Make the bobbing bubbles interesting by placing a love note in each balloon before you blow them up. Tie an envelope containing instructions and a pin on the 'bouquet', and get ready for a big *bang* of romance!

Play a card or board game designed for just two players.
Look for games designed for only two players. You may find a shop that specializes in amusing items for couples, including adult games. There are also fun 'quizzes' to test your relationship! If your loved one prefers 'artistic' fun to regular games, try that body-paint set!

Take a course on wines and discover an intriguing new 'language' that will encourage the one you love to be wined and dined.

If an extensive course is not available, try a wine-tasting class! Wine jargon – particularly when French wines are involved – is quite suggestive! You will learn to speak of the 'perfume' or the 'bouquet', and the depth of the 'robe', which refers to the colour. You will also learn how to make wine 'waltz' in your glass, how to 'revel in its body'! Impress your dinner guests with your familiarity with wine varieties and their subtleties, with your ability to choose from a wine list, and with your knowledgeable comments as you properly 'taste' wine that has been presented to you in a restaurant!

When choosing a wine for an intimate dinner, at home or in a restaurant, try to find one with a love-inspired label – such as Nights of Love or Passion Valley – or one that is decorated with a lovers' scene. Your efforts to make the occasion 'visually' romantic are sure to be appreciated!

Choose spirits with romantic names.

Be different when choosing cognac, brandy, and other after-dinner or late-evening 'sippers'. Amaretto is known as the 'lovers' liqueur' for its sweetness and distinctive flavour of almonds. Napoleon brandy suggests romantic 'conquests'. You may even discover those with romantic names like 'Le Parfait Amour' – The Perfect Love!

A lovely prelude to a romantic interlude!

An amusing or romantic telephone 'speaks' of love!

It is amusing to see a telephone in the shape of a heart, lips, a golf bag, or even a high-heeled shoe! Today, such telephones are widely available. Besides being great conversation pieces, they are romantic reminders for your loved one to phone you often!

Is the love of your life working late? Take supper to her!
Take a supper hamper to your hard-working sweetie. Keep the
menu simple and non-messy: no jellied eels to melt all over the
report she is working on! Splurge on the accessories: a lace
serviette for a placemat, lovely dishes and silverware, and a
nice goblet for juice or water. You might even slip in a few
flowers. If possible, bring a bite for you to share, then make a
quick exit so she can get back to work. No doubt such a lovely
supper-break will be greatly appreciated . . . as well as an
incentive to hurry home to you!

Offer your love partner a mystical gift.
Even people who don't believe in astrology or in fortune-telling
have fun listening to their future. We all want to know what is
in store for us! So send your love partner to a reputable psychic:
she may tell him he has met the love of his life! Or the psychic
may tell her she has a dark-haired admirer who will stay in her
life forever! Most people love to hear about their future at the
beginning of the year or near their birthday. Dare to give your
love a glimpse of destiny – with you!

A gift of a massage is a love message that says 'I care'.
Give your loved one an especially caring message with a gift
certificate for a massage by a professional masseur. You might
even find someone who will come to your home and massage
both of you!

**You're engaged – and your ring is beautiful! Why not buy
an engagement ring for *him*?!**
The woman of the nineties can be romantic, too! Why should
the privilege and thrill of wearing an engagement ring be
reserved only for women? An elaborate, jewelled ring is not
required, but a tastefully-designed band inscribed with the date

and both your initials or with a lovely quotation would be worn with pride!

Take your love partner to an unfamiliar place.
Make your next date an exotic adventure. Nothing refreshes the dreary monotony of everyday life like a change of scenery! You don't have to charter a plane, just go to an ethnic restaurant! Sample spicy Spanish tapas or paella; explore the pungent pleasures of a Middle-Eastern mechoui! Choose a restaurant with an elaborate décor: leather ottomans and luxurious pillows trimmed with provocative tassels, perhaps even an exotic belly-dancer to entertain you during dinner! Completely immerse yourselves in the adventure of having dinner in 'another country'. Pretend you are James Bond and his beautiful companion . . . drink in the atmosphere . . . and at the end of the evening, emerge into the starry night filled with the passion and romance of a faraway land.

OUTRAGEOUS AND EXPENSIVE ROMANTIC SUGGESTIONS

The following suggestions would interest lottery winners or people who have high incomes, as several of these are outrageously expensive romantic fantasies. You might manage to indulge in one of them once in a lifetime – unless you or your love partner have the resources to grant any wish! Even if you can never actually do these things, here are some fairy-tale romantic scenarios and grand gestures of love to dream about.

Offer your love a first-class airline ticket to anywhere in the world.
Her mother – or her sister – lives overseas? Wouldn't a first-class plane ticket from you be generously romantic? Be imaginative and send her the ticket attached to a bunch of balloons on a Wednesday, with the departure date on that Friday, so she can spend at least the whole weekend with her family. Send her by Concorde and she will have even more time to spend with her loved ones. Of course you will assure her that you will water her plants and take care of her cat . . . and miss her immensely! You are generous to a fault, for you have even included traveller's cheques for a little shopping in the city of her choice!

Charter a plane for an unusual adventure!

Here's one way to find yourself in seventh heaven! Have a caterer prepare an elegant assortment of canapés, caviare, strawberries with a kiss of pepper, and a chilled bottle of the best champagne. Add a package of exquisite chocolates and have it all delivered to the airport where you have chartered a plane and pilot. Of course, you haven't said a word about all this to your love! Have a stretch-limousine whisk your love to the tarmac and the waiting plane and usher him up the steps and into the luxurious interior.

When you are airborne, hand him an envelope in which you have placed a card and a rather nice sum of money! The card reveals the destination; the money is to buy clothes to suit this spectacular adventure. The destination could be an exclusive island resort, a famous city, or your chalet in the Swiss alps! Of course, you have handled all the details of passports, immigration requirements, and the like. You will have a long enough flight and enough privacy to get to know each other better – a true 'in the clouds' romance!

Is fear of flying a problem? Then charter a luxury yacht and sail calm, blue waters under starry nights and sun-kissed days, stopping in exotic ports along the way. The idea is to do something ultra-luxurious and romantically stimulating – an exciting adventure for two!

A memorable weekend!

Send your love a card several days in advance of your planned adventure. Only indicate the time and day she is to be ready to go away for a weekend. Have a limousine arrive at the appointed hour. The excitement will mount during the drive to the elegant resort hotel or fabulous villa complete with servants and a double jacuzzi you have booked for the two of you. As the limousine arrives, have a small chamber orchestra play your love's favourite music. But you still haven't appeared. Arrange for the hotel manager to have the 'star of the show' shown to a beautifully appointed room where a fabulous array of clothing awaits in the large closets and bureaus. An outfit, suitable for the next location in your plan, is in a prominent spot.

Once dressed in these clothes, your dazzled love will be escorted to a secluded area of the beach, to the best view in the area, or to a yacht, depending on the resort. In any of the locations, you will have had a beautiful table set with shimmering linens, china, and crystal, and decorated with flowers and candles. Two comfortable chairs have been arranged and draped with silk. There are a hundred lighted candles of all sizes and colours glowing softly in the sand. As your loved one arrives, you appear – dressed as elegantly as the occasion requires.

After a divine gourmet dinner, when the last candle has sputtered out in the sand, a spectacular fireworks display lights up the sky. The final burst is a love tribute that flashes the message 'I love you' as the orchestra plays 'Moonlight and Roses' or 'Starlight Serenade'. As the last note fades away, a prancing white horse with a beautifully decorated saddle and bridle is led to your side. You whisk your loved one up into the saddle and hold him tightly as the two of you gallop off to your waiting suite at the resort!

The rest of the romantic weekend is up to the two of you to invent and enjoy!

Pressed for time? Charter a luxury yacht for a weekend. You don't know a thing about sailing? Not to worry; the captain, crew, French chef and every possible convenience is included! You and your loved one arrive on a Thursday or Friday evening – casual dress and soft-soled shoes are recommended – and begin the weekend with a delightful lobster and champagne dinner. Weather permitting, you sail – or most likely, motor – through long, enchanted days of gentle breezes softly caressing your sun-warmed skin, along with star-bright nights of romance, anchored in a calm bay surrounded by the scent of flowers and the rustle of palm trees on the nearby shore. Perhaps the two of you will go for a midnight swim!

Declare your love with a banner in the sky!

Have an airplane pull along a banner that says, 'I love you!', or declare your love in sky-writing!

   Many small airports offer these services, so let your imagination run wild and be recklessly romantic! The sky's the limit!

Buy advertising space on a bus or tube, or in the newspaper, to declare your love!

A man did this after his girlfriend told him she wanted an official marriage proposal. The man in question took out a full-page spread in the local newspaper to declare his intentions. Of course, his love noticed the huge advert, which concluded with, 'Is this official enough?' Needless to say, she passionately accepted his proposal of marriage! The next week the newspaper in which the ad appeared carried a feature story about the couple and their amusingly romantic gimmick!

A hoarding in front of your love's house is a constant reminder of your love.

From Paris comes a story of a lovesick man who could not seem to win the heart of the woman he adored. In order to keep his name and his message in her thoughts, Pierre had a hoarding set up across the street from her front door. On it he had written, *Je t'aime, Marie!* It worked! A week after the hoarding went up, Marie went out her front door, walked straight over to the hoarding, and left a big red lip-print on it!

Tell the entire city of your love: have your love declarations painted on a bus!

Although actual costs depend on your city, in Montreal the costs of having a bus decorated with your message of love would be around $75,000 (Cdn.) for a year. Then there is a

$10,000 (Cdn.) fee for removing the declarations when the publicity contract is up. This is just an example. The text is up to you!

Take your love for a ride in a chauffeured stretch limousine, stopping at top gourmet restaurants for the various dinner courses!
Inquire about a service that puts fine food and fine cars together. Some offer a stretch limo complete with chauffeur, flowers, music, and a video of shows from Le Moulin Rouge and the Crazy Horse Saloon in Paris – to put you in the mood! Your limousine will tour your city, stopping at the finest restaurants to pick up your appetizers, entrées and desserts, which have all been ordered ahead of time. Fine wines and champagne are naturally included!

If the city you live in does not offer such a service, you can improvise by hiring a chauffeured limousine – or a Rolls Royce – and organizing the restaurant 'pit stops' yourself! A great idea for a mid-week pick-me-up or a romantic prelude to a lovely weekend!

Commemorate special occasions with a specially-designed gold charm bracelet.
Gold bracelets can be charmingly romantic – when you have your jeweller design little charms that have special meaning for the two of you. A skyline of the city where you met, a tiny candelabra for that special dinner when you told her you loved her, a dancing couple – whatever you consider the main theme of each month or year you two have been together. The ideas are endless and the result is very special. Your gift will be cherished forever, and you can add charms as events and years go by!

Create a paradise in the middle of nowhere.

There are still many deserted areas in the world that you can escape to – all you have to do is choose your favourite setting and arrive there with your love via hot-air balloon! In advance of the Big Day, arrange to have a huge tent installed at your choice location and have a decorator arrange a dreamy interior décor – perhaps an *Arabian Nights* theme with opulent Persian rugs, cushions, silken draperies, and elegant low tables bearing baskets of fruit and vases of flowers. You may need a generator to furnish electricity for the lavish lamps, or you could use a multitude of oil lamps and candles instead. Have a banquet prepared and ready to be served on a beautifully appointed table. Contrast the ruggedness of the setting with the opulence inside your tent! Create a romantic world of passionate delight for the love of your life, and invite him to enter . . .

It is not necessary to use up your life savings to show your love!

Carlos Eduardo, a man from Sao Paulo, Brazil, had been crazy about his beautiful neighbour for the last four years. Still, he could never bring himself to declare his love. When he found out that she had just broken up with her boyfriend, Carlos decided to show Elaine his love. Although he was not a rich man and he earned a modest income, Carlos took his life savings of £2,000 and bought 100 kilograms of roses and wild flowers which he jettisoned from a helicopter over Elaine's garden. Through the mist of her delight, Elaine remembered having danced with Carlos at a neighbourhood festival. She agreed to a date with her young admirer, and that is the beginning of their romantic history!

A romantic gesture need not be so elaborate that it will put you in the poor house! Use your imagination to create an incredible experience for you and your loved one. The off-beat, out of the ordinary, madcap adventure is what will endear you to each other and give you memories to strengthen your bond of romantic love!

SINGLES AROUND THE WORLD!
THIS CLUB IS FOR YOU

Marie Papillon's International Singles' Club – For *all* singles *everywhere!*

As a reader of the highly popular, best-selling *A Million and One Love Strategies*, you are invited to become a member *free of charge* and to have the opportunity of subscribing to an exclusive *Singles Newsletter* PLUS access to specialty catalogues featuring items of particular interest to singles. Write *now* for full details! Simply complete the form below and send it to:

International Singles' Club
255 Boul. D'Anjou
Suite 211
Châteauguay
Québec J6J 2R4
Canada

First name _____

Surname _____

Address _____

_____

_____

_____

Country _____

Post code _____

Age _____   Sex [   ] Male   [   ] Female

Of further interest:

THE ART OF KISSING

William Cane

♥ Are your kisses ever too wet? Too dry? Too monotonous? Too noisy?
♥ How long do the best kisses last?
♥ Should you *always* keep your eyes closed?
♥ What's the best way to kiss someone for the first time?

In *The Art of Kissing*, lovers will find all they need to add tenderness and technical know-how to all their kisses – from quick, teasing pecks to complicated continental kisses. It contains practical, lips-on advice including dos and don'ts, personal anecdotes and a unique 'kissing encyclopaedia' that details the techniques for more than twenty-five kinds of kisses. You'll find advice on kissing underwater, ideas on what to do with your hands, rules for playing kissing games, plus safety tips for kissing in movie theatres and in cars.

If you've been privately striving to perfect this highly intimate and sensual craft, *The Art of Kissing* is sure to unseal lips, untie tongues, and revive both new and old love lives, mouth-to-mouth. Try it and see if it doesn't make every kiss as tender, fun, passionate, thrilling, and unforgettable as your very first.

SEXUAL POWER

What is it? Who's got it? And how to use it to succeed in love and life!

Sandra Sedgbeer

We all envy people who seem to have more – and better – relationships than us, and we particularly admire and envy those people who seem to have it all, though it's often difficult to work out why they do. The secret is sexual power!

But what is the essence of sexual power? And where does it come from? Few of us can define it in words, but we easily recognize it when we see it. If you have it, the world can become your oyster. And if you haven't, the big question is: how can you get it?

Sexual Power is a charismatic guide for men and women who want to maximize their untapped reserves of magnetism, sexuality and desirability.

Discover the subtle uses of

- Body language
- Flirting
- Self-esteem
- Neuro-linguistic programming

to achieve amazing success with the opposite sex: whether as lovers, colleagues, or just friends.

You'll never envy anyone's sexual appeal again, because this book shows you that you don't have to be slim, you don't have to be a superstar, and you don't even have to be rich or good-looking – for with *Sexual Power* you can have it all.

SECRETS ABOUT MEN
EVERY WOMAN SHOULD KNOW

Barbara de Angelis

If you have ever wished that men came with instruction booklets, you need despair no longer. Barbara de Angelis' best-selling *Secrets About Men Every Woman Should Know* is the book you've been waiting for since your first date!

Revealed in this book:
- Secrets about men and sex that men will never tell you
- The six biggest mistakes women make with men
- What men say . . . and what they really mean
- Men's top twenty turnoffs
- The five biggest mysteries about men
- How to spot – and avoid – the men who will give you the most trouble
- How to get the man you love to open up
- Techniques for becoming a more powerful woman

Barbara de Angelis is America's foremost expert on love and relationships. This book will give you the tools you need to create the relationships with men that you always dreamed were possible.

THE GOOD SEX DIET

How to use food to transform your sex life

Arabella Melville

Here's how to create a sexy dinner for two, and how to use food to stimulate your sexual appetite.

Here, too, is revealed the subtle art of creating the atmosphere and mood for love, and you will also find a guiding hand to help keep you and your partner in peak condition with sex drives that can switch swiftly and tirelessly into top gear.

With her sensuous food making, her dreamy mood making, and her performance-improving tips, let Arabella Melville tantalize your taste buds and transform your sex life.

AROMATHERAPY FOR LOVERS

Holistic sex through the magic of scent

Maggie Tisserand

Aromatherapy For Lovers opens up a whole new world of sensual lovemaking for you and your partner, showing you how to make the act of love truly holistic: mentally, physically and emotionally.

- how to make up sexy massage oils and 'love potions'
- how to soothe and relax your partner with touch and fragrance
- ideas for scented lingerie, pillows and sheets
- essential oils to stimulate erogenous zones
- how to use finger pressure and reflexology to cure sexual dysfunction
- oils for beautifying your skin and making it silky to the touch
- aromatic remedies for improving and prolonging your sexual performance.

Full of practical techniques and inspiring ideas, this book – by the author of the best-selling *Aromatherapy for Women* – will enhance your love life, excite your partner and bring out your hidden sensual depths.

THE ART OF KISSING h/b	0 7225 2650 0	£8.99	☐
THE ART OF KISSING p/b	0 7225 2601 6	£4.99	☐
SEXUAL POWER	0 7225 2142 1	£5.99	☐
SECRETS ABOUT MEN	0 7225 2776 4	£4.99	☐
THE GOOD SEX DIET	0 7225 2485 4	£4.99	☐
AROMATHERAPY FOR LOVERS	0 7225 2762 4	£4.99	☐

All these books are available from your local bookseller or can be ordered direct from the publishers.

To order direct just tick the titles you want and fill in the form below:

Name: _____

Address:_____

_____ Postcode: _____

Send to: Thorsons Mail Order, Dept 3, HarperCollins*Publishers*, Westerhill Road, Bishopbriggs, Glasgow G64 2QT.
Please enclose a cheque or postal order or your authority to debit your Visa/Access account —

Credit card no: _____

Expiry date: _____

Signature: _____

— to the value of the cover price plus:
UK & BFPO: Add £1.00 for the first book and 25p for each additional book ordered.
Overseas orders including Eire: Please add £2.95 service charge. Books will be sent by surface mail but quotes for airmail despatches will be given on request.

24 HOUR TELEPHONE ORDERING SERVICE FOR ACCESS/VISA CARDHOLDERS — TEL: **041 772 2281.**